CW01502453

TABLE OF CONTENTS

Bharata
Before
the British
and other essays

TOWARDS A NEW INDOLOGY

SHONALEEKA KAUL

Vitasta

Śrīkṛṣṇārpaṇamastu

In loving memory of
Jim
(2012–2022)
Lionheart

Published by
Renu Kaul Verma
Vitasta Publishing Pvt Ltd
4348/4C, Ansari Road, Daryaganj
New Delhi-110 002
info@vitastapublishing.com

ISBN: 978-81-19670-23-9
© Shonaleeka Kaul
First Edition 2024

MRP ₹ 750

Edited by Abhijit Baroi
Layout and Cover by Somesh Kumar Mishra
Printed by Chaman Enterprises, New Delhi

PREFACE

The Indian Constitution famously begins with the words "India, that is Bharat". The title of this book then, *Bharata Before the British,* is not only for alliterative effect, but is also a nod to the reclamation of selfhood that our Independence from British rule in 1947 symbolised and for which it set the stage. This book, or rather the essays that it brings together, addresses in one way or another a number of fundamental questions regarding the history of early India. It is written expressly for the lay person and brings exciting new insights and in-depth explorations from the arena of scholarship out into the world of the general reader who is curious and invested in knowing authentically about the early career of Indians as a people.

How far back does the idea of Bharata, that is India, go? Did the British bring India into existence or is she an ancient nation? Was Kashmir historically 'unique' and isolated from the rest of India or thoroughly connected with it? How was Islamisation culturally experienced in medieval Kashmir? Is myth the antithesis of history or a historical mode in its own right? What is the antiquity of Krishna worship at Mathura? How did Shakti veneration shape the identity of a people and their land? On a different plane, is there only one way of time-keeping or did premodern India host multiple temporal visions and worldviews—ways of knowing and being—that have been suppressed by an unequal world order? Did ancient Indians write history? Was there an Indic vision of the discipline as different from modern Western notions? Was Sanskrit an elitist language or a literary culture with public reach and relevance? Did it speak only for the rich and the powerful or did it recover the voices of marginalised Others, including non-human animals? What was the purpose of architecture in ancient India? Could it be an instrument of liberation (*moksha*)? On the other hand, what was the ancient idea of erotics (*kama*) and how did it relate to society? How did it feel—smell, sound, touch, appear—to live in an ancient Indian city? Does Sanskrit poetry contain merely stereotyped and idealised depictions of ancient times or have we been reading it wrong? What were the overarching goals of Indic knowledge systems and how far have we come from them today?

In engaging these varied issues, in filling gaps in our knowledge about ancient India or its regions, in correcting misplaced perspectives, and in offering culture-sensitive methods with which to work through our texts and traditions, *Bharata Before the British and Other Essays* invites us to rethink our understanding of India and Indology. It challenges, in particular, the hold on the profession of history of colonial and neo-imperial approaches, on the one hand, and political ideologies, on the other. These have taken us considerably away from developing a robust emic understanding of ourselves—our nation, our thought, our practices and patterns of belief and behaviour. The diverse essays in this book, penned over the years and bringing together history, literature, philosophy, anthropology and art, attempt to reclaim such an understanding in ways that do justice to our historical sources on their own terms rather than compromise them in the service of extra-academic imperatives.

We live in a time of fake narratives and social media-fuelled disinformation, on the one hand, and hubris of some professional historians towards 'public' histories, on the other. Fittingly perhaps then, the last two essays in this book discuss the state of Indian history today and also what the way forward may be to ameliorate the ills of the academic establishment, the associated stasis in the field, and its disconnect with the masses.

Several of the essays carried here are revised versions of a popular invitation column that I used to do for *The New Indian Express*. Some of these pieces going viral and the enthusiastic feedback that I received in my inbox from readers every time the column appeared, were proof of the thirst and need for transmitting rigorous historical research and revelations to the public in a digestible and engrossing manner. History did not have to be boring and heavy and abstruse! It could and should speak to people of all backgrounds and their concerns while yet retaining its classical literary form (rather than only the current rush to videos and podcasts!). This book is an extension of that belief. Without diluting historical detail and referentiality, nor falling for populism, it draws the audience into a whole new world of stimulating questions about India and Indology and offers cutting edge answers to them.

I wish to thank Prasanna R S, Assistant Resident Editor of *The New Indian Express*, for inviting and nudging me to do the column and being a supportive and involved editor over the two years that I wrote for his paper while battling multiple attacks of Covid and other challenges. My gratitude is also due to the publishers (especially Routledge) of my earlier books, as well as the IGNCA journal *Kalakalpa*, on which I have drawn for the content of a few essays. A special thanks to Arpita Biswas for executing the lead map carried in chapter one. Ravi Dhar, B R Mani, Mayank Pandey, Ananta Vrindavan Das, Shailendra Bhandare, Iqbal Ahmed, Todywalla Auctions, Classical Numismatic Group CNG and the Tallenge Store are all warmly acknowledged for their help with other illustrations. Aishani Shrivastava assisted with re-formatting a few of the essays. My thanks to Renu Kaul Verma, the dynamic Director of Vitasta Publishing, who when she requested this book, convinced me this labour of love would be in the best of hands.

My revisionist journey in history is a quarter of a century old now and I would be remiss if I did not acknowledge the teachers, colleagues and friends in this time who gave me the freedom and applause to tread new paths and critique, often radically, old ways of the history academy. To be sure, this freedom is not to be taken for granted in Indian academia where, despite the lip service, neither dissent nor autonomy of scholarship is encouraged. Similarly, a large number of my students in Delhi University and JNU over more than two decades have given abundantly of their devotion and enthusiasm for their teacher and the new histories she did with them.

I owe my lessons in professional independence and integrity as well as pride in the country to my beloved father and prodigious journalist, the late Sumer Kaul. With my husband, Nachiketa, I have shared a love of Indian philosophy. My canine kids Jim, Kalli, Vito and a host of others have brought me joy and sustained me through life's many ups and downs.

For these people and this book, and for the singular honour of being born an Indian, I thank God.

Shonaleeka Kaul
13th April 2024, Baisakhi

LIST OF ILLUSTRATIONS

Bharata before the British: The Idea of India in Precolonial Times

In an ancient, continuous living civilisation like our own, the past is never past but an important completive and context to situating the present. This is not only because national identities typically form in the *longue durée*. This perspective is important to reclaim also—and all the more so—for societies that have undergone the colonial disjuncture: the irruptive epistemic violence that colonial modernity wreaked on much of the non-west, including Bharata or India, forcing a break with the endogenous in the service of Empire, and making necessary today a fresh, decolonised engagement with our past and ourselves. A prime example is the question: how old is the idea of India?

Of course, 75 years into independence, we should not have had to still be wondering whether and what the idea of India in premodernity was and yet here we are. One of the reasons why this remains an enduring question rather than a long-clarified one is that mainstream ancient Indian historians, but for exceptions such as R K Mookherji and B D Chattopadhyaya,[1] have shown reticence in engaging with this fundamental question, as if there were something inherently reactionary or chauvinistic about it. Indeed, in today's deeply antagonistic political climate, if you even make a claim about an ancient idea of India, you can in certain circles be villainised for it!

You can be subjected to invective and slander and accused of having a certain sectarian ideological motive.[2]

This is deeply unfortunate because it attempts to sabotage the query from being what it is: an impulse to know our past on its own terms, on the strength of irrefutable historical testimonies. But the irony is that while all founding fathers of modern India swore by the Indian 'nation' and 'nationalism', today these seem to have become swear words for some. To speak of India's unity through all her vibrant diversity may invite abuse in these quarters. And to refer to her antiquity and ancient texts evinces a condescension (oh what do these Puranas know!) and worse, a communalised hostility (again a throwback to colonial mindsets) that ancient Indian texts speak for only one denomination or faith, which is an unhistorical supposition.

Broadly, reactions today to the question 'How far back does the idea of India go?' range from taking India as an unexamined, given, eternal category at one end, to denying its very existence before the British colonised us. The latter is perhaps a more serious historiographical problem because, as we will see, it chooses to ignore or silence rather too vast a body of evidence that does attest the existence of a clear premodern idea of India.

Why is there this denial? One reason is modern myopia and hubris that pre-empts looking back beyond the colonial experience, which is seen as defining of everything we are today – as great an irony as there can be for a 5,000-year-old civilisation. A second reason is clearly a hangover of imperialist politics and historiography, which prided itself in this instrumentalist disinformation that there never was an India. For instance, in 1880, Sir John Strachey, British administrator who trained the Imperial Civil Services of India, would begin his lectures saying: "The first and most important thing to learn about India is that there is not and never was an India"![3] Coming from a representative of the colonial state then, whose political conquest of the land had indeed been piece by piece, this divisive statement uninformed by historical insight should perhaps not surprise. What is surprising, however, is that nearly a century and a half later, there is still epistemic confusion over the question of how far back India as a territorial entity and unity goes and it is not uncommon to find some leading scholars deny the very possibility.

Thus in his authoritative book *India after Gandhi*, Ramachandra Guha called India "an unnatural nation", implying that modern developments such as British rule and the Freedom Movement forced a diverse and disconnected bunch of regions and peoples into one artificial and unhistorical entity called the Indian nation.[4] It was understood that this happened, for instance, on account of the British bestowing on this ancient land such institutions as the railways and the civil services, which supposedly did not just 'modernise' India but also unified it for the first time by building a common locomotive and bureaucratic framework that we had otherwise lacked.

Others such as Partha Chatterjee, concerned perhaps with countering eternalising claims, declared that "there are no ancient nations anywhere in the world. All nations (rashtra) are modern. . . . The Indian rashtra as a nation-state has only been in existence since the middle of the twentieth century" [sic].[5] Ironically, *rashtra*, the Sanskrit word used here for the concept of nation (which then confusingly becomes nation-state in this work), is in fact a very ancient term. It occurs multiple times in later Vedic texts from the 10th to 5th century BCE (for example, *Vajasaneyi Samhita* 10.2, *Shatapatha Brahmana* 5.3.4.5, *Atharvaveda Samhita* 7.109.6), in the *Mahabharata* from the 4th century BCE (for example, 5.40.7, 12.279.25),[6] in the *Arthashastra* from the 4th century BCE (?) (for example, 1.6.5)[7] and in the *Manusmriti* from the 2nd century CE (for example, 7.65).[8] But while Chatterjee does not entirely dismiss vast premodern Indian empires such as the Mauryas and the Mughals, he prefers to insert a new element in any understanding of nation, namely, popular sovereignty, which he admits "is a very modern idea which emerged in Western Europe and North America in the late eighteenth century". He then concludes in circular fashion: "Without the claim to popular sovereignty, there can be no nation-state or rashtra. Therefore all nations are modern."[9]

Clearly, in operation here is a teleology—the presupposition that the modern period is more influential in shaping a people than the ancient or medieval could ever be. These positions also show the persistent hold of colonial and Western thought worldwide. For so deep is the dependence on European models of historical development and vocabulary, such as that of German and Italian unification or the French Revolution, that the fundamental difference between a nation and a nation-state is lost sight of in these denials of the ancient idea of India.

To be sure, unlike a nation-state, which is a formal and political arrangement, a nation is first and foremost a notion: The jointly held sense of belonging to a common territorial and cultural entity that a people name and assert; a community of emotion, of belief and of praxis; "a felt community", as Rajat Kanta Ray called it,[10] and a classic 'subjective region', as Bernard Cohn may have said.[11] Now, even a working acquaintance with what are known as the master texts of Indic civilisation and the cultural geography contained in them yields the presence of this notion of a felt community and a common bounded entity which are affirmed and named. Moreover, there are astonishing convergences over two millennia in the way a disparate set of historical commentators and observers attest this readily recognisable idea of Bharata or India. And further, remarkably, this idea is seen to embrace, with no apparent unease, both India's spatial unity as well as her incredible diversity. This will sound familiar to those conversant with the claims ("Unity in Diversity!") of India's nationalist movement leading up to 1947 and after; however, it is not the invention of that movement. We have premodern Indian texts that put out ages ago this inclusive vision of what India is and it is time we acknowledge and substantiate this remarkable phenomenon.

Perhaps the earliest text to define India as 'Bharatavarsha', broadly yet resonantly, as the land between Himalayas and the sea, is the hoary *Mahabharata* (conservatively dated to between the 5th/4th century BCE to 4th century CE). In particular, its sixth book, the *Bhishma Parva*'s tenth chapter, details in more than 70 verses first the historical geography of India—all the many mountain ranges and rivers of this land running from north and north-west to the south and from north-east to the west, including Ganga, Sindhu, Vitasta or Jhelum, Saraswati, Yamuna, Chandrabhaga or Chenab, Gomti, Sarayu, Godavari, Narmada and Mahanadi (*Mahabharata* 6.10.1–74). It then documents the ethnography of the land, namely, the *janapadas*

Not to scale. For broad representational purposes only.

Figure 1.1 Bharatavarsha as revealed in the *Mahabharata*:
Select *janas*. Courtesy: Author.

or territories occupied by variegated communities (*janas*) that peopled Bharatavarsha.

Significantly, in a so called 'mythological' text, the *janas* included are all historically attested people, from those of Kashmir, Gandhara (Peshawar), Kamboj (Afghanistan) and Punjab in the north to Vidarbha and Malava in central India and from Kashi, Magadha, Odisha, Bengal and Assam in the east to Dravida, Kerala, Karnataka, Kuntala (Telangana) and Chola in the south. (This should urge a reconsideration of the myth versus history binary. See Chapters 9 and 11.) Those named also included *mlecchas* and *yavanas*, on the one hand, 'outsiders', so to speak, and 'tribes' such as the Nishadas, Shabaras, Kiratas and Abhiras, on the other. There is also an explicit reference to all four castes (*varnas*) inhabiting Bharatavarsha.

In this way, as per the Indian epic's testimony, no conflict is seen between the spatial unity and identity of Bharatavarsha and its inherent diversity. Instead, a frank acknowledgement of its geographic and ethnic complexity obtains rather than any exclusionary vision of the land. Thus to see this unity as only a "retrospective thrust of hegemonic [modern] nationalism", as some scholars suggest,[12] is to miss the capaciousness and pluralism within the most ancient ideas of India. Bharatavarsha emerges here as a singularity that subsumed rather than erased the many.

Further, while the focus of our discussion here will be this ethnic and cultural idea of India, let me just say a little bit about the political, because this is something that some scholars like to insist is missing before the British. But the truth is even politically, Bharatavarsha is already seen in the *Mahabharata* as this singular aspirational realm for all kings to want to bring under one rule, as the conversation between Dhritarashtra and Sanjay in the same *adhyaya* tells us.[13]

Moreover, this idea of Bharatavarsha as *chakravartin kshetra* or the area of the great conqueror is echoed many times in historical inscriptions from across the country. For example, the Hathigumpha inscription of King Kharavela of Kalinga (Odisha), dated as early as 1st century BCE, mentions how this king went out to conquer all of Bharatavarsha ('Bharadavasa' in Prakrit).

The Satavahana king Shri Pulumayi's Nasik inscription and the Shaka king Rudradamana's Girnar inscription, both from the 2nd century CE, as well as Samudragupta's 4th century CE Allahabad *prashasti* (eulogy) enumerate the two halves of the subcontinent, the *uttarapatha* (northern route) and the *dakshinapatha* (southern route), thereby presuming the larger whole, just like in ancient Buddhist literature from the 6th century BCE where these names are first mentioned. The 9th

Figure 1.2a Hathigumpha Cave, Udayagiri, Odisha. Courtesy: Author.

Figure 1.2b Inscription of King Kharavela of Kalinga, 1st century BCE, naming 'Bharadavasa' in Hathigumpha Cave. Courtesy: Wikimedia Commons.

century CE Pala king of Bihar and Bengal, Devapala's rhetoric of conquest also included the land "bounded by the snowy mountains in the north, Setubandha-Rameshvaram in the south and the two seas in the west and east".[14]

So clearly, right across a millennium and a half, India *is* present as a term of political reference and aspiration. And occasionally, it showed up as not just political reference but political reality too, for we know that the first pan-Indian empire in our history, that of Asoka Maurya in the 3rd century BCE, covered nearly the whole of the subcontinent. And much later, under Akbar and his successors, the Mughal Empire displayed a similar vastness.

With that point made, and before we return to textual testimonies, please note that a number of other inscriptions also refer to Bharatavarsha, be it the Rishthal inscription of western Madhya Pradesh from 515 CE, which refers to a temple built as a symbol of Bharatavarsha, or the Rashtrakuta king Govinda IV's 918–933 CE inscription and the Chalukya king Someshvara IV's 1038 CE inscription, both of which show Kuntala (Telangana) to be in Bharata, the Shravanabelagola epitaph of Mallishena dated to 1129 CE where the entire extent of what we know as India is meant, or the Handala grant of Vijayanagara king Harihara in 1356, where Karnataka is described as in the south of Bharatavarsha.[15] So, the idea spouted by some, that only one kind of idealised literary sources in antiquity refer to India and not the supposedly more pragmatic, everyday sources such as inscriptions, is untrue.

❧ ❧

Now, returning to chronology in our story, after the *Mahabharata*, in the 4th century BCE, the Greek ambassador to India, Megasthenes, in his book *Indika* also named 'India' as bounded by the sea to the east, west and south, by Mount Hemodos ('Abode of Snow') to the north, where it was separated from Central Asia (Scythia), and by the Indus to the west.[16] The extent of the whole country is said to be 28,000 stadia (ancient Greek measure of length) from east to west and 32,000 stadia from north to south. He adds for good measure: "It is said that India, being of enormous size when taken as a whole, is peopled by races [sic] both numerous and diverse, of which not even one was originally of foreign descent, but all were evidently indigenous."[17]

After him, Ptolemy, the celebrated 2nd century CE geographer from the Roman Empire based in Egypt, described India and her regions in copious detail. He claimed in similar fashion that India was bounded by the ocean in the south and the snowy mountains in the north; further, he fascinatingly spoke of an India that went east of the mouth of the river Ganga right up to China, thereby including perhaps what is known as the North East today as well as Bangladesh. He cited the Hindukush as this country's western boundary, much like Xuan Zang after him (see below).[18]

At about the same time, in the far south, Tamil Sangam texts such as the *Patirruppattu* and the later epic *Shilappadikaram* (5th century CE) were also invoking the same geographic imagery of the space between the snowy Himalayas and Cape Kumari (Comorin) in the oceanic south.[19]

Meanwhile, in the 5th century CE, the *Vishnu Mahapurana* (2.3.1, 8) mapped not just Bharata's geographic but also ethnic and cultural boundaries thus:

> *Uttaram yatsamudrasya himadreshchaiva dakshinam*
> *Varsham tadbharatam nama bharati yatra santatih.*
> *Yojananam navasahram tu dvipoayam daksinottarat*
> *Purve kirata yasyante pashcime yavanah sthitah.*[20]

This translates to "the country north of the sea and south of the Himalayas is Bharata and her children are Bharati. Nine thousand yojanas from north to south, it has kiratas in the east and yavanas in the west". Kiratas referred to denizens of Assam and the eastern Himalayas, while Yavanas at this point in history referred to those settled in Greater Punjab. On view then is an explicit and inclusive self-understanding of the land whose other features, including being a *karmakshetra,* are also elaborated in the text. As per the text, it is the only land of karma (*karmabhumiriyam*) on the entire planet—the land of action and its fruits by which people can ascend to heaven or hell, that is, where they can realise their own destinies.

Explicitness and inclusivity in the idea of India are found articulated again in the 6th century CE encyclopaedia *Brhat Samhita* composed by the polymath Varahamihira. This text (14.1–31) exhaustively enumerates the many regions and peoples that were part of India, displaying, yet again, clarity and detail of this idea of a unity through plurality.[21]

This would resonate with Xuan Zang, the Chinese Buddhist pilgrim's testimony in the 7th century CE. Zang travelled all over India and left a detailed account of the land. Writing in his memoirs *Si Yu Ki*, Zang says that standing at Langham, not far from ancient Nagarahara (modern Jalalabad, Afghanistan), west of the Khyber Pass, he felt he stood at the gateway to the country called 'Indu'. He described Indu, again, in classical terms as bounded by the snowy mountains to the north and the sea on three sides, extending to an area of 90,000 li (Chinese mile) and inhabited by 70 different kingdoms.[22]

He tells us the meaning of the name Indu, calling it the Sanskrit word for 'moon' since the country was luminous like the moon from the collective radiance of its sages.[23] He says Indians liked this name best, even though the Chinese had earlier other names for this country, such as *Tien chu kuo*, which meant Country of the Heavenly Bamboo, or *Hsi-yu*, the Western Domain. So the idea of India in Chinese perceptions went back much further than Xuan Zang.

What all of this suggests is that well before the 7th century CE, there was in place a clear notion of India as a conceptual and lived place. Moreover, the modern view that this land was too vast and diverse to ever have been one country or nation ignores the fact that the ancient Indian concept of 'nation' could well recognise and embrace that vastness and diversity and acknowledge, alongside, a common unified sphere of cultural circulation.

It should come as no surprise, then, that clear geographic and circulatory horizons would inform the itinerary of any premodern traveller seeking to circumambulate this robust cultural sphere. Indeed, through their movements, such travellers would have simultaneously enacted this sphere and its routes and pathways, fortifying what Diana Eck called (in a narrower ritual context) a pilgrims' nation.[24] Thus, notwithstanding its endemic pluralism, India was also acknowledged as a common unified sphere of cultural circulation and a singular episteme.

Perhaps there is no greater illustration of this idea of India as both many and one, both diverse and unified, than the stellar example of Adi Shankaracharya, the seer-intellectual who in the 8th century CE established the supremacy of trans-sectarian Vedanta *advaita* i.e. unified consciousness beyond multiplicity and form. Let us dwell on this remarkable case at some length.

The 13th century CE *Shankara Dig-Vijaya* narrates that Shankara, together with his disciples and king Sudhanva, undertook a great tour of the land (*digvijaya*), debating a great variety of schools of thought.[25] He set out from Kaladi (Kerala) and traversed first to Rameshvaram, then Kanchi (Tamil Nadu), then Andhra, Vidarbha and Karnaṭaka, defeating in particular Tantric Shaivas such as the Bhairavas and Kapalikas. Thereafter he reached the shores of the western sea and then Gokarna

Figure 1.3a Shankaracharya temple, Srinagar, Jammu and Kashmir, 8th century CE. Courtesy: Wikimedia Commons.

(Maharashtra), Saurashtra, Dvaraka (Gujarat), defeating along the way Vaishnavas, Shaivas, Shaktas and Sauras. He is then said to have moved onwards to Ujjayini (Madhya Pradesh), Bahlika (Bactria?), Shurasena (Mathura), Darads (Gilgit Baltistan) and Kuru and Pañchala (Punjab and Haryana).

Following that, he is described as taking his exegetical endeavours to Kamarupa (Assam), Koshala (Uttar Pradesh), Anga, Vanga and Gauda (Bengal), defeating Shaktas, Pashupatas, Baudhas and Kshapanakas (Jainas) (*Shankara*

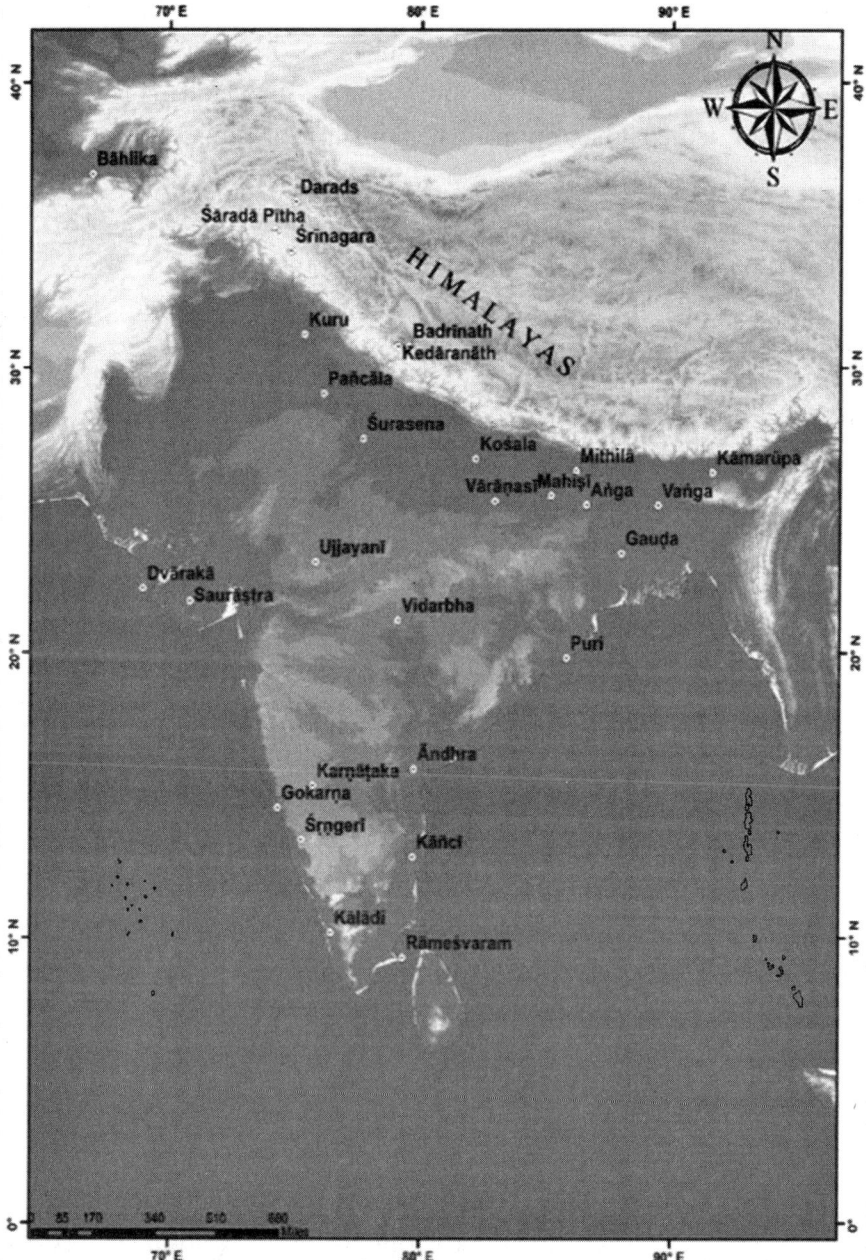

Figure 1.3b Some places associated with Adi Shankaracharya and his *digvijaya* around Bharatavarsha, 8th century CE. Courtesy: Author.

(Map for broad representational purposes only.)

Digvijaya 15.166–185). This phase of his *digvijaya* would have included his momentous debate with Mandana Mishra, the famed Purva-mimamsaka ritualist, and his scholar-wife Abhayabharati at Mahishi (Bihar) (*Shankara Digvijaya* 8). Shankara also went to Badrinatha and Kedaranatha later (*Shankara Digvijaya* 16). The text tells us:

> The doctrine of *brahmavidya* that Shankara preached, which confers liberation through the elimination of all duality, reigns victorious over the country—from Rameshvaram in the south, where Rama built his bridge dividing the seas, to the northern boundaries marked by the Himalaya mountains which bowed down with its peaks to Shiva at the time of the conquest of the Tripuras; and from the eastern mountains where the sun rises, to those of the west where it sets. (*Shankara Digvijaya* 6.106–07)

The culmination, as it were, of these advaitic travels was, we are told, all the way in north Kashmir where the ultimate victory of Shankara's intellect was symbolised in his ascension of the throne of omniscience (*sarvajñapitha*) at the renowned Sharada *peetha* (*Shankara Digvijaya* 16.186–195) on the banks of the river Kishenganga, today in Neelum Valley (Pakistan Occupied Kashmir), just north of the Line of Control. We know independently from the 12th century CE history of Kashmir, Kalhana's *Rajatarangini* (IV. 325), that the Sharada *peetha*, the seat of the goddess Shakti-Saraswati, was a pilgrimage of subcontinental renown and draw in the 8th century CE. Al beruni also informs us that it continued to be among the top three shrines of entire Hind in the 11th century CE.[26] (See Chapter 2 for the intensely connected histories of Kashmir and the rest of India.)

The *Shankara Dig-Vijaya* narrates that, gathered on the banks of the Ganga while on his *digvijaya*, the *acharya* was exhorted by a voice in this manner:

> In the world, Jambudvipa is the most famous region. In that region Bharata excels all others. In Bharata, Kashmir is the most famous place. For there, it is said, Mother Sharada is present. In that region there is a temple with four gates dedicated to Sharada. Within is the Throne of Omniscience. . . . Scholars from the east, west and north, who could prove their omniscience, have in the past opened the three gates pertaining to their respective directions. It is said that till now there has been no learned man from the south who could open the southern gate. (*Shankara Digvijaya* 16.54–61)

Note how the symbolic unity of Bharatavarsha's directions as coming together in Kashmir is self-consciously stated here. Hearing this, Shankara headed towards Kashmir and successfully passed the test that the goddess Saraswati herself set him and thereafter he ascended the *sarvajñapitha*.

Commemorating this association with Kashmir appears to be the 8th century CE Shankaracharya temple, a landmark till today in Srinagar city, built atop a hill at the site of the old temple of Jyeshtheshvara, which is said in the *Rajatarangini* (I. 124) to have been founded by a descendant of Mauryan King Ashoka circa 3rd/2nd century BCE.[27] Shankara's connection with Kashmir and his strong local memory there indicate the remarkable centrality of the far north of India to the imagination of its far south and vice versa, pointing again to coherent territorial assumptions.

Furthermore, tradition, as recorded in some late

hagiographies such as Chidvilasa's *Shankara-vijaya*, maintains that Shankara established *matha*s, or monastic institutions, in the four extremities of Bharatavarsha, among other centres. These *caturamnaya pitha*s were/are Badrinatha in the north, Puri in the east, Shringeri in the south and Dvaraka in the west, which are also associated with the Advaitic orders of Dashanami Sannyasins. It needs no labouring to see that not only these four centres but the entire itinerary of his peregrinations, his *digvijaya*, corresponds to the extent of India as it was mapped in premodernity.

This prompted Sarvapalli Radhakrishnan to suggest that Shankara was being "a shrewd political genius and patriot" in his choice of the location of these *matha*s.[28] I believe that his peregrinations were not exactly "patriotism", nor were they only polemics; they were also pedagogy. For, Shankara's *digvijaya* simultaneously effected and demonstrated a sphere peopled by great diversity of praxis and thought, such as India, but unified by trans-sectarian *advaita*, which pierced through the 'illusion' (*mithya, maya*) of multiplicity. Bharata thus provided a laboratory, as it were, for Shankara, one that in its own diversity and unity mirrored both the bewildering variety of *samsara* (the material world) and the ultimate oneness (*ekatmata*) of *brahman* (pure consciousness). The singularity—whether *brahman* or India—that subsumes rather than erases the many was recognised only through its realisation.

We are still not done with the evidence! To continue our story in chronological order: In the 11th century CE, the Persian traveller Abu Raihan Al beruni in his *Kitab ul Hind,* describes India ('Al Hind') thus: "Limited in the South by the above mentioned Indian Ocean and on all three other sides by the lofty mountains, the waters of which flow down to it". He goes on to say: the inhabitable world extending southwards from the Himavant is Bharatavarsha, which is the centre of Jambudvipa. The parts named and ascribed to it are located in Al Hind alone.[29] Note that we come across *Bharata kshetra* or *Bharata khanda* in southern Jambudvipa in Jaina cosmological literature as well from this early medieval period.

There are still more examples: In the 14th century, Indo-Persian poet Amir Khusrau in his *Nuh Sipihr* (3.5.69–72) resoundingly speaks of Hind as his *watan* (nation) and cites Hind's dozen diverse languages (*hindawi*) to include Sanskrit, Kashmiri, Sindhi, Punjabi, Bengali, Gujarati, Kannada and Tamil. His understanding of Hind, then, was co-extensive with this entire area peopled by these languages.[30]

Further, throughout the same Chapter 3, Khusrau praised Hind as the one country that was paradise on earth (*firdaus*) and superior to other countries thanks to its temperate climate, its abundant flora with special reference to its luscious mangoes and bananas, condiments such as cardamom, cloves and betel nuts, and also because of its classical language of learning, Sanskrit, which he describes as a pearl amongst pearls.

According to Khusrau, the intellectual wealth of Hind was incomparable and the world's scholars came to India to gain knowledge whereas Indians had no need to go to the world for the same. He goes on to name all the knowledge systems that thrived in India, traditions of wisdom (*danish*) and philosophy (*hikmat*) including logic, astronomy, mathematics and the physical sciences. Khusrau affirms that India invented the numerals (today ironically known as Arabic numerals!) and especially the zero and also the game of chess (*shatranj*).

He also singled out for mention Indian music, animals and feminine beauty. In his own words:

> How exhilarating is the climate of this country
> Where so many birds sing melodiously.
> Poets composers and singers rise from this land
> As abundantly and as naturally as the grass.
> How great is this land which produces men
> Who deserve to be called men!
> Intelligence is the natural gift of this land
> Even the illiterate are as good as scholars.
> There cannot be a greater teacher than the way of life of
> the people here.
> It is the gift of the almighty, this cultural environment,
> very rare in other countries that
> If perchance any Iranian Greek or Arab comes by
> He will not lack for anything
> Because they will treat him as their own![31]

This son of a Turkish settler from Uzbekistan clearly knew and admired his adopted country!

Then, in the 16th century, the famed Mughal historian Abul Fazl writes in the *Ain i Akbari*: "The sea borders Hindustan on the east, west and south. In the north, the great mountain ranges separate India from Turan, Iran and China ... Intelligent men of the past have considered Kabul and Qandahar as the twin gates of Hindustan... By guarding these, Hindustan obtains peace from the alien raiders."[32] Note the reference to Kabul also resonates with Ptolemy and Xuan Zang. Interestingly, however, Fazl claims that Hindustan also included Sarandip (Sri Lanka), Achin (in Sumatra), Maluk (Malaya), Malagha (Malacca) and many islands, "so that the sea cannot really demarcate its limits". He probably referred to the spread of Indic culture here.

Fazl, much like Khusrau, further writes of the inhabitants of Hindustan: "the people of this country are God-seeking [all acclaim the oneness of God], generous-hearted, friendly to strangers, pleasant-faced, of broad forehead, patrons of learning, lovers of asceticism, inclined to justice, contented, hardworking and efficient. True to salt, truth-seeing and attached to loyalty."

The Tibetans, on the other hand, called India rGya-gar (Vast Land?) or Phags-Yul (Noble Country), the source-country of their Buddhist masters. Their works such as Lama Taranath's 16th century *History of Buddhism in India* and the later *Jewel Garland of Buddhist History* mention gurus from Phags-Yul belonging to Kashmir and Peshawar (N), Andhra and Kanchi (S), Saurashtra (W) and Bengal (E).

❧❧ ❧❧

Thus on view, again and again, is staggering evidence, over an enormous span of time and variety of contexts, of astonishing convergences in the perception or knowledge of what India—Bharatavarsha, Indu, Hind, Indoi, rGya-gar, Phags-Yul, Hindustan—was. Though not necessarily identical in every respect, nor coterminous with present day boundaries or concepts, the fact that there seems to be a great deal that continued to be held in common in the idea of Bharata across the centuries by Hindus, Buddhists, Muslims and Jainas, by residents as well as foreign travellers, by pilgrims, poets and chroniclers, should have a sobering effect on modern debates that deny traditions of continuity where they may exist in an ancient living civilisation such as India even in the midst of much historical movement and change.

Notes

1   R K Mookherji (1914) *The Fundamental Unity of India.* Calcutta: Longmans; B D Chattopadhyaya (2017) *The Concept of Bharatavarsha and Other Essays.* Ranikhet: Permanent Black.

2   When I first wrote about the ancient idea of India in *The New Indian Express* on 14th August, 2020, I was instantly subjected to *ad hominem* slander by two Indian academics based in Toronto. They could not, however, for all their baseless invective, demolish any of the wealth of historical evidence I presented. They were exposed by a widely-read rejoinder from me on the news platform that had published them, thereby escaping a legal suit but not the ignominy of being shown up for the poverty of their hit-and-run 'scholarship'/ journalism. See Shonaleeka Kaul (2020) 'The Empire Strikes Back: Ad Hominem as History', *The Wire*, https://thewire.in/history/ the-empire-strikes-back-ad-hominem-as-history Last accessed 27.03.2024.

3   Cited in Diana Eck (2012) *India: A Sacred Geography.* New York: Harmony Books, p. 47.

4   Ramachandra Guha (2007) *India after Gandhi: The History of the World's Largest Democracy.* New York: Harper Collins, p. 7.

5   Partha Chatterjee (2022) *The Truths and Lies of Nationalism as Narrated by Charvak.* Delhi: Permanent Black, pp. 5–6.

6 V S Sukthankar edited (1947) *Mahabharata*, Pune: Bhandarkar Oriental Research Institute.

7 R P Kangle edited (1969) *The Kautilya Arthashastra: A Critical Edition*, published by the University of Bombay. http://gretil.sub. unigoettingen.de/gretil/1_sanskr/6_sastra/5_artha/kautil_u.htm. Last accessed 31.03.2024.

8 J L Shastri, edited (1983) *Manusmṛti with the Sanskrit Commentary Manvartha-Muktavali of Kullūka Bhaṭṭa*, Delhi: Motilal Banarsidass. http://gretil.sub.uni- goettingen.de/gretil/1_sanskr/6_sastra/4_ dharma/smrti/manu2p_u.htm Last accessed 31.03.2024.

9 Partha Chatterjee, *The Truths and Lies of Nationalism*, pp 6–7.

10 Rajat Kanta Ray (2003) *The Felt Community : Commonalty and Mentality before the Emergence of Indian Nationalism*, New Delhi: Oxford University Press.

11 B Cohn, 1987 [1967] 'Regions subjective and objective: Their relation to the study of modern Indian history and society' *In:* B Cohn, edited, *An Anthropologist among the Historians and Other Essays*, Oxford and New York: Oxford University Press, pp.100–135.

12 B D Chattopadhyaya (2017) *The Concept of Bharatavarsha and Other Essays*, Ranikhet: Permanent Black, book jacket.

13 This runs right in the face of the following statement by Ishrat Alam: "There is little evidence of Bharata being the explicit object of conquest for every aspiring chakravartin". 'Names for India in Ancient Indian Texts and Inscriptions' in Irfan Habib edited (2005) *India: Studies in the History of an Idea*, Delhi: Munshiram Manoharlal, p. 44.

14 Hathigumpha Inscription: D C Sircar (1965) *Select Inscriptions bearing on Indian History and Civilization*, vol. 1, Calcutta: p. 213–21. Nasik and Girnar inscriptions: cited in Ishrat Alam, 'Names for India in Ancient Indian Texts and Inscriptions', p. 39. Allahabad Prashasti: J F Fleet (1888) *Corpus Inscriptionum Indicarum*, vol. 3, Calcutta, pp. 7–13.

15   Rishthal inscription: *Epigraphia Indica* vol. XIII, pp. 326–327.
     Govinda's inscription *Epigraphia Indica* vol. XIV, p. 244.
     Someshvara's inscription *Epigraphia Indica* vol. XIV, p. 282. Handala
     grant: *Epigraphia Indica* vol. XIV, p. 88. Mallishena cited in Ishrat
     Alam, 'Names for India in Ancient Indian Texts and Inscriptions', p.
     43.

16   J W McCrindle (1877) *Ancient India as Described by Megasthenes
     and Arrian.* London: Trubner and Co., Calcutta: Thacker, Spink and
     Co., Bombay: Education Society's Press, p. 30.

17   Ibid., p. 35.

18   J W McCrindle (1885) *Ancient India as Described by Ptolemy*,
     London: Trubner and Co., Calcutta: Thacker, Spink and Co., p. 33.

19   A S Menon (1987) *Kerala History and Its Makers*, Kottayam:
     DC Books, pp 24-25. R Dikshitar translated (1939) The
     Shilappadikaram, London : Oxford University Press, p. 327.

20   T Upreti, edited (2003) *Vishnu Mahapuranam of Maharshi
     Vedavyasa*, Vol. 1. Delhi: Parimal Publications.

21   V S Sastri and M Ramakrishna Bhat edited (1946) *Varahamihira's
     Brihat Samhita*. Bangalore: V B Subbiah & Sons.

22   S H Wriggins (2003) *The Silk Road Journey with Xuan Tsang*,
     Boulder, CO: Westview Press, p 56.

23   Cited in Tan Chung (2018) *China: A Five Thousand Year Odyssey*,
     Sage, Kindle location 2041.

24   Diana Eck, *India: A Sacred Geography.*

25   Swami Tapasyananda, translated (2008) *Sankara-Dig-Vijaya: The
     Traditional Life of Sri Shankaracarya* by Madhava Vidyaranya,
     Chennai: Sri Ramakrishna Math.

26   Qeyamuddin Ahmed edited (1983) *India by Al-Beruni*, Delhi:
     National Book Trust, p. 53.

27 R S Pandit translated (1935) *Rajatarangini: River of Kings, Saga of the Kings of Kashmir,* New Delhi: Sahitya Akademi.

28 Swami Tapasyananda, *Sankara-Dig-Vijaya,* p. 24.

29 Athar Ali (2006) 'The Evolution of the Perception of India' in his *Mughal India: Studies in Polity, Ideas, Society and Culture,* Delhi: Oxford University Press, p. 110.

30 R Nath and Faiyaz 'Gwaliari' translated. (1981) *India as Seen by Amir Khusrau,* Jaipur: Historical Documentation Research Programme.

31 Syed Ali Nadeem Rezavi (2005) 'The Idea of India in Amir Khusrau' in Irfan Habib edited *India: Studies in the History of an Idea,* Delhi: Munshiram Manoharlal, pp. 121–28.

32 Athar Ali (2006) 'The Evolution of the Perception of India', pp. 113–14.

Kashmir and the Rest of India: A Forgotten History

2

Despite Kashmir's prominence in public discourse in this country, her stark absence from historical discourse—from course curricula, textbooks and research programmes in university departments across India—tells a tale. This astonishing academic neglect of a region which, over the millennia, played an extraordinary role in Indian civilisation, has, in no small measure, given rise to a host of misconceptions and misrepresentations. Some of these have dovetailed with separatist politics, which may go a considerable way in explaining the silence on Kashmir's historical identity, especially her long and rich ancient past.

Indeed this country as a whole, not to say Kashmiris themselves, seem to be far more invested in Kashmir's politics than her history. Even when history is invoked, typically commentators speak only about the last 30 years of armed insurgency, or the last 70 years since 1947, or the last 170 years, i.e. 1846, the Treaty of Amritsar when the Dogras took over as the rulers of Jammu and Kashmir. Somehow, it is thought to be adequate to go thus far back and no further to understand Kashmiri identity.

This is very short-term and myopic, and the problem with that is that historical identities of regions do not form in the short term! Typically they are accretionary and cumulative, emerging out of a myriad processes of interfacing with other regions, and form in the long term. But there has been little engagement in public discourse with this *longue durée* identity of Kashmir. We hear a great deal about the relatively recent and constructed political identities of Kashmiris, but we don't hear about their historically evolved selfhood. In this essay, let us attempt to redress this knowledge vacuum by delving into some essential but little-known aspects of 2,000 years of the formative history of this prodigious land.

It bears repetition that the identity of a community or a region is not constructed overnight but formed organically over the *longue durée*. Further, as the 'connected histories' paradigm tells us, regions do not emerge or exist in isolation but in a network of shaping interactions with other regions or a supra region. But when the historical identity of a region so formed is forgotten or denied in the service of conflict, the community involved may disintegrate. Kashmir in recent decades has been in the grip of a similar process of loss through violence. Terrorism in the Valley unleashed, and was predicated on, a denial and erasure of the open, plural and dynamic history of Kashmir, deracinating in the process the Kashmiri community and propping up a fundamentalist narrative and an agenda which, in their closed and exclusionist character, were far removed from the history of the land and its people, as we will see.

One of the pillars of this false narrative has been the refrain that Kashmir was never a part of India historically or culturally. Even among the handful of scholars who did write on ancient Kashmir and should have known better, the deep-rooted assumption has been that Kashmir was somehow hermetically sealed off from the Indian mainland and therefore developed a cultural insularity and 'uniqueness'. Indeed, Kashmir is as unique as any and every region of this most diverse country called India. But the assumption that this uniqueness derived from an isolation from the Indic mainstream is simply unhistorical. In ironic corollary, every aspect of Kashmiri culture was thought, retrojectively, to have non-Indic origins and influences. Nothing could be further from the truth.

One look at cultural markers of identity and mobility in Kashmir from at least the 5th century BCE onwards till the early medieval period— material culture, textual representations, foreign accounts, inscriptions, language, art, religion and philosophy—attests overwhelmingly to how early Kashmir was never isolated or insular, but incredibly open and cosmopolitan, and heavily Indic in her genesis and composition rather than 'unique'. In other words, despite the fact that Kashmir bordered multiple cultural regimes— Iranian, Sogdian, Tibeto-Burman and Indic—she was hardly a cultural hybrid, but epitomised the Indic for two millennia. What follows are the connected histories of Kashmir and the rest of India, which the world has conveniently forgotten.[1]

❧ ❧

First the macro picture. As we saw in Chapter 1, there was a clear idea of India in existence long before the British colonised us—and Kashmir was always a part of it! Thus it will surprise many that the earliest Sanskrit text to define 'Bharatavarsha', the *Mahabharata* 6.10.52 (dating to at least

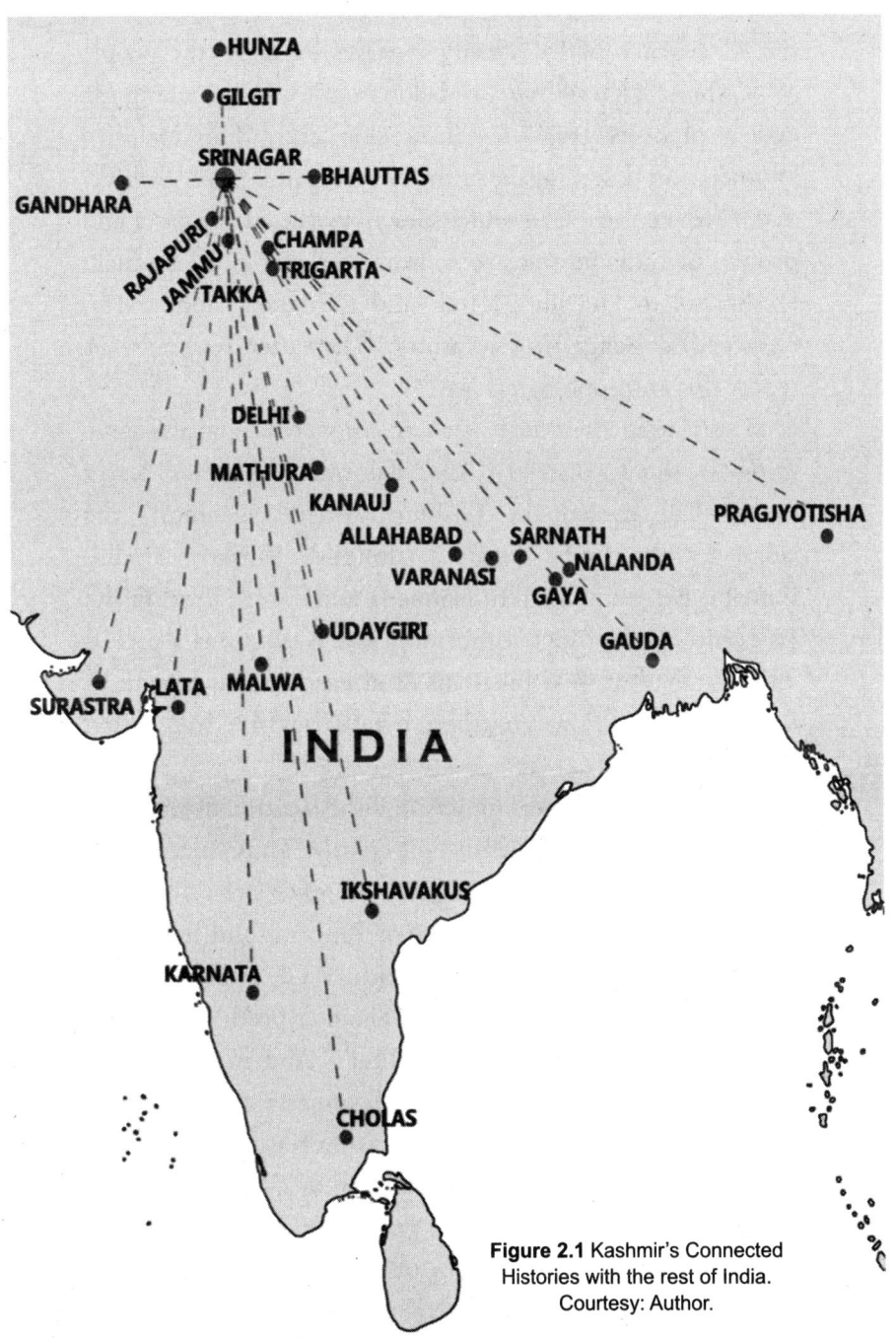

Figure 2.1 Kashmir's Connected
Histories with the rest of India.
Courtesy: Author.

the 4th century BCE), already includes by name the people of Kashmir (*Kashmirah*) as belonging to India, alongside dozens of other *jana*s inhabiting this land.[2] This inclusive enumeration is seen again in the encyclopedic *Brhat Samhita* V. 70 (6th century CE) which describes the many parts and peoples of India in one sweep, from Kashmir and Gandhara (Peshawar) to Dravidas, Kerala and Karnataka, and Assam, Odisha and Bengal to Saurashtra.[3] Thereafter *mahapuranas* repeat this anthropological feat.

Later, resident Indo-Persian voices were saying the same thing. In the 14th century, Amir Khusrau in his *Nuh Sipihr* (3.5.69–72) named the Kashmiri tongue as among the languages of 'Hind' (*hindawi*), alongside Sanskrit, Sindhi, Punjabi, Bengali, Gujarati, Kannada and Tamil.[4] And in the 16th century, the Mughals not only saw Kashmir as a part of 'Hindustan', but their historian Abul Fazl made it a point to distinguish Hindustan's northern boundaries from Iran, Turan and China.[5]

If this is how insiders understood the location of Kashmir, outsiders to India believed no differently. Thus Xuan Zang, the 7th century CE Chinese pilgrim, in his first person account of travels through 'Indu', speaks of Kashmir and its capital Srinagari at length.[6] In the 11th century CE, the Persian Al biruni described north Kashmir's Sharada peetha as among the top three shrines of entire 'Hind'.[7] And in the 16th to 18th centuries, Tibetan Buddhist chroniclers such as Lama Taranath named their ancient gurus from Kashmir as coming from India, which they called 'rGya-gar' or 'Phagsyul'.

And yet perhaps the most graphic historical testimony remains the pan-Indic voyages of Shankaracharya. This 8th century CE Indian seer-intellectual undertook, we are told, a famous tour of philosophical conquest of the land, intensely debating the varied local scholarship across the length and breadth of this country. Setting out from his home in Kaladi, Kerala, he consciously chose none other than Kashmir—specifically the Sharada peetha known as the seat of all learning (*sarvajñapeetha*)—as the fitting culmination and validation of his scholarly travels. (*Shankara Digvijaya* 16.186–195).[8] The ancient Shankaracharya temple at Srinagar still stands witness to the memory of this epic visit as also to the breathtaking centrality of Kashmir in the far north of India to the imagination of its far south, and vice versa.

Thus, textual testimony after testimony from observers outside Kashmir—from the rest of India and foreign chroniclers—established a clear understanding of her belonging well within 'India' from at least the 5th century BCE onwards. It is only natural then that evidence from inside early Kashmir—archaeology, linguistics, script, politics, art, literature, philosophy, religion—also attests to a constant synchronicity with the Indic mainland. Yet this has been completely overlooked in the modern narrative on the Valley. Let us look at some of these cultural markers from Kashmir's founding history.

Civilisation arises in Kashmir at the same time as in the rest of India circa 6th century BCE, and in the same form, designated as the Northern Black Polished Ware culture. NBPW is associated with the rise and spread of cities, punch marked coinage, commerce, and state society in the Ganga Valley and central India, and then over most of the subcontinent, in a phenomenon known as Second Urbanisation. The site of Semthan, 44 kilometres south of Srinagar, has yielded important evidence of this diagnostic NBPW material culture from 500 to 200 BCE, including the same deluxe pottery, silver and copper punch marked coins (including a type associated with the Mauryan empire and belonging to Bihar!), building construction, copper and iron objects, and stone and terracotta beads.[9]

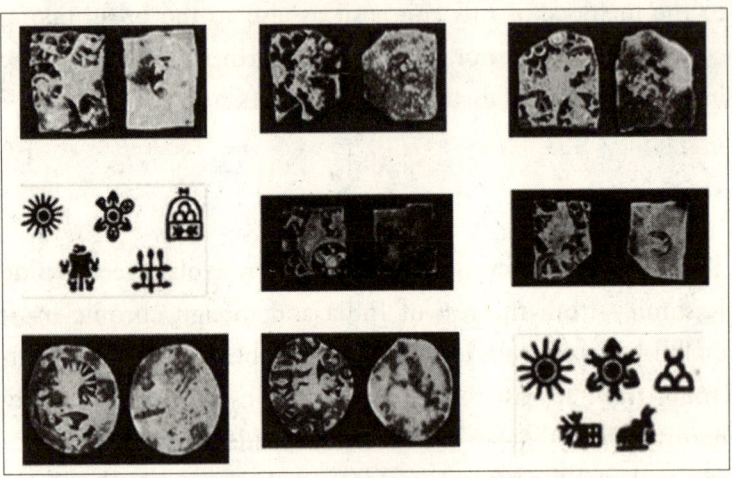

Figure 2.2 Magadhan punch-marked coins found at Semthan, Jammu and Kashmir, 4th century BCE. Courtesy: SPS Museum, Srinagar.

All these appearing in the Valley simultaneously with the rest of India is significant—but should not be surprising. For Kashmir was in fact within reach of one of the two great pan-Indic trade and communication routes of the time, the northern Uttarapatha, which ran from Peshawar to Bengal, and in turn connected with the southern Dakshinapatha, which extended from Bihar into peninsular and coastal India.

Now, Kashmir was geographically and historically proximate to two of the northwesternmost cities of the

Uttarapatha: Takshashila in the Peshawar plains via the Baramulla Pass, and Shakala (Sialkot) in Punjab through the Sidau, Toshamaidan and Pir Panjal Passes. So, the great ancient Indian travel and communication network was connected through Shakala and Takshashila to Srinagar, in the process no doubt transmitting Indic culture—material and intellectual—back and forth. In fact Takshashila and Shakala themselves were great centres of Sanskritic learning.

🌿

Speaking of Sanskrit, it is among the earliest historical languages we have in Kashmir, just like the rest of India. This is seen in the first Kashmiri texts, *Nilamata Purana* (7th century CE) and *Rajatarangini* (12th century CE), composed in Sanskrit; in the long list of Kashmiri place-names that are all derived from Sanskrit (Anantnag, Srinagar, Sopore, Harwan, Baramulla, Tulmul, Kanraz, Maraz and so on); and in a large number of the coins and inscriptions recovered, not just from Kashmir but also from Gilgit-Baltistan, Jammu, Ladakh and Peshawar, which mention the Indic epithets of local kings such as *maharaja* and *shri,* and their Sanskritic names such as Meghavahana, Navasurendradityavarman and Lalitaditya. Iconic historical documents from this wider culture region, such as the Buddhist Gilgit manuscript and the mathematical Bakhshali manuscript, are also in Sanskrit.

Indeed, it is through Kashmir and Gilgit-Baltistan that Sanskrit, which was described by the 7th century CE Chinese traveller Xuan Zang as "the language of India", spread in the trans-Himalayas, that is, in Khotan, Kucha, Turfan and Sogdia, along with Buddhism. There is abundant epigraphic and manuscript evidence for this in those lands from the fifth to the tenth centuries CE.[10]

But what about Kashmiri, the vernacular tongue? Though there is little evidence of it being written before the 13th century CE, literary references suggest that it was spoken from early on. The origins of Kashmiri is a significant question, since language is deemed an important indicator of ethnic and cultural identity. So where did Kashmiri come from?

George Grierson's view from 150 years ago that Kashmiri was a Dardic language, and not an Indo-Aryan (IA) one such as Sanskrit, has long been rejected. After the work of linguists George Morgenstierne and Colin Masica, it is now known that the so-called Dardic languages such as Kashmiri and Shina cannot be distinguished from IA languages at all, but are simply "a bundle of aberrant IA hill languages".[11] Moreover, as S S Toshkhani and others have demonstrated, Kashmiri can be traced to a form of speech that closely resembles archaic or Vedic Sanskrit, sometimes mediated through Prakrit.[12] Thus Kashmiri and Sanskrit—and indeed the vast majority of Indian languages from the IA family—would then be cognate languages, so that we are looking at a horizontal continuum between Kashmir and the rest of India linguistically as well.

❧ ❧

Apart from Kashmir's early archaeology, historical geography and linguistic roots, which proved to be deeply Indic, another telling cultural marker is script or the writing system of early Kashmir. After a brief appearance by Kharoshti on coins in Kashmir and other parts of north-west India, by the 3rd century CE the Brahmi script—from which the vast majority of Indian scripts today are derived—had taken over completely, not just in the Valley but in the wider culture region. In fact in Kashmir, the earliest inscribed letters in Brahmi dating much earlier to 150 BCE have been found from the walls of Sultan Zainul Abidin's mother's 15th century tomb in Srinagar, while in Kishtwar, the Bathishtal cave inscription, dating to 3rd century CE, is the earliest to be found in Jammu. This is followed by a number of coins issued by Kashmiri kings carrying Brahmi legends. Also, 80% of the 5,000 ancient inscriptions found in Hunza, Gilgit, Chilas and the Karakoram Highway in PoK are in this quintessential Indic script. And, as the epigraphist Oskar von Hinüber tells us, the writing style here shows affinities with, remarkably, Western Mathura Brahmi![13]

Similarly, when Sharada, the script par excellence of Kashmir, evolved from Brahmi circa 8th century CE, it was under the influence of Eastern Allahabad Brahmi, pointing again to astonishing connectivity.[14] Sharada, in turn, was used beyond Kashmir across NWFP, Peshawar, Ladakh, Kangra, Chamba and Punjab right up till Delhi and Mathura.

All in all, it is obvious that Kashmir partook of shaping material and cultural formations of early India. But that's not all. From the beginning, she was also a part of pan-Indian political formations such as the 3rd century BCE Mauryan Empire, which stretched across the subcontinent. Emperor Ashoka is believed to have founded the capital city of Srinagari, a local memory we hear of not only in the *Rajatarangini* I.104 (12th century CE), the 'first' history of Kashmir, but even earlier in the Chinese traveller Xuan Zang's account of his visit to the Valley (7th century CE).[15] Recall that numismatists identified Mauryan imperial issues among the punch-marked coins found in Semthan, and that the iconic

Shankaracharya temple at Srinagar is located at the site of the Jyestheshvara temple said to be erected by Ashoka's putative son and successor in Kashmir.

Kashmir was also a part of trans-regional Indic kingdoms of the Kushanas (2nd–3rd century CE) and Hunas (6th century CE), which extended at different points in time till Banaras and Malwa respectively. Further, kings, queens and ministers of Kashmir were drawn from and in alliance with different parts of India across the centuries. Would you believe it that Kashmir and Gandhara (Peshawar) were known to be political allies of Magadha or ancient Bihar! (*Harivamsa* II. 34. 20).[16] Indeed, Kashmir had complex marital and political histories with regions very far away and deep within the Indic mainland such as Pragjyotisha (Assam), Gauda (Bengal) and Tamilakam.

For example, Meghavahana (5th century CE), the great-grandson of an exiled king of Kashmir, was given asylum by the king of Gandhara who, in time, sent him across the length of the Himalayas to Pragjyotisha for the *svayamvara* of its princess. Winning her hand, Meghavahana returned loaded with wealth and the royal Vishnu parasol of the Assamese king. He was then invited by the ministers of Kashmir to ascend the throne (*RT* II. 145–51; III. 3–15). Similarly, Bhikshachara (12th century CE), a prince of Kashmir cast away at birth, grew up in the Malwa king's court in the Deccan as his adopted son. Eventually he returned to Kashmir and won back the crown (*RT* VIII. 224–8; VIII. 842–8).

Still, other rulers from Malwa such as Pratapaditya and Matrigupta (6th–7th century CE), believed to be descendants of the legendary emperor Vikramaditya, were invited by Kashmiris to be their king. This was due in part to their lineage, showing Kashmir's subscription to the north Indian politico-mythic universe. Several queens of Kashmir were also drawn from remote regions including Cholamandalam (Tamil Nadu), Assam (as we saw before in Meghavahana's case), Andhra, Jalandhara (Punjab) and Kalanjara (Madhya Pradesh).[17] Complementing the diverse nature of Kashmiri royalty was the eclectic composition of other ruling elites over the centuries. King Lalitaditya (8th century CE), known as the universal ruler (*sarvabhauma*), had a Tuhkhara spiritual advisor, Ston-pa; Jayapida's (6th century CE) chamberlain was the ruler of Mathura; Anantadeva's (10th century CE) jester was from the Ganga plains, while his ministers were from Kangra and, again, Malwa (*RT* IV. 246; VII.189, 190–3, 204).

Interestingly, in the service of King Harsha (11th century CE) were people from Punjab and also from far-off Karnataka. Indeed the dynamic, if quixotic, Harsha spectacularly introduced Kannada couture in the royal court at Srinagar, and also a new coin type depicting the elephant—an emblem far removed from Kashmiri ecology and imagination— under inspiration from the same type issued by the Gangas of Karnataka (RT VII. 675, 926, 1207)! What an incredibly open and cosmopolitan land Kashmir was!

Figure 2.3 Gold coin with elephant motif issued by King Harshadeva, 11th century CE, inspired from coins of the Ganga dynasty of Karnataka. Courtesy: Cunningham Collection of the British Museum.

Not just that, the *Rajatarangini* tells us that several Kashmiri rulers undertook military expeditions deep into the subcontinent. Most notably, Lalitaditya undertook conquests in north and east India, including against Kanyakubja (Kanauj, Uttar Pradesh), the symbol of imperial sovereignty in early medieval times which was coveted also by the Rashtrakutas of Maharashtra, Pratiharas of Rajasthan and Palas of Bengal. But while we famously hear in history textbooks of this "tripartite struggle" over Kanauj, Kashmir is never mentioned! This is despite the fact that Lalitaditya's 'Shripratapa' coins have been found in large hoards from half a dozen places in Uttar Pradesh and Bihar such as Sarnath, Bhitare, Aunjhar and Nalanda, reaffirming the political and commercial presence of Kashmiris in the Ganga valley.[18]

Figure 2.4a King Lalitaditya Muktapida, 8th century CE. Artist's Impression. Courtesy: Wikimedia Commons.

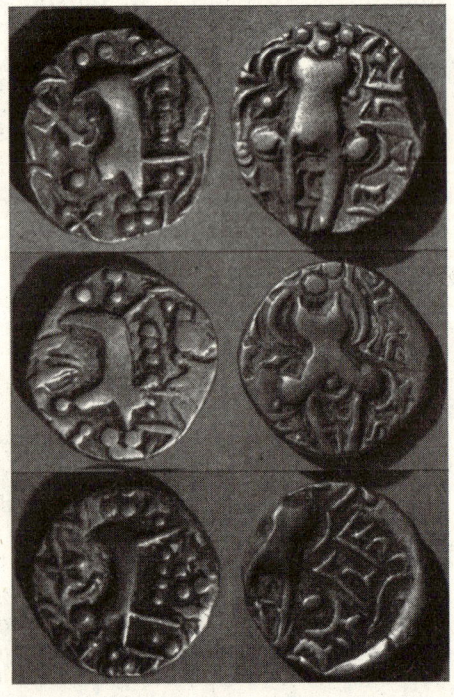

Figure 2.4b King Lalitaditya's alloy 'Shripratapa' coins found in Banda district, Uttar Pradesh. Courtesy: SPS Museum, Srinagar.

Thus, Kashmir's internal politics did not exist in isolation at all, but was a porous process from the beginning, inextricably tied up with other regions of the Indian subcontinent, near and far. This squares with, and must have flowed into and out of, the social and cultural interconnectedness of early Kashmir and the rest of India that is on view.

We have so far surveyed Kashmir's early archaeology, historical geography, linguistics, writing systems and political foundations, all of which demonstrates her participation in seminal Indic material, cultural and political formations. We will continue to see more evidence of the same, but let us first turn to the remarkable historical process that seems to have underlaid this intense connectivity between Kashmir and the rest of India. This is a process crucial in history, yet virtually ignored by scholars of Kashmir, namely, migration. Of course we often hear of the influx of groups from west and central Asia as late as the 14th–18th centuries, bringing Islam to the Valley and shaping what is understood as Kashmiri popular culture today. What we never hear of is the fact that long before this, people from different corners of India travelled to and settled in Kashmir over some two millennia.

We saw how a number of kings and queens of Kashmir were drawn from other parts of India, as near as Punjab on the one hand and as far as Assam, Andhra and Tamil Nadu, on the other. In similar fashion, ministers at Srinagar could hail from Kangra, Mathura, Malwa and even Karnataka. They no doubt brought with them their own customs and traditions.

However, while regional courts attracting men from far

and wide may not be exceptional, in Kashmir we seem to be looking at a society-wide phenomenon. For, in the 12th century CE *Rajatarangini*, we hear of not only courtiers but commoners, in fact a mixed bag of individuals and groups migrating to Kashmir in pursuit of their vocations. Thus we find students from Gauda (Bengal), traders from Rauhitaka and Takka (Haryana and Punjab), magicians from Dravidadesha (South India), graziers from Khasha (Nepal), artisans and horse dealers from the Gangetic plains and sex workers "from different regions". Kings Jayapida, Lalitaditya, Avantivarman and Harsha (6th–11th centuries CE), in particular, are said to have gathered from many lands various learned men. And of course there are common references to brahmans and *bhikkhus* from Madhyadesha (Gangetic plains), as also from Gandhara in one instance, from Dravidadesha, and from Saurashtra and Lata (Gujarat), being settled in large numbers by several kings in the Valley or flocking to it on their own (*RT* I. 307–12, I. 341–3, VI. 300, VI. 300, VIII. 2444; III. 3–15, IV. 244).

On view then are not only state but also non-state actors in Kashmir's remarkable prehistory of immigration, and a host of pursuits—education, commerce, pilgrimage, art and employment—that brought them there from other parts of the subcontinent. Not only does this attest to an open and dynamic society, the demographic implications of this little-noted phenomenon may also be fundamental. Who is the Kashmiri ethnically—this becomes a moot question now and far removed from the exclusionist and separate status that has been claimed in modern times.

What's more, as if in historical corollary, we see Kashmiris moving to other parts of India as well, though the exact scale remains to be determined. This included, again, kings and ministers who turned India-ward on abdication or retirement to live in cities such as Banaras and Prayag (*RT* III.297; IV.414–20; VII.646, 1007–8; VIII.13); and Kashmiri generals on the one hand, and scholars and litterateurs on the other, who took employment in courts as far south as the Deccan and as far east as Mithila (Bihar). One need only recall the renowned Sanskrit poet Bilhana (11th century CE) in the service of the Western Chalukyan King Vikramaditya VI of Kalyana (Karnataka), or Mahapandita Shakyashribhadra (13th century CE), who headed the universities at Vikramshila and Odantpuri (Bihar). The latter was known as Kache Panchen ('Kashmiri Pandit') in Tibet, where also he taught Buddhism.

Further, 12th–15th century CE Chola and Pandya inscriptions from Shrirangam, Chidambaram, Tirruvoruyur (Tamil Nadu) and Kalahasti (Andhra), among other places, fascinatingly speak of original natives of *Kashmiradesha* as resident, landed persons holding high official posts (*rayan*) there![19] They also mention donations by and to Kashmiris centred on the Shaiva and Vaishnava temples. Beyond individuals, it is also popularly believed that Saraswat Brahmans migrated from Kashmir to other parts of India, especially the Konkan coast.

Similarly, we hear of Kashmiri merchants plying their trade at Bhrigukachchha (Bharuch), the famous ancient port on the Gujarat coast, while Kashmiri pilgrims frequented the holy site of Gaya (Bihar) for obsequies in such numbers that, as the *Rajatarangini* (VI.254, VII.1008) tells us, a Kashmiri minister in the 9th century CE sought tax exemption for them from the local ruler there!

This episode perhaps aptly symbolises early Kashmiri identity, which seemed to consist in a distinct regional self-

Figure 2.5 Ranganathaswamy temple, Srirangam, Tamil Nadu, where a 12th century CE inscription refers to a 'gift of land in association with Aryan Vasudeva Bhattan alias Brahma Rayan from Kashmiradesham'. Courtesy: Wikimedia Commons.

awareness in the midst of an overarching subscription to all-India beliefs and practices. Indeed, as all the evidence surveyed suggests, for the first two thousand years or more of their history, Kashmiris never seemed to see a conflict between their local and pan-Indic affiliations and wore both with ease and pride.

We saw how early Kashmir's archaeology, historical geography, linguistics, writing systems, political formations and even demography were dynamically shaped in sync with other regions of India—a connected history long silenced and conveniently forgotten by the rush to separatist politics. It is no wonder then that for the first two millennia, Kashmiri culture—art, religion, philosophy and literature—also resonated with the Indic and vice versa.

Thus, as John Siudmak has shown, Kashmiri stone art or sculpture, in every one of its stages from the 4th century CE onwards at Bijbehara, Baramulla and Pandrethan, displayed a constant and concrete synchronicity with Gupta, post-Gupta and Pala art styles of three centres thousands of miles away, namely, Sarnath (Uttar Pradesh), Udayagiri (Madhya Pradesh) and Nalanda (Bihar).[20] The shared idiom was possibly because of itinerant artists from these places coming to work in ateliers in Kashmir. This repertoire included all-India icons such as the Buddha, *Boddhisattva, Trimurti, Vaikuntha Vishnu, Vasudeva, Ekamukhalinga, Maheshvara* as *Bhuteshvara, Brahma,* many-armed *Durgamahishasuramardini, Kali, Surya, Ganesha, Kartikeya, Harihara* and *Matrikas* such as *Indrani* and *Chamunda,* complete with ensigns such as *yajnopavit* (sacred thread), *vanamala* (garland) and *vahana* (vehicle).

Figure 2.6a Ganesha, Kashmir, 9th century CE, Bronze. SPS Museum, Srinagar. Courtesy: Author.

Figure 2.6b Nataraja, Kashmir, 9th century CE, Bronze. SPS Museum, Srinagar. Courtesy: Author.

Figure 2.6c Ekamukhalinga, Kashmir, 6th century CE, Stone. Courtesy:
Metropolitan Museum of Art Cultural Commons.

Figure 2.6d Vaikuntha Vishnu, Kashmir, 9th century CE, Stone. Courtesy:
Metropolitan Museum of Art Cultural Commons.

Figure 2.6e Brahma, Kashmir, 9th century CE, Stone. SPS Museum, Srinagar.
Courtesy: Author.

Figure 2.6f Buddha, Kashmir, 9th–10th centuries CE, Bronze. SPS Museum, Srinagar. Courtesy: Author.

Figure 2.7a Gold coin of Kushana King Huvishka showing Shiva (Oesho) and Uma (Ommo). Kashmir, 2ⁿᵈ century CE. Courtesy: Classical Numismatic Group CNG.

Figure 2.7b Gold coin of King Meghavahana showing Shiva with trident, lion sprawled at his feet, and seated Shri Lakshmi, Kashmir, 5ᵗʰ century CE. Courtesy: Toddywalla Auctions.

In fact, even the beautiful iconography on standard Kashmiri gold coins, right from the Kushanas (2ⁿᵈ century CE) and Kidaras (5ʰ century CE) for the next 1200 years, depicts Shiva with his *trishula* (trident) on the obverse and a seated Sri Lakshmi, lotus in hand, on the reverse, a motif familiar from other North Indian dynastic issues as well.

Famed Kashmiri bronzes, preserved in the monasteries of Ladakh and Tibet, also show the influence of the late Buddhist Pala school of Bihar and Bengal. Fascinatingly, the *Rajatarangini* (IV. 259) narrates how King Lalitaditya (8ᵗʰ century CE) brought back with him to Kashmir from Magadha (Bihar) colossal Buddha statues gleaming in bronze, strapped on the backs of elephants—a local memory of a momentous transfer of artwork that evokes the artistic and religious interconnectedness of the two regions. The technique used for the bronze making, called *cire purdue*, was also pan-Indian.

Indeed from the very beginning, Kashmiris worshipped the same deities as the rest of India, be it Shiva, Shakti, Vishnu or the Buddha, and their respective pantheons. It is Kashmiris, such as Kumarajiva (4th century CE), son of a Kashmiri brahmana and a Kuchean princess, who took Buddhism to China and Central Asia, on the one hand, and esoteric Shiva Advaita (Kashmir Shaivism) to the Deccan, on the other. While preserving their own special rituals, Kashmiris observed all the same festivals as the rest of India, be it Ganesh Chaturthi (*Pann*), Shivaratri (*Herath*) or Janmashtami (*Zaram satam*), even as the Devi remained central to Kashmiri selfhood (see Chapter 3).

It is no wonder then that, dedicated to Shakti-Saraswati, the Sharada temple, at present lying derelict in PoK, was once thronged by devotees from as far as Bengal in the 8th century CE (*RT* IV.322–33), and was listed by Al biruni in the 11th century CE as among the top three shrines of all of Al Hind (India). And till today, daily Hindu prayers in Tamil Nadu intriguingly begin with the invocation *sharadadevi kashmir-puravasini namastute* (salutations to the goddess Sharada of Kashmir). Premodern Indic connectivity, and Kashmir's role in it, are truly mindboggling!

And finally, we are not to forget the long line of virtuoso Kashmiri grammarians such as Patanjali and poets such as Kalhana, Bilhana, Somadeva and Kshemendra, linguists and rhetoricians such as Vamana, Udbhata, Mammata and Anandavardhana, musicologists like Sharangadeva, and philosophers and yogis like Utpaladeva and the doyen Abhinavagupta. These scholars from the Valley revolutionised Sanskrit literature, ethics, aesthetics and metaphysics, virtually monopolising the intellectual scene across the Indian subcontinent from the first into the second millennium CE. Their works circulated widely and were studied as learned models as far as, again, the deep South, something that a scholar has colourfully described as saffron in the *rasam*![21]

So thoroughly Indic thus was Kashmir's foundational history and so crucial was Kashmiri participation in the subcontinent's affairs in the *longue durée*. How did this happen if Kashmir was never a part of India? And yet thousands of lives have been lost over this question. I believe the erasure of this history from living memory is the root of disinformation and conflict in the Valley. The Kashmiri today may not know from where they come and what their rich Indic legacy is, thanks to the fallacious identity discourse of the separateness of their land—a discourse that has done great epistemic violence most of all to the Kashmiri community, severing them from their own illustrious past. However, history cannot be wished away simply because it does not suit politics. Instead, it is perhaps in the reclamation and acceptance of her plural, open and cosmopolitan histories that the path to peace and reconciliation in Kashmir may yet lie.

Notes

1   Attempts to suppress this history are still on. See for example this recent publication that brazenly plagiarised the title, paradigm and approach of my book *The Making of Early Kashmir: Landscape and Identity in the Rajatarangini* (2018) only to repeat the hackneyed misrepresentation of early Kashmir as anything but Indic in culture. See Mohammad Ashraf Wani and Aman Ashraf Wani (2023) *The Making of Early Kashmir: Intercultural Networks and Identity Formation,* Delhi: Routledge. For other attempts to discredit this powerful history, see Chapter 16 in *Bharata Before the British.*

2   V S Sukthankar edited (1947) *Mahabharata,* Pune: Bhandarkar Oriental Research Institute.

3   Panditabhushana V Subrahmanya Sastri and Vidwan M Ramakrishna Bhat translated (1946) *Varahamihira's Brihat Samhita* Bangalore: MBD Electric Printing Works.

4   R Nath and Faiyaz 'Gwaliari' translated (1981) *India as Seen by Amir Khusrau,* Jaipur: Historical Documentation Research Programme.

5   Athar Ali (2006) 'The Evolution of the Perception of India' in his *Mughal India: Studies in Polity, Ideas, Society and Culture.* Delhi: Oxford University Press, pp.113–14.

6   Sally Hovey Wriggins (2003), *The Silk Road Journey with Xuan Zang* USA: Westview Press, p. 56.

7   Qeyamuddin Ahmad edited (1983), *India by Al-Beruni,* Delhi: National Book Trust, p. 53.

8   Swami Tapasyananda translated (2008) *Sankara-Dig-Vijaya: The Traditional Life of Sri Shankaracharya,* Chennai: Sri Ramakrishna Math.

9   G S Gaur (1987) 'Semthan Excavation: A Step towards Bridging the Gap between the Neolithic and the Kushan Period in Kashmir' in B M Pande and B D Chattopadhyaya edited, *Archaeology and History: Essays in the memory of A. Ghosh,* vol. I, Delhi: Agam Kala Prakashan. pp. 327–37. Iqbal Ahmad (2013) *Kashmir Coins,* Delhi: Dilpreet

Publishers, p. 13; and *Indian Archaeology: A Review*, 1980–1.

10 Lore Sander (1989) 'Remarks on the Formal Brahmi of Gilgit, Bamiyan and Khotan' in Karl Jettmar edited, *Antiquities of Northern Pakistan: Reports and Studies*, vol. I, *Rock Inscriptions in the Indus Valley*, Mainz: Verlag Phillip von Zabern, pp. 114–15. K Warikoo (2014) 'Karakoram Himalayas and Central Asia: The Buddhist Connection', in K Warikoo edited *The Other Kashmir: Society, Culture and Politics in the Karakoram Himalayas*, Delhi: Pentagon Press, pp. 19–22.

11 George Morgenstierne (1961) 'Dardic and Kafir Languages', *The Encyclopaedia of Islam*, vol. 2, Fasc. 25, Leiden: E J Brill, pp. 138–9. Colin P Masica (1991) *The Indo-Aryan Languages*, Cambridge: Cambridge University Press.

12 S S Toshkhani (1985) 'Some Important Aspects of Kashmiri as a Language', in K.L Kalla edited, *The Literary Heritage of Kashmir*, Delhi: Mittal Publications, pp. 18–23.

13 Jason Neelis (2006) 'Hunza-Haldeikish Revisited: Epigraphical Evidence for Trans-Regional History' In Herman Kreutzmann edited, *Karakoram in Transition: Culture, Development and Ecology in the Hunza Valley*, Karachi: Oxford University Press, pp. 164, 167.

14 Lore Sander, 'Remarks on the Formal Brahmi of Gilgit, Bamiyan and Khotan,' p. 110.

15 R S Pandit translated (1935) *Rajatarangini: River of Kings, Saga of the Kings of Kashmir*, New Delhi: Sahitya Akademi.

16 A Purushothaman and A Harindranath translated (1936) *Harivamsa Purana* based on the Chitrashala Press edition edited by Pandit Ramachandrashastri Kinjawadekar. Source: http://mahabharata-resources.org/harivamsa/harivamsa-cs-index.html.

17 See Shonaleeka Kaul (2018) *The Making of Early Kashmir: Landscape and Identity in the Rajatarangini*, Delhi: Oxford University Press for all details.

18 Iqbal Ahmad, *Kashmir Coins*, Srinagar: Dilpreet Publisher, p. 38.

19 *South Indian Inscriptions*, vol.24 (1982) No. 84, *Annual Report of Indian Epigraphy* vol. 369 (1911); vol. 146 (1922), vol. 600 (1926), vol. 345 (1928–29), vol. 14 (1936–7) [sic] as cited in S Chandni Bi (2013) 'Kashmir in Tamil Epigraphs' in *Epigraphical Society of India Annual Proceedings*, vol. 39, pp. 74–83.

20 John Siudmak (2013) *The Hindu–Buddhist Sculpture of Ancient Kashmir and Its Influences*, Leiden: E.J. Brill, p. 211.

21 Whitney Cox (2006) 'Saffron in the Rasam', in Y Bronner, W Cox, and L McCrea, edited, *South Asian Texts in History: Critical Engagements with Sheldon Pollock*, Delhi: Primus Books, pp. 177–201. Tenth century CE Kashmiri texts being studied in south India in the 15th century has also been acknowledged by Sheldon Pollock (2004) 'Sanskrit Literary Culture from the Inside Out', in his edited *Literary Cultures in History: Reconstructions from South Asia*, New Delhi: Oxford University Press, p. 112.

Shakti Worship and Selfhood in Kashmir

3

While Shakti worship is iconic in Bengal, and the more convivial forms associated with it, such as the *garba* dance, exist in Gujarat, few know that, historically, it is in Kashmir that the Goddess has been central to the definition of regional identity and selfhood.

The feminine divine can be studied in different ways: one would be the theological perspective, looking at the nature and functions and symbolism of the Goddess, often esoteric; the other related way is iconological, looking at how the Goddess was represented in a variety of media like stone, bronze and clay, and why. In this essay, however, we shall not go into the theology or the iconology of the Goddess. I shall instead try to show that at the level of popular conceptualisation and practice, goddess worship in Kashmir was not just iconographic but topographic.

In other words, I will look at the geo-mythologies within which god and goddess cults were conceived in early Kashmir both textually and on the ground. I will argue that Shakti is tied up intimately with the way the land of Kashmir itself has been culturally understood and mapped over time as seen in her founding texts *Nilamata Purana* (7th century CE), Kalhana's *Rajatarangini* (12th century CE) and *Bhringisha Samhita* (17th century). I will focus on river, spring and hill goddesses, with a detailed reference to the three paramount *devi*s of Kashmir worshipped to this day—Sharada, Sharika and Ragnya. This is because, true to the pan-Indian pattern, mythology and geography in Kashmir were, as Diana Eck would put it, "a joint imaginative and descriptive undertaking".[1] Geographical knowledge was "grounded in the mythical apprehension of the world's meaning and order",[2] even as myth-making and religion itself were resonant with the natural markers of the land, which generated a sense of place and rootedness in the Valley.

❧ ❧

All major Hindu gods and goddesses have been worshipped in Kashmir for millennia. This is well attested, not just in the ancient texts but in the plethora of iconographic representations of these pan-Indic deities found all over the Valley from early on. These include not only colossal Shiva lingas, Bhuteshwaras and Vaikuntha Vishnus, but resplendent images of the Goddess as both Durga Mahisasuramardini and Parvati with family, as also Kali and *matrikas* such as Chamunda.

Figure 3.1a Kali, Kashmir, 8th century CE, SPS Museum, Srinagar. Courtesy: Author.

Figure 3.1b Durga Mahishasuramardini, Pulwama, Jammu and Kashmir, 8th century CE, SPS Museum, Srinagar. Courtesy: Author.

Alongside this *saguna* (theistic) tradition, a *nirguna* (monist) Shaiva-Shaktism emerged in Kashmir known as Trika. Built up by a series of scholar-*siddhas* such as Utpaladeva, Abhinavagupta, Lalleshwari and Lakshmanjoo (8th–20th centuries), Trika became emblematic of Kashmiri belief, shaping even Islamic Sufism when it arrived in the 14th century.

According to this yogic/tantric school, the universe is replete with one supreme consciousness called Parama Shiva, and Shakti, primeval energy, is its principle of creation. Realising this truth is *moksha* and Kashmir was literally the place to attain it since liberation suffused its very ecology, as it were.

For example, Harmukh ('mouth of Shiva'), the towering holy mountain approximately 45 km north of Srinagar, is also the name of the point in the human body at which the *kundalini shakti* lies coiled in the *muladhara chakra*, and, when awakened, can ascend to pure consciousness. Further, see this verse from Lal Ded or Lalleshwari, the iconic Shaiva yogini of 14th century Kashmir, invoking the hydraulic origins of the Valley (discussed later), and describing Kashmir as a bridge to salvation:

I saw, once, the waters that flowed
From the mouth of Shiva (Harmukh)
To the Foot of Vishnu (Vishnupad)
Becoming a bridge across the illusory world (samsara)[3]

Vishnupad or Konser Nag is approximately 65 km south of Srinagar. This allegorical verse thus beautifully captures not just the north-south extent of Kashmir but the complete overlap between her physical and spiritual domains. Goddess Parvati too is associated with the vicinity of Konser Nag at Naubandhana peak, having transformed herself into a great boat (*nau*) to save life forms during the deluge.

Indeed Shakti worship defines Kashmiri identity through a close association with the very land and waters of Kashmir. The *Nilamata Purana* (verse 172–80) and Kalhana's *Rajatarangini* (I. 25–27), the 'first' history of Kashmir, speak of a special land that was not just born of the Goddess but embodied her as well.[4] Thus the originary myth of the formation of Kashmir from the *Satisaras* or the lake of Sati, Shiva's wife. This lake was said to be inhabited by a demon to kill whom, on the request of the sage Kashyap, the gods drained the water, revealing a land fit for human settlement. There is thus a founding association of the land with the Goddess. The very name Kashmir is said to carry within it the syllable for water, 'ka', as the *Nilamata* (verse 227) tells us. This is the first of several myths which combine geology and tradition in Kashmir. For we know that the geomorphological formation of the Valley did occur from a primordial lake many thousands of years ago, evidently a memory preserved in this myth.

Moreover, the valley did not drain out completely and a number of residual lakes, pools and springs have remained in Kashmir, inaugurating a wetland ecology. These are known as *kunda* or more commonly *naga*, which is also the term for serpent and refers to both the lakes and their tutelary deities in Kashmir. And so, in the *Rajatarangini* (I.28) too, Kashmir is described as "the land of the *naga*s which is under the protection of Nila, the king of the *naga*s, whose parasol is the swelling Nila *kunda* (modern Verinag) with the flowing waters of the Vitasta for his staff".

After this opening statement enshrining the river and its lake as central to the idea of Kashmir, significantly, in both the *Nilamata* (verse 260, 1426) and the *Rajatarangini* (I.29), the river Vitasta is declared the goddess Parvati (*vitasta yatra parvati*). But that's not all. Kashmir herself is Parvati! The *Nilamata* (verse 245–46) has no less than lord Vishnu declare: "*Kashmirah parvati raja tatra haranshajah jneyo*" (Kashmir is Parvati; know her king to be a portion of Hara [or Shiva]). So, Kashmir is instated as the very embodiment of Shakti again.

Indeed, the many perennial rivers with which Kashmir is blessed constitute the first and ubiquitous form of the feminine divine. These were the Saraswati, Sindhu, Trikoni, Vishoka, Krishna, Madhumati and Paroshni, among others, all of which merged with the boon-giving and celestial Vitasta (*NP* 1446–7). A sacralising of the complete riverine network of Kashmir is seen in a fashion that both appropriates the pan-Indic goddess Shakti and rivals the iconic rivers of the Indic supraregion such as Ganga and Yamuna, which were long invested with boon giving and celestial powers. Thus it is said in the *Nilamata*: "The Ganga does not excel the Vitasta. The Vitasta supercedes the Ganga as the Ganga only leads to heaven, while the Vitasta paves the way to liberation" (*NP* 1427–29, 322).

One also hears of the *sapta Ganga* or seven Kashmiri rivers deemed as venerable as the Ganga (*NP* 621–22). In keeping with the deemed sanctity of rivers that were the Goddess incarnate, a host of pious ceremonies such as *homa, vrata, upavasa* and an entire ritual economy was founded on the banks of Kashmir's rivers at the numerous redemptive *tirtha*s that emerged there. The river banks also became the locus of river festivals, *nadi maha*, an age-old practice across the Indian subcontinent. The worship of Vitasta was undertaken in a week-long festival in the lunar month of Shravan, end-July to end-August; it began with the propitiation of Varuna, the god of water, and of Uma (Parvati) and Dhanada (giver of wealth) on the fifth day of the new moon; on the sixth and seventh days, virgins (*kumari*), representing both the Goddess and the river, were bathed and anointed; on the ninth day, people offered flowers, food prepared from sugar, incense, bedding and blankets; on the tenth day, Uma was worshipped as a bride with incense, food, earthen lamps, garlands, curd, grain, sugar, safflower, saffron, collyrium and bangles, and on the thirteenth day the birthday of Vitasta was observed with people fasting and performing vocal musical performances (*NP* 784–792).

The confluences (*sangama*) of rivers such as of the many boon-giving and sin-bearing tributaries of Vitasta like Saraswati, Trikoni, Vishoka, Chandravati and Paroshni, when they joined the Vitasta, were deemed especially sacred among *tirtha*s. The river goddesses became the motif for purging sins and attaining purity, and by all of these rivers of the region ultimately merging into the Vitasta, who is the goddess Uma, all of Kashmir was deemed to be purified.

⚘ ⚘

In a remarkable instance of cultural continuity, further exemplifying Shakti's role in Kashmir's place-consciousness, the three paramount *kula devis* of the Valley worshipped to this day, also manifest as river, spring and hill goddesses. Thus, at the confluence of the rivers Kishenganga and Madhumati, atop an alpine spur, stands the ancient shrine of goddess Sharada, who lent her name to Kashmir as *Sharada desha*.

Dedicated to Shakti-Saraswati, or the goddess of learning, the Sharada peetha was built over a subterranean spring, which is the Goddess herself. According to tradition narrated in the *Bhringisha Samhita*, when the war was to break out between

Rama and Ravana, Parvati was relocated from Lanka to the Himalayas by Hanuman, in the form of water in a *kamandala* (jar). Wherever drops spilled *en route* in the Valley, a sacred lake formed. Thus came into being all along the route to the Sharada shrine and visible to this day: the Masanag in Gushi, a pond 700 sq. feet in area; some miles ahead the Devibalnag in Tikri with its colour-changing waters; further above, the Krishnag where pilgrims would stop to bathe, followed by the spring in Tehjan or Tejavan as mentioned in the *Mahatmya*. And finally, where the goddess-bearing *kamandala* was put down is where the sanctum of the Sharada shrine lies. The Goddess exists in the form of a spring or *kunda* that is marked by the presence of a rough slab of stone 6' by 7' and half a foot thick. All the other spring waters are believed to be connected to this subterranean Sharada *kunda*. According to another myth, this is also the spot where the goddess Sharada revealed herself to Rishi Shandilya.

Figure 3.2a Sharada peetha, end 19th century, North Kashmir.
Courtesy: Wikipedia.

Today lying in ruins just beyond the Line of Control (LOC) in village Shardi, the Sharada peetha was once thronged by devotees and scholars from as far as Bengal, on the one hand, and Kerala, on the other, as early as the 8th century CE. The most famous of these would be the great Adi Shankaracharya whose hagiography describes the *peetha* as *sarvajñapeetha* or the seat of omniscience. The Sharada peetha was listed by Al biruni even in the 11th century CE as among the top shrines of all of Hind (India), alongside Somanatha and Thaneshwar. And till today, some daily Hindu prayers in Tamil Nadu fascinatingly begin with the *Sharadastotram,* an invocation that goes '*sharadadevi kashmir-puravasini namastute*' (salutations to the goddess Sharada of Kashmir). This underlines the complete identity between this form of Shakti and the land of Kashmir in the imagination of the rest of the Indian subcontinent in ancient times. It also demonstrates astonishing premodern Indic connectivity and Shakta Kashmir's place in it.

Figure 3.2b Sharada peetha in ruins today, Neelum Village, Pakistan Occupied Kashmir. Courtesy: Wikimedia Commons.

Another outstanding example of a great goddess cult that is centred on a spring is that of Ragnya devi or Kheer Bhawani at Tulmul (ancient Tulyamulya mentioned in the *Rajatarangini*), 22 kilometres from Srinagar. Here Shakti or Durga appears in her *sattvic* form, that of tranquility or bliss, not *raudra* or the furious form. This is Ragnyadevi who is worshipped with milk and rice, in strictly vegetarian ways, hence the name Kheer Bhawani, which is derived from the Sanskrit word *ksheer* for milk. The *Zyeth Atham* (Jyeshtha Ashtami) celebrations in May or June are held by Kashmiri Hindus at this shrine. Her shrine is located on an islet in the middle of a septagonal holy pond (said to resemble the Om in Sharada script). Its waters are deemed miraculous, for they are said to change colour – from milky white to red or pink, blue, orange, to the 'worst of all' black, which is believed by Kashmiris to portend some evil occurrence. This phenomenon is attested by Abul Fazl in the 16th century and again by Swami Vivekananda in the end of the 19th century.[5] In recent history, it is said that the waters of Kheer Bhawani blackened at the time Kashmir was invaded by marauding tribals from Pakistan on 23 October, 1947.

Figure 3.3 Kheer Bhawani, Tulmul, Jammu and Kashmir. Courtesy: Wikimedia Commons.

Mention should be made of yet another spring *tirtha* of Goddess Saraswati who, as the *Rajatarangini* (I.35) mentions, appears as a swan in a lake atop the Bheda hill. Here, Saraswati appeared before Rishi Pulastya, who prayed for Ganga to arise there, leading to the name of Gangabheda *tirtha* (modern Budbror). The Bheda hill, though 7,800 feet high, is remarkable in that snow does not fall within 350 feet of the sacred lake atop it, even as the area all around is covered with snow. This ancient legend is again attested by Fazl.

And then there is the highly revered goddess Sharika Bhagawati, the *ishta devi* of Srinagar, who may be described as a hill goddess. She resides atop the iconic hill Hari Parbat. On the Ashad Shukla Paksha Navami, the Goddess assumed the form of the sharika bird (*hari*, in Kashmiri) and, lifting a celestial pebble in her beak, dropped it on an evil demon in the Valley, crushing it to death. This pebble then came to rest on the hill and became the goddess incarnate—a giant rock (*shila*) smeared in vermilion and bearing the natural mark of the *shrichakra*. She is fervently venerated as Chakreshwari even today.

Figure 3.4
Sharika Bhagawati, Hari Parbat, Srinagar, Jammu and Kashmir. Courtesy: Author.

Everywhere, then, in Kashmir, its past and present, history and myth, geography and spirituality, fold into one another to yield an extraordinary identity rooted in the land and based on Shakti. This was an identity which was birthed through the medium and idiom of pan-Indic Sanskrit, but which remained nonetheless closely rooted in the local world. Indeed, Hinduism has always been a highly locative religion, one that typically constructed geo-biographies or geo-cults which offered a universal template within which regions such as Kashmir could infuse and express their own special character and traditions of belief and worship.

Notes

1   Diana Eck (2012) *India: A Sacred Geography*, New York: Harmony Books, p. 53.

2   Ibid.

3   This is my reworking of the verse cited in B N Kachru, *Lalla's Voices of the Everyday Wild: A Brief Introduction to the Translations* https:// kashmirasitis.com/wp-content/uploads/2020/08/Tirthas-in-J-K-CL-Gadoo.pdf. Last accessed 30.03.2024.

4   References are from Ved Kumari Ghai translated (1973) The *Nilamata Purana* vol. II, Srinagar: J&K Academy of Art, Culture and Languages; Marc Aurel Stein edited and translated (1960 [1892, 1900]) *Kalhana's Rajatarangini or Chronicle of the Kings of Kashmir*, 2 vols. Delhi: Munshiram Manoharlal.

5   Chaman Lal Gadoo *Tirthas of Jammu and Kashmir*, Delhi: Vidya Gauri Prakashan https://kashmirasitis.com/wp-content/uploads/2020/08/Tirthas-in-J-K-CL-Gadoo.pdf, p. 18. Accessed on 30.03.2024.

Lal Ded and A Thousand Years of Kashmir Shaivism: In Historical Perspective

The year 2020 marked the 700th anniversary of the revered Kashmiri *yogini* Lalleshwari or Lal Ded ('Granny Lal'). Though iconic in Kashmir, she is little known outside the Valley. This is despite the fact that the much older metaphysical tradition she represents—Shiva *advaita* or trans-sectarian monist consciousness—and some of its expressive forms share a good deal with other monist/gnostic traditions across India.

For example, Shankaracharya (Kerala), Kabir (Banaras), Guru Nanak (Punjab), Namdev (Maharashtra) and Akka Mahadevi (Karnataka) all variously espoused, like Lal, devotion to God culminating in realisation of, or union with, the supreme Absolute. Lal Ded is, then, as Indic as she is Kashmiri and offers yet another instance of Kashmir's deeply connected histories with the rest of India. More on this later. Let us reprise first the life of this extraordinary saint and her significance for our times.

Though little is known about Lal, except that she was perhaps born in Pandrethan, near Srinagar, in the early 14th century and left her marital home at a young age in pursuit of God; her many sayings (*vaakh*) that seeped far and wide into popular usage in Kashmir speak for her. They also deeply influenced the local Sufi saint, Sheikh Nooruddin or Nund Rishi.

As I explain in my book *Looking Within*, Lal's *vaakh*s are often in the first person and addressed to herself. Seen in other mystics as well, this is a technique that points to Lal Ded's central teaching of turning inwards to arrive at life's greatest truths. Thus she says:

> I rejected every false belief
> Immersed myself in my inner voice alone.
> Ultimately I saw my Self looking deeply into my Self.
> And knew it to be You, God, in every speck.[1]

Lal takes you on an individual's journey through the woes of the human condition, disillusionment with the world, an anguished search for God and, ultimately, to the realisation of the highest truth that liberates. Her teachings are universal: the transience and futility of material pursuits, human attachments, and the emotions they generate such as greed, anger, pride and fear of loss and death.

Her humanism thus makes it easy to relate to Lal. This might explain why her sayings were preserved, till as late as the 19th century, not in any text but through popular collective memory, in songs, proverbs and hymns recited by all strata of Kashmiris. They also constitute one of the earliest compositions in Kashmiri, pioneering the emergence of literature in that tongue.

As her *vaakh*s suggest, Lal belongs to the Trika school of Kashmiri Shaivism, which was represented earlier by scholar-*siddha*s such as Bhatta Narayana, Utpaladeva, Abhinavagupta and Shitikantha (8th–13th century CE), and after Lal, by Roopa Bhavani (17th century) and Lakshman Joo (20th century), among others.

Simply put, according to Trika, all of creation is suffused

by one indivisible supreme consciousness called *Parama Shiva* or *Omkara*. But human beings do not realise this truth since their intellect is clouded by delusions induced by a sensory or materialistic life. This makes them mistakenly identify with their worldly forms and roles, causing a great deal of suffering in the process, and obscuring their real identity, which is one with God, who is formless, pure consciousness.

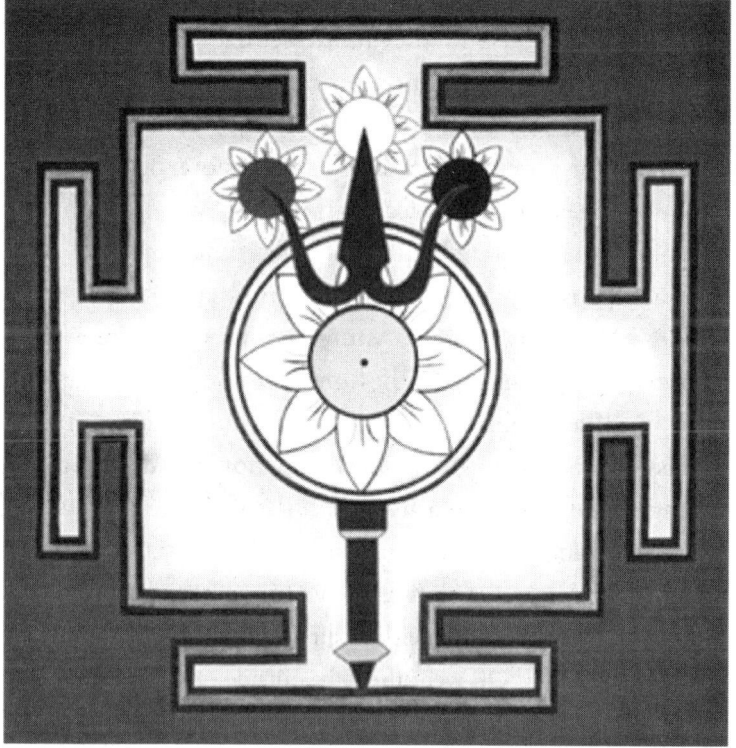

Figure 4.1 *Trishulabijamandalam yantra* of Parama Shiva. Courtesy: https://www. anuttaratrikakula.org.

Lal urges a simple and spontaneous (*sahaj*) understanding or recognition of this ultimate reality by turning inwards. This is because *Parama Shiva* himself is subtle and spontaneous and resides within each of us.

> Shiva is the sole reality and witness
> In whichever direction you look.[2]

Thus, people were not to be discriminated on the basis of their outward faith or customs. The inclusivism of Kashmiri Shaivism was great indeed.

Lal, like most bhakti saints, also rejected external rituals, ostentation and extreme asceticism. She prescribed instead a passion for God and the quintessential yogic technique, namely, intense concentration on the Self through observing the inflow and outflow of one's breath, which leads to the direct experience of pure consciousness. One who experiences this state no longer knows any fear or grief, not even of death, and hence becomes liberated within one's lifetime (*jivan mukta*).

Lal's life is inspiring for not only spiritual but also ethical reasons. Here was a brave, young, solitary woman, with a profound understanding of the human condition, striving with acuity and determination to find a way out of the confusing morass of everyday life, social relations and emotional entanglements to the clarity and bliss of self-discovery. She stood alone and aloof in the face of apparent social censure for being such an intrepid and unconventional woman.

> When the inner light lit up within me
> Off went the light outside.

> Let people abuse and taunt me!
> Or let them shower petals in adoration!
> Nothing affects me.
> I am pure consciousness!

Only when I can withstand censure
Will my inhibitions break down.
Let my pride be torn asunder!
Let not attacks bother me![3]

No ordinary person is capable of such exceptional self-awareness and fortitude.

In our consumerist and hyper-connected modern world, we are ironically disconnected from our own inner selves, and suffer great violence and turmoil as a society consequently. Today therefore, more than ever before, Lal Ded's utterances shine brightly from across the centuries as a beacon of salvation, beckoning us to reclaim our Self and sanity.

❦

Let us now place Kashmir Shaivism as a whole in its historical-geographical context rather than a theological or metaphysical one. This is not only because there is already a surfeit of scholarship on the philosophical content and details of this tradition, but also because apart from the details and the micro picture, there is a need to remind ourselves of the big picture, the wider context which perhaps produced Kashmir Shaivism and in which context Kashmir was not alone.

We ought to begin, however, by noting that while Kashmir Shaivism or devotional *Shivadvaita*, as it is also called, originated no later than the 8th century CE, Shiva-Shakti worship, or Shaiva Shaktism in Kashmir, dates back to much earlier. Even if we go only by extant material evidence, then Shiva-Shakti worship was reigning in the Valley from at least the 2nd century CE, as glimpsed in Kushana gold coins of the period that clearly depict Shiva, trident in hand and a tiger sprawled at his feet on the obverse and the seated goddess on the reverse. The legends on the coins name them as Oesho (Shiva) and Ommo (Uma). Beautiful gold coins from the Kidara dynasty (5th century CE) continue the striking tradition. Colossal *banalinga*s and *ekamukhalinga*s as well as sculptures of Maheshvara as Bhuteshvara, the Kashmiri iconographic innovation, and images of Shiva's divine family, comprising Parvati, Ganesha and Kartikeya, are also to be found in the Valley from at least the 5th century CE. So also are representations of Harihara (conjoint Shiva and Vishnu), trimurti (the three *rupa*s of Shiva), Ardhanarishvara, the 18-armed Durgamahisasuramardini, Kali and assorted *matrika*s such as Chamunda, in gorgeous green-grey chlorite stone and later in bronze.[4]

In fact, the *Nilamata Purana*, composed in Sanskrit in the 8th century CE and the earliest extant account of Kashmir's origins and sacred geography, tells us that Kashmir was founded from a primordial lake —Satisaras—that embodied Sati, the consort of Shiva (Shakti herself). The *Nilamata* as well as Kalhana's *Rajatarangini*, the earliest surviving history of Kashmir from the 12th century CE, unambiguously state that the Valley of Kashmir is Parvati herself and the king of Kashmir but a portion of Shiva (*kashmirah parvati raja tatra haransajah jñeyo*). Chapter 3 discusses this embeddedness of Shaiva-Shaktism in the land of Kashmir and its implications for her selfhood and place-consciousness.

But alongside this theistic and iconographic or *saguna* form of Shaiva-Shaktism, there developed a deeply monist or *nirguna* strand of philosophy in Kashmir that identified Shiva as pure consciousness. This school, which came to be variously called *Pratyabhijna* (Recognition), *Trika* (triad of Shiva, Shakti and Nara) or *Krama* (Succession of stages), was represented in the works of great scholar-*siddha*s such as Bhatta Narayana (8th century CE), Utpaladeva (9th century CE), Abhinavagupta—the doyen synthesiser of aesthetics and metaphysics in the late 10th and early 11th centuries CE—and Shitikantha (13th century CE). As mentioned before, Lal Ded belonged to this line of realised souls, as did Roopa Bhavani in the 17th and Lakshman Joo in the 20th century who espoused the same continuous tradition well into our own times.

Figure 4.2 Trika Yogini Lalleshwari or Lal Ded, 14th century. Courtesy: Ravi Dhar.

Figure 4.3 Kashmir Shaiva master Swami Lakshman Joo, 20th century.
Courtesy: Wikimedia Commons.

As explained briefly above, according to *Trika*, all of creation is replete with one indivisible super consciousness called *Parama* Shiva, and Shakti, the primeval energy, is its principle of creation (*vimarshini*). Spontaneously realising this truth, this unsurpassed (*anuttara*) reality, is *moksha*. But human beings do not realise this, since their intellect is clouded by delusions (*maya)* or amnesia induced by a sensory and material life which obscures their real identity, which is one with God, who is formless, nameless, pure consciousness.

Trika recommended a simple and spontaneous (*saral, sahaj*) recognition of this ultimate reality by turning inwards into the Self, because Shiva himself is subtle and spontaneous and resides within each of us. Thus the path of *Trika* was *nishpath path*, a pathless path. On this path, through God's grace, an intent concentration on the Self via observing the inflow and outflow of one's breath—*ajapa gayatri*, the natural *mantra*—led to the direct experience (*anubhava*) of ultimate consciousness, which is first envisioned as the union of Shiva-Shakti. Thus, *moksha* was Self-realisation—an expansion of the indivisible self to include the whole of creation by seeing beyond all dualities and differences (*bheda*). Hence, Trika was *abheda,* the ultimate *advaita* (non-duality). Pure consciousness thus experienced was a state of blissful and radiant nothingness (*shunya atishunya)*. As Lal Ded put it:

> Practices *(tantra)* gave way to knowledge *(mantra)*.
> Knowledge dissolved into consciousness.
> When consciousness dissolved, nothing remained.
> Nothingness dissolved into Nothingness.[5]

❧❦

Now, let us consider the hugely influential, some would say defining, Indic tradition of monist Vedanta, which goes back to at least the *Upanishad*s, conservatively dated to 1000 BCE, and the *Brahma Sutra*s from about 500 BCE. These were the first texts to speak of consciousness, *cit* or *brahman,* and liberation as realisation of the unity of the Self (*atman*) with *brahman.* Later, commentaries (*bhashya*s) on these texts and on the syncretic *Bhagavad Gita* were composed by Adi Shankaracharya, the *advaitin* par excellence, in the 8th century CE. Shankara, as we know, travelled to and taught in Kashmir, and his hagiographic traditions record very self-consciously the symbolic unity of *Bharatavarsha*'s four directions coming together in the pinnacle of learning, Kashmir (see Chapter 1).

Still later, in remarkable continuity, came about the popular *nirguna* gnostic traditions associated with the *Nathapanthis* such as Matsyendranatha and Gorakhanatha in the Ganga plains, starting again in the 8th or 9th century

CE, the Virashaiva Akka Mahadevi in Karnataka in the 12th century CE, Kabir in 15th century Banaras or even Nanak in Punjab (15th century) who spoke of *ek omkara,* and Namadeva in Maharashtra (13th century CE) who saw Vithal (Vishnu) as supreme. All of them espoused simple, spontaneous, deep devotion to God, culminating in union with the Absolute, who is formless consciousness.

Now, anyone familiar with these traditions will have no difficulty in identifying that Kashmir Shaivism, its doctrinal and expressive particularities apart, was but a regional offshoot or efflorescence of a vast and prodigious, pan-Indic monist consciousness. And this is the larger historical context within which this essay began by urging that we understand the emergence of Kashmir Shaivism. For while there has been no dearth of metaphysical studies on Trika, it may be fair to say that some of this scholarship has tended to treat it in a historical vacuum, making of it something of an esoteric exhibit or a self-contained cultural isolate in all its Kashmir-bound uniqueness.

I dare say this emphasis on uniqueness converges with the manner in which the region of Kashmir herself has been misrepresented in historiography for some 200 years now as a secluded, insular and thereby unique cultural formation that somehow had no truck with the supra region, the Indic mainland. However, as I have shown in my book *The Making of Early Kashmir*, it is simply unhistorical and untrue to speak of an isolated and 'unique' Kashmir. This is because, as we saw in Chapter 2, there is an overabundance of evidence, material and textual, empirical and discursive, to urge our moving away from what I call the 'unique history' paradigm to the 'connected histories' paradigm for Kashmir and the rest of

India. This transition is necessary if we are to truly understand the emergence of Kashmir as a culture region and indeed the birth of Kashmir Shaivism.

To summarise the evidence, from the 5th century BCE onwards, that is, from the dawn of civilisation in the Valley till at least the 12th century CE, all cultural markers in Kashmir— archaeology, textual representations, foreign accounts, inscriptions, coins, languages, art, religion and philosophy— speak to a Kashmir that was open, plural and cosmopolitan, and overwhelmingly Indic in her genesis and composition. In fact, we see a constant synchrony with other regions of India, near and far, and deep and extensive, very real connections and mutual entanglements, not just with neighbouring areas such as Punjab and Himachal Pradesh but also with centres of Indic civilisation in the deep interiors such as Patna, Nalanda, Gaya, Banaras, Allahabad, Mathura, Malwa, Gauda (Bengal), Assam, Karnataka, Kuntala (Telangana) and Tamil Nadu.

Kashmiris looked to these other parts of India for politics, trade, education, asylum, employment, art, religion, philosophy, aesthetics, fashion (!) and pilgrimage, while people from different parts of India turned to Kashmir for the same reasons. And underlying this intense connectivity between Kashmir and the rest of India was the crucial historical process of migrations, both into and out of Kashmir, vis a vis other parts of India over the centuries. This had singular implications for the transfer and intermingling of demography and culture, both material and intellectual. Not only were kings, queens and courtiers at Srinagar drawn variously at different points of time from Punjab, Assam, Andhra, Tamil Nadu, Kangra, Mathura, Malwa and Karnataka, bringing with them their own traditions, but a mixed bag of commoners—students, poets, pilgrims, *baniya*s, graziers, ritualists and of course *brahman*s and *bhikku*s from *Madhyadesha* (Ganga plains), Dravida desha (South India), Gaud (Bengal), Gandhara (Peshawar), Saurashtra and Lata (Gujarat) are found settled in numbers in the Valley.

In corollary to this forgotten history, we also see Kashmiris moving to other parts of India. This included, again, kings and ministers who chose to go and live in Banaras and Prayag on abdication or exile, and Kashmiri generals, on the one hand, and scholars and litterateurs such as Bilhana and Mahapandita Shakyashribhadra (described as *kache pachen* or 'Kashmiri Pandit' by the Tibetans), who took up employment in courts as far south as the Deccan at Kalyan or in universities as far east as Vikramshila and Odantpuri in Bihar, on the other.

We also have 12th–15th century CE inscriptions from Shrirangam, Chidambaram (the Shaiva centre par excellence) and Tirruvoruyur in Tamil Nadu and Kalahasti (Andhra), among other places, fascinatingly speaking of original natives of Kashmiradesha now resident as landed persons holding high official posts (*rayan*) in the South! It is also popularly believed that Saraswat Brahmanas migrated from Kashmir to other parts of India, especially the Konkan coast.

Here was cultural transmission and communication of astonishing reach and multilinear character—the very context in which we have to understand the birth of something like *Trika*. When you take all of this evidence and phenomena together, is there any wonder that Kashmiri culture for over 2000 years resonated with the Indic and vice versa?

The result was a Kashmiri identity that consisted in a distinct regional self-awareness in the midst of an overarching subscription to all-India beliefs and practices. And it is at this historical intersection, this intense mix of the Indic universal and the Kashmiri local, that the origins of Kashmir Shaivism can be understood.

Notes

1   Shonaleeka Kaul, edited and translated (2022) *Looking Within: Life Lessons from Lal Ded*, Delhi: Aleph, p. 42.
2   Ibid., p. 109.
3   Ibid., pp. 45, 48–49.
4   Shonaleeka Kaul (2018) *The Making of Early Kashmir: Landscape and Identity in the Rajatarangini,* Delhi: Oxford University Press, pp. 145–52, 155.
5   Shonaleeka Kaul, *Looking Within,* p. 71.

Thoughts on the Kathakautukam and Islam in 15th Century Kashmir

A few years ago, in preparation for a book discussion of a translation into English of poet Shrivara's *Kathakautukam*, I had the occasion to reflect on this curious little text. It belongs to a region, Kashmir, which, as I discovered in the course of my own lectures on Kashmiri history around the country and the world, people knew precious little about. It is also a text that hails from and speaks to a moment of defining disjuncture in Kashmiri history.

Composed in 1505, well over 100 years into the advent of Islam and West/Central Asian groups and rulers into Kashmir, the *Kathakautukam* is a Sanskrit reworking—not mere translation—of a Persian original. The original was a *masnavi*, a mystical romance called *Yusuf wa Zuleikha,* written in 1483 by Maulana Abdul Rehman Jami from Herat, Afghanistan, just a couple of decades before Shrivara's work. *Yusuf wa Zuleikha* was, in turn, adopting a story with Biblical and Quranic precedents.

Therefore, in being a classic Sanskrit *kavya*, yet engaging with a text, a language, and a belief system that were essentially external to the Sanskrit ecumene at that point, the *Kathakautukam* can be seen as performing two historical functions: One, it demonstrates the prodigious persistence or continuity of Sanskrit literary culture in straddling, transcending or outlasting major historical change and the resultant social and cultural challenges. And two, it also responds to that historical rupture in ways that entail greater complexity and agency than we perhaps imagine. Let us see how.

❦

It may not be a coincidence that the author of the *Kathakautukam*, Pandit Shrivara, was also the author of the *Tritiya Rajatarangini* or *Zaina Tarangini*. This text covered the period 1459–1486 of Kashmiri history, after the earlier *Dvitiya Rajatarangini* composed by his guru, the historian Pandit Jonaraja (b.1389–d.1459). To those who may not be familiar with the Rajatarangini tradition, these texts were the sequels to the iconic *Rajatarangini* by Kalhana.

Written circa 1148–1150 CE, Kalhana's magnum opus is the earliest extant history of Kashmir and of its royal dynasties. It was not the first history of Kashmir, however, as is mistakenly supposed by scholars and lay people alike. Kalhana himself enumerated nearly a dozen predecessors of his work (*purva grantha*) that attempted the same thing, seemingly over several preceding centuries. Much like early Kashmiri culture itself, Kalhana's *Rajatarangini*, as I have demonstrated in my book *The Making of Early Kashmir*, represented a prodigious amalgam of pan-Indic Sanskrit traditions such as *shastra*, *itihasa*, *vamshavali* and *kavya*, and local Kashmiri content, to document more than two thousand years of regional history in a universal idiom. This was in keeping with Kashmir's intensely connected histories with the rest of India (see Chapter 2).[1]

As a legatee to this remarkable tradition of regional history-writing, Shrivara was intently familiar with precisely the centuries that separated Kalhana from him, having chronicled these in part. These centuries brought to a Hindu and Buddhist Kashmir not only a new religion, Islam, but a new demographic and a new cosmopolitan literary medium, Persian, that effectively took over from Sanskrit as the preferred language of the court, administration, elite education and *belles lettres*.

Crucially, these centuries also brought a new ruling class and new policies of state some of which distinguished the Kashmiri subjects on the grounds of their faith, not to say perpetuated violence against them and their culture and practices. The 14th century in particular belonged to the likes of Turko-Mongol invaders such as Dulacha (1320) and kings such as Sikandar 'Butshikan' ('idol-breaker'), of the Turko-Persian Shahmiri dynasty, who ruled from 1389–1413 with his Kashmiri convert-minister Saifuddin (formerly Suhabhatta) under the impress of Iranian Kubrawiya Saiyyid proselytisers. Their reigns and personal dispositions are associated in traditional accounts and memory with oppression, trauma and tumult in the Valley.

Based on medieval chronicles such as Jonaraja's *Dvitiya Rajatarangini,* which was contemporaneous to these events, and the later Sayyid Ali's *Tarikh I Sayyid Ali* (1569), historians such as R K Parimu, Mohibbul Hasan, G M D Sufi and P M K Bamzai have noted the systematic persecution of Kashmiris based on their faith and the destruction of their places of worship. R K Parimu writes: "During the reign of Sikandar and Ali Shah (1386–1420)...force and compulsion were employed by the second convoy of missionaries who came [from Persia]...The Hindus were compelled to embrace Islam. Those who refused either died or quit the country. Cremation of dead and wearing of Hindu symbols [the *tilak* on the forehead] [and idol worship] were interdicted, and *jaziya* [cess on non-Muslims] was levied. Many Hindu temples were pulled down and their images were broken...."[2]

These historians tell us that Shariat was sought to be enforced with strictness in the land; a special office called 'Sheikh ul Islam' was instituted to ensure the same. S A A Rizvi writes: "Sultan Sikandar demolished ancient temples in Pampor, Vijabror, Martand, Anantnag, Sopor and Baramula. Many puritanical laws were implemented...The persecution of Brahmans, their exclusion from the top echelons of government, and their replacement by Iranian migrants, accelerated the process of the conversion of the Brahman elite."[3]

To quote Jonaraja himself:

Due to the ill luck of the subjects, the king became addicted to *yavana darshana* just as the wind destroys the trees and locusts the paddy crop, *yavana*s decimated the religious traditions and practices (*achara*) of Kashmir. Prompted by the gifts of honours and bounties which the king bestowed on them, *mlecchas* [outsiders] entered Kashmir...(*DRT* 572, 575–76).[4]

Further:

Struck by fear, some Brahmans killed themselves by means of poison, some by rope, others by drowning, jumping off cliffs, or burning themselves. The country was contaminated by hatred and thousands committed suicide...There was no city, no town, no village, no wood, where the *turushka* [Turk] left the temples of gods unbroken...Polluted by the evil practices of *mlecchas*, the brahmanas, *mantras* and *deva*s of Kashmir were deprived of their prowess. (*DRT* 591–603).

The *Tarikh I Sayyid Ali* corroborates this, adding that mosques were built over the razed temples and the manuscripts of the Hindus, "which the ancient kings had got written and over which the people of this land had faith," were piled high like a *minar* by Sikandar and thrown into the Vatalanmarg lake, and dirt piled atop them, forming a barrage.[5]

Of course, by the time Jonaraja and then Shrivara were writing, these kings had been succeeded by the likes of the broader-minded and compassionate persona Sultan Zainul Abidin (1395–1470), born Shahi Khan, the son of Sikandar. Zainul Abidin has been enshrined in popular Kashmiri narrative as 'Budshah' or 'Great King' for his lenient and solicitous treatment of non-Muslims and their culture in his realm. But the memory of cultural trauma is still writ large in the works of the medieval chroniclers of Kashmir.

༺ ༻

This then is the historical background against which Shrivara composed a cross-cultural text like the *Kathakautukam*. How is this to be understood? Historically, rare would be the cultural interface that is or can be a simple process free of the stresses of its time. It is more plausible to envisage a complex phenomenon of tensions and negotiation instead. I argue that our text, Shrivara's *Kathakautukam*, represents such a statement of the stresses involved and a self-conscious attempt at negotiating them from a position of strength.

A close look at the rather ambivalent *prayojana* or preamble to the text bears out this contention. It is framed, true to a Sanskrit *nandi* and *prashasti*, with the frequent invocation of Shiva, Ganesha and Saraswati thus:

> That all surpassing radiance
> Of Shambhu, I first salute:
> That to which homage is paid
> By the sages and the lord of gods;
> On beholding it in the heart
> Through yoga do the yogic masters
> With all joy then understand
> That emptied minds, though feeling pained,
> Have mastery on all the world;
> And on that, having meditated
> Even for a single moment,
> One always gains felicity (*Kathakautukam* [henceforth *KK*] 1.1).[6]

Shrivara goes on to say: "After obeisance to Ganesha, the remover of all obstacles, and to Bharati, the goddess of speech, in her triple form, I have put together in our immortal language this tale recounted in the *yavana shastra* [the foreign scriptures]"(*KK* 1.2–3).[7] He repeats this assertive observation about Sanskrit later, saying that, given that this tale (*Kathakautukam*) was received from a celestial being, it was appropriate that he was rendering it in the language of the gods (*KK* 1.38–40).[8]

Shrivara's opening pages also have frequent references to the Vedas. And they then go on to elaborate, quite unexpectedly, the quintessential Kashmir Shaiva or *Trika* monist theology of the union of Shiva and Shakti thus:

> Without love for the Ultimate, there is nothing at all in

the world. That alone engenders renunciation, [and] can lead to happiness. With the mind's attachments under control, that love is the lord Shiva himself and, in union with Shakti, or energy, creates all that is. Duality is indeed to be shunned in the world... The supreme perfection is only one, and in it is but a single great lord... Perceiving himself also within that noble and ideal wholeness, the king of gods too was filled with joy (*KK* 1.49– 53).[9]

To whom can I reveal all this? Shiva wondered. And born of this desire was manifested the charmer, his Mohini... He was the Mahadev, the great god. The energy that was his wish united with the receptacle that was his love to bring forth the world. (*KK* 1.54–57).[10]

Here appears to be a rather self-confident assertion of the poet's cultural location. Though a retelling of a Sufi Islamic composition, Islam finds no mention in the dedication of the *Kathakautukam*. The prophet Muhammad, however, called *paigambar shiromani* (crown jewel among prophets) is certainly spoken of as the one who received this poem from a divine messenger (*KK* 1. 16).[11] Hinting at inherent contradictions, the poet cryptically writes: "Conscious of its [the tale's] power and majesty, I now speak of its greatness, and let not that sublime intent be affected by doubts caused by contrary scriptures"(*KK* 1.18).[12]

More prominently, the ruling Muslim king of Kashmir, Mohammad Shah, third in line from Zainul Abidin, is praised for his virtues in an idiom that is no different from what was used by other Sanskrit *kavya*s to praise Hindu or Buddhist kings (*KK* 1.20–35). Listen closely, however, and some references to tense experiences also creep in. Thus, Shrivara writes:

> This world is passing through and filled with hundreds of worries. May the lord of Gods lead me from its darkness into light. And may my mind forever be in Shambhu's service... For without words radiant with homage to Shambhu and praised by good people, the world's stability itself could be in jeopardy.

At another point, he refers to "the slavery of the world and terror dwelling in the heart" (*KK* 1.4–10).[13]

Elsewhere, he says about Muhammad Shah: "He is an abode of virtue and conscious of the original unity of things [monism]. And out of his regard for cows, he has exempted them from slaughter" (*KK* 1.30).[14]

☙❧

In a court that was perhaps still hung over on Budshah's catholicity in having Sanskrit works translated into Persian, much like the Mughal Emperor Akbar did later, Shrivara's reverse gesture of retelling a Persian text in Sanskrit may be seen as mirroring that catholicity in a sense. Or perhaps it was simply undertaken at the king's orders. Shrivara's own ambivalence, as seen earlier, is hard to miss. He writes:

> The twofold nature of expression is described by the learned as truth and untruth. Both can be agreeable and are hard to attain. For *duty, more true than proper, is not auspicious or pleasing for everyone. To insist on speaking the truth may also be less preferable* than the wish for the accomplishment of all things. Adornment of the world with both truth and

prosperity is best for good-minded people, in *speaking with a forgiving nature, both little and the truth* (*KK* 1.91–94. Emphasis added).[15]

Be that as it may, working even within the bounds of what he hints at being a certain ideological awkwardness, Shrivara's choice of text represents a certain cultural curiosity and felicity. After all, the colophons of the text describe Shrivara as adept in the *yavana* language (Persian).[16] But his choice also points to an astute inclusivism. For, *Yusuf wa Zuleikha* was a Sufi work of the mystic kind that emphasises and adulates the love of God and the suffering and craving of the individual soul for union with God, much like a romantic lover's craving for their beloved—in this case, the beautiful Zuleikha's for Yusuf. As A N D Haksar puts it: "Zuleikha is part of a parable of the soul in search of god."[17]

It is this common ground of *tauhid i wajudi* or unity of being, Islam's mystic monism which aspires to divine union, that clearly resonated with the homegrown mystic monism or non-dualism of Kashmiri Trika Shaivism, also known as Shiva *advaita*, which Shrivara was not just familiar with but actually followed. This is seen in his articulation of Trika in both the prologue (quoted above) and the epilogue of his poem.

꧁ ꧂

As we saw in the last chapter, non-dualism or *advaita* has a long history in the Indian subcontinent, going as far back as the Upanishads that first gave the call circa 1000 BCE of *rupam rupam pratirupo bhavuh,* that is, from the multiplicity of forms (in the world) to the unity of consciousness (see

Chapter 4 for more details).[18] Kashmir Shaivism, in particular, dates back to at least the 8ᵗʰ century CE and a long line of sages. Of these, the great *Trika* yogini and poetess, Lalleshwari or Lal Ded, lived during the 14ᵗʰ century. Through her hugely influential renderings (*vaakh*) in the local dialect, the gnostic philosophy of liberation centred on spontaneous experience of pure consciousness (*parama shiva*) via self-realisation by the soul, seeped far and wide through Kashmiri society. Lal's path required an intense, all-consuming love and longing for Shiva. This is not unlike the sentiment that Shrivara chooses to express at the end of the *Kathakautukam*:

> Arise in prayer and seek shelter with the great god in whom there is joy. Who can attain fulfillment without serving him?... He is the sole shelter... the god of all the gods and the lord of all the world. Seek his refuge.... We bow to that lord, the eternal soul, the cause of creation, sustenance and dissolution.... Dwelling on him in pure meditation, the yogis do not ever see any fears.... They have but a single flavor in their words. It is the name Shiva.... May my singing of his names with joy, devotion and a tremulous voice not go waste in this our world (*KK* 15.5–19).[19]

For Lal, *moksha* was an expansion of the individual self to include the whole universe by seeing beyond all dualities and differences. Her words thus seem to be echoed by Shrivara's position in the *Kathakautukam*. She says:

> Shiva is the sole reality and witness
> In whichever direction you look.
> *Don't distinguish the Brahmin and*
> *the Muslim then.*
> If you are a trika, go within,

Know only yourself.[20]

That is where Shiva resides. Look no further.[21](Emphasis added.)

Immersed in Shiva, stable of breath,
Constant in contemplation.
He whose heart
Knows no duality or attachment,
With him alone is the lord of all gurus,
Shiva, delighted.[22]

He is Shiva, Keshava, and Brahma,
Eternal and unborn.
May He take away the births and deaths
Of this poor woman!
He, Hara, just Hara, the only One!![23]

That's not all. Among the defining figures of 14th–15th century Kashmiri thought, echoing Lal Ded closely, and indeed believed to have been her disciple, was the Kashmiri saint, Shaikh Noorudin Noorani or Nund Rishi, born 1375, a local convert. He has been enshrined in memory as the 'Flag bearer of Kashmir' (*Alamdar-e-Kashmir*). Even as he maintained a distance from the Islamic Sultanate and the Kubrawiya Persianate order in Kashmir, his *shruk*s (verses) in the local tongue, Kashmiri, exercised huge sway over the masses of the Valley, much like Lal's *vaakh*s.

Non-dualism, or spontaneous realisation of one absolute godhead (who Nund interchangeably calls Allah and Shiva), who was pure, formless consciousness, through a concentration on the Self or soul (*ruh*), marks Nund Rishi's teachings as well. So does the emphasis on the *guru*, on divine grace, and on rising above differences and worldly attachments. The Kashmiri sacred geography (Harmukh, Gangabal) and spiritual technology (yogic breath work, called *ham-sa*) are also stunningly the same in the works of the two saints. In fact it is this continuity with local beliefs that explains Nund and his disciples in Kashmir, who were Muslims, adopting the title of Rishi, which is the Sanskrit word for a Hindu sage. They also deferred to a host of pre-Islamic spiritual practices. It is a continuity and a lineage that Nund himself owns and which kept him in tension vis-a-vis the Sultanate in Kashmir. It inaugurated what a scholar has called the "vernacularisation of Islam for Kashmir" and the creation of a "breakthrough thinking of an inclusive Kashmiri community".[24] Though the Rishi movement was in time subsumed by the more orthodox Suhrawardis, nonetheless witness some of Nund Rishi's utterances to get a sense of the essential similarity with Kashmir Shaivism and its breadth of outlook:

> Having seen God,
> How can I conceal the fact?
> United with my self
> Is the Universal self! (134)[25]
> What qualities appeal to you in the world
> To allow your body such indulgences?
> *The Musalman and the Hindu sail in the same boat!*
> Finish this game and then let's go home (*ghar*) [to God]
> (81).[26] (Emphasis added)

> He does not judge you by your dialectics.
> The spiritual condition (*halas*) does He observe.

Meditate on God with tongue stuck to your palate [Yogic
kriya]
Thus will the Raaz Honz [Royal Swan/pure consciousness]
Be drawn into your net! (136)[27]

Having ferried across the Gangabal lake
For the whole night the shepherd did wait
For how else was he destined to meet Shiva?!
O Lord, bestow a similar boon on me! (109)[28]

The shepherd followed Shiva.
How did he come by the trail?
Entering Harmukha, he disappeared there!
O Lord, bestow a similar boon on me! (110)[29]

Lalla of Padmanpora
Drank in long draughts, nectar divine.
A beloved *avatar* (incarnation) she was to us all.
O Lord, bestow a similar boon on me! (105)[30]

Thus, as opposed to the frictions and fractures inflicted
by state-sponsored conversions in medieval Kashmir, it is this
common ground laid by *Trika* and extended by the Rishi order
that could have facilitated—and makes deep sense of—the
apparent act of cross-cultural passage that the *Kathakautukam*
represents, albeit with all its ambivalence intact. It seems
clear that in adapting as he does a Sufi tale of romantic love
(*ishq*) sublimated to the love of God (Allah), and interpreting
it fearlessly in terms of the love of Shiva Shambhu, Shrivara
demonstrates not only a catholicity but a cultural self-belief
and resilience against the odds. He is subtly, in his own words,

"speaking little and the truth with a forgiving nature"! And in doing so, he is acting in the tradition of the home-grown sages of his land who had seen and spoken the ultimate truth: the unity of consciousness. Reading the *Kathakautukam* in these ways is to unravel the little-known intricacies of cultural encounter and redemption that 15th century Kashmir experienced.

Notes

1   Shonaleeka Kaul (2018) *The Making of Early Kashmir: Landscape and Identity in the Rajatarangini*, Delhi: Oxford University Press.

2   R K Parimu (1969) *History of Muslim Rule in Kashmir*, Delhi, p. 393, cited by RL Hangloo in Aparna Rao edited (2008) *The Valley of Kashmir: The Making and Unmaking of a Composite Culture*, Delhi: Manohar, p. 101.

3   S A A Rizvi (1977) 'Islamic Proselytization' in G A Oddie edited *Religion in South Asia*, Delhi, p. 33, cited by R L Hangloo in Aparna Rao edited (2008) *The Valley of Kashmir*, p. 103.

4   All quotations from the *Dvitiya Rajatarangini* are from Srikanth Koul edited (1972) *Rajatarangini of Jonaraja*, Hoshiarpur: Vishvesharananda Institute Press.

5   Cited in R L Bhat (2023) *Kashmir under Shariyat: Muslim Rule as per the Primary Persian Sources*, Srinagar: Gulshan Books, pp. 84–86.

6   A N D Haksar translated (2019) *A Tale of Wonder: Kathakautukam*, Delhi: Penguin, p. 3.

7   Ibid., p. 4.

8   Ibid., p. 9.

9   Ibid., p. 10.

10 Ibid., p. 11.

11 Ibid., p. 5.

12 Ibid., p. 6.

13 Ibid., pp. 4–5.

14 Ibid., p. 7.

15 Ibid., p. 16.

16 Ibid., p. 193.

17 Ibid., p. xvii.

18 *Katha Upanishad* cited in Kapila Vatsyayan edited (1991) *Concepts of Space, Ancient and Modern*, Delhi: IGNCA, p. xvi.

19 A N D Haksar, *A Tale of Wonder*, pp. 189–91.

20 Shonaleeka Kaul edited (2019) *Looking Within: Life Lessons from Lal Ded*, Delhi: Aleph, p. 115.

21 Ibid., p. 99.

22 Ibid., p. 61.

23 Ibid., p. 62.

24 Abir Bazaz (2023) *Nund Rishi: Poetry and Politics in Medieval Kashmir*, Delhi: Cambridge University Press, pp. 28, 247.

25 B N Parimoo translated with an introduction (1984) *Nund Rishi: Unity in Diversity*, Srinagar: J&K Academy of Art, Culture and Languages, p. 127.

26 Ibid., p. 90.

27 Ibid., p. 129.

28 Ibid., p. 108.

29 Ibid., p. 108.

30 Ibid., p. 106.

From Space to Consciousness: Architecture as Advaita

6

Part of a quest for a culturally rooted practice of architecture is asking fundamental questions such as: What did the act of building mean beyond the act itself? 'Architecture', from the Greek *architecton* ('prime builder'), is fundamentally articulated space. Or, as Aldo van Eyck evocatively called it, "outlined emptiness", the outlining performed via the act of building, which encloses and contains space.[1]

In Indic conceptions, however, right from the first millennium BCE, the word for space is *akasha,* which implies vastness, transcendence and a phenomenon as all-encompassing as the sky. Clearly then, space as *akasha* was the opposite of anything finite, bounded or enclosed. So in this understanding, architecture would be the paradoxical attempt to limit the limitless, enclose the unenclosable. Which begs the question: Is architecture a contradiction in terms?

And yet, humankind *has* been building and enclosing space for millennia. So what does this transition from the unlimited to the limited, from the transcendent to the contingent, do to space? In generating an interior and an exterior, does building not also generate an artificial divide and duality or splitting asunder of experience? In forcing a separation between the world within and without, and ushering within the built interiors the bulk of our activities, has civilisation and its prime force, architecture, contracted and narrowed down rather than expanded our lives and our sense of reality? This is a question of both physics and metaphysics. Ultimately, however, it is perhaps a question of ethics: What *is* the practice of architecture meant to effect in human terms? A separation or a continuum? A split or equipoise? Alienation or belonging?

৵৵ ৵৵

These are questions that have agitated the minds of some thinker-architects in the West such as van Eyck and Christopher Alexander, who perceived a growing crisis of mindlessness and disembeddedness in contemporary architecture, and went on to exhort a style of construction that felt like a built homecoming, "places where we can be what we really are", or which tapped into the eternal truth in the ordinary and every day.[2]

In doing so, these architects rightly apprehended the connection between the surrounding built environment and the psycho-social life of the individual. They believed in the transformative potential of architecture in facilitating the overcoming of contradictions that people and indeed societies felt within themselves, and their attainment of a relaxed equipoise instead. They emphasised the overcoming of dualities—the forced separation of interior from exterior— as the key to wholesome and harmonious buildings and communities.

These issues are as relevant to modern India where building appears as a heedless, profiteering business. Indian urban architecture today displays an overwhelming functionalism and monotony, apart from a confused poverty of form—the predominant impression one gets from the mushrooming jungle of skyscraper-slums that the urban core and peripheries alike have become. While there is nothing wrong with function and it is a necessary and sufficient impetus for building, the question really is: What is the *nature* of the function that is aimed at? Is it that of mere utility, or is it that of purpose, a "lasting human validity"?[3] The two are vastly different in terms of their social and spiritual potential.

What may ancient history tell us in this regard? Scholars speak of two broad types of public architecture: sacred and secular. The great temples and stupas of early India and the cities and palaces can be respectively assigned to these types. However, this binary is itself a separation imposed by European modernity, which expects the sacred nowadays to have a minimal role and the secular, perhaps, minimal soul. This may not be quite how the ancients thought. They professed perhaps far more integrated life-goals.[4]

In early India, form and consciousness were considered inseparable, regardless of the character of the building, and their union was invested with cultural meaning and efficacy. Architecture was a self-consciously undertaken project which, like a *yajna*, was believed to be transformational, both for its practitioners and its clientele. This essay draws on a couple of central concepts of space from early India, *mandara* and *mandala*, to explore how form and spirit fused synergistically with a view to transforming the individual partaker and ultimately the community.

Returning then to the concept of *akasha*, while retaining its essential qualities of infinitude and transcendence, *akasha* could be of three different kinds: in the middle, *citakasha*, mindspace that gave rise to all activity and perception; above it, *paramakasha*, the infinite space of nameless consciousness; and deep within, *hrdayakasha*, the space of the human heart. What's more, appearing to confound all notions of scale and hierarchy, *paramakasha* was exactly replicated in *hrdayakasha*, or rather it reposed deep within the latter.

In the *Taittiriya Upanishad* (II. 1) (circa 1000 BCE), this was expressed as *nihitam guhayam parame vyoman*: "deep within the cave-[like heart of] man lies infinite consciousness".[5] Here was the microcosmic paradox: the secret of outermost space is to be found in the innermost! As the *Chhandogya Upanishad* (8.1.1–3) described it: "Within the city of *brahman* (infinite consciousness) is a small lotus flower. Within that is a still smaller space, the human heart (*hrdayakasha*). Within that space is the deepest truth."[6]

In metaphysical terms, the individual *atman* (soul) mirrored the universal *brahman* (pure consciousness), and true knowledge was the realisation of their unity, or the true nature of reality *was* their unity. Indeed *moksha* (liberation), was not some other-worldly pursuit but *jivan mukti* (liberation in one's lifetime) or the realisation in the here and now of that state of bliss arisen from union with the infinite. Known as *advaita* (non-dualism), this trans-sectarian philosophy established itself as influential from very early, finding expression first in the *Upanishads*, then the syncretic *Bhagavad Gita* (2nd century BCE), down to Adi Shankara and Vedanta (9th century CE onwards) and the *nirguna* bhakti saints (14th–17th centuries).

Of course one does not have to be an *advaitavadin* to see that it is to make manifest a culturally validated idea of reality that most knowledge systems of early India strove in great epistemic unison. Architecture was no exception. *Vastu* texts from the first and second millennium CE, in the midst of the plethora of technical specifications they offer, were ultimately about architecture not as an end in itself but as a means to an end greater than itself—architecture as meditation on the true nature of reality. Thus whether it was building a sacrificial altar, a temple or a city, architecture at its highest became an instrument of liberation.

❦

To recap: We ask what is the ultimate purpose of architecture? Is it mere utility or a "lasting human validity"? Dividing our experience of the world into an interior and exterior, what does the act of building effect in human terms? A separation or continuum? A split or equipoise? Alienation or belonging? Here we explore two central architectural concepts from early India, *mandala* and *mandara*, in which form and spirit fused synergistically with a view to transcending divides and transforming the partaker. In metaphysical terms, the *hrdayakasha* (human heart) and *paramakasha* (cosmos) or the individual *atman* (soul) and universal *brahman* (pure consciousness) mirrored each other, and true knowledge was the realisation of their unity. So Indic architecture, too, at its highest, became a meditation on this true nature of reality, which led to *moksha*.

How did this happen actually? One of the powerful techniques evolved for this was the concept of *vastupurushamandala*. Note the portentious homology between the human body (*purusha*) and architecture (*vastu*)—an understanding of space in the image of man,[7] a parallel that extended between the body and the universe too, as we will see. The *mandala* is a square grid design or plan, consisting of 64 or 81 squares radiating outwards from the centre, on which ritual altars, temples, *chaityas*, houses, palaces or cities were meant to be founded in early Indian architectural thought. It is a configuration of square base, surrounding enclosure with apertures/exits, and a real or projected vertical axis.

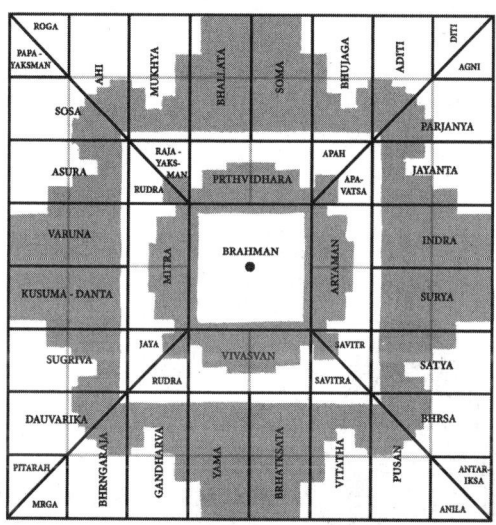

Figure 6.1 *Vastupurushamandala* with superimposed temple plan expanding outwards from the centre. Courtesy: Author.

In the temple specifically, this "axis of access", as Michael Meister called it, was visualised stemming from the centre of the diagram or sanctum, called *garbha grha* (womb), *guha* (cave), or *hrdaya* (heart).[8] It rose through graded tiers as high as the devotee's vision could rise, to form a spire called *shikhara* (peak) or *vimana* (tower), culminating in a finial or summit called *bindu* (point).

The *bindu* served literally as the point of contact between the immanent, concealed, recessed consciousness deep within the *garbhagrha* or *hrdayakasha*, on the one hand, and the transcendent expansive infinite consciousness without, i.e. the *brahman* or *paramakasha*, on the other. The temple plan thus symbolised the "descent and ascent of consciousness", to quote R. Nagaswamy,[9] and provided for the merger of exterior with interior, or of eternal consciousness with that of the devotee. Duality was thus overcome; reality was thus realised. Further, it is by the spatial plan of the temple, via the *mandapa* or verandah, which led straight up to the sanctum, that the devotee was inexorably drawn to the *garbhagrha* to experience this self-transcendence.

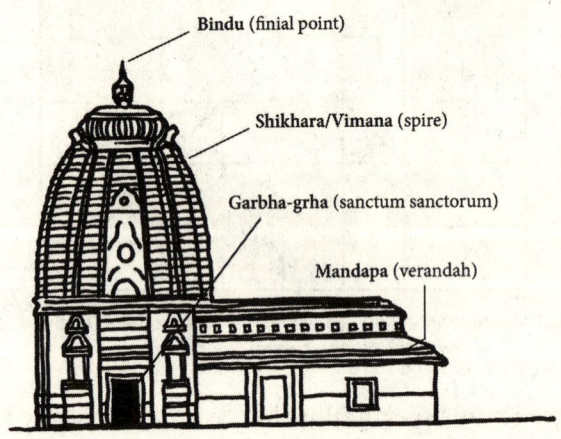

Figure 6.2 Cross-section of North Indian (*Nagara*) style temple (*mandara*).
Courtesy: Author.

As if that wasn't transformative enough, the temple also served as a participatory creation myth. The reference to *purusha* harks back to the celebrated Vedic *Purusha Sukta* or creation hymn, wherein the cosmos was born from the body of the primeval or supernal man. But "in the beginning was

Figure 6.3 Pillared *mandapa* leading straight up to dark *garbhagriha*. Courtesy: Wikimedia Commons.

darkness, swathed in darkness; all this was but unmanifested water," as the *Rig Veda Samhita* (X.129.3) narrates. From this cosmic ocean of darkness, using the inverted heavenly mountain named Meru or Mandara, the gods and demons conjointly churned into existence all of creation. Mount Mandara is veritably the *axis mundi*, then, that rent or pillared apart the heavens and the earth, holding up the former, connecting it to the latter, and lending to the Hindu temple its name, *mandara*, and its analogy with a mountain.

Here is, interestingly, how the astrophysicist McKim Malville describes the transformative experience of entering a temple:

> Moving inward in space and backward in time, one proceeds from brightly lighted exterior space to darkness, from large open spaces to confined small space, from richness of carving and decoration to the simplicity of the unadorned centre... Enshrouded by a darkness pierced only by a few lamps, lies the *garbhagrha* ... symbolic of the chaos, potentiality, and undifferentiated wholeness out

of which the universe emerged. Spreading outward from the centre along cardinal and inter-cardinal directions, the stones of the temple [and the rich iconography on them] symbolize the [diversity of] creation into which the universe transformed itself.[10]

The underlying unity is thus never lost. As the *Katha Upanishad* tells us: *rupam rupam pratirupo bhavuh* ('the formless takes many forms').[11] Further: "Decorated with symbols of water like images of Ganga and Yamuna, the doorway of the [womb chamber] is a transformational symbol, like water itself. When entering ... the devotee undergoes a transformation and a death: He dies to time. For he can travel back in time by moving to the temple centre, and experiencing or re-experiencing [there] the birth of the cosmos."[12]

The temple plan thus set eternity in motion, as it were! Can there be a more profound reminder to humankind of being at one with creation? And can there be a more powerful argument for overcoming the fragmentation and alienation that plague modern humans and society?

❧ ❧

What may we take away from all this? One, we must acknowledge the transformative potential of architecture and the veritable power of architectural space when it is true to, and in harmony with, qualities of the human spirit in equipoise. Therefore modern architecture must rediscover such meaning and purpose for itself as is greater than itself. And, two, we must infuse contemporary building practice with culturally specific possibilities and solutions to the perennial problems of the human condition. In other words, we must restore to the practice a communitarian knowledge and vision of a better way of life. Far from a contradiction in terms, early Indian architecture appears to have been meant to overcome contradictions of the inner and the outer, the subject and the object, mind and matter, unity and multiplicity, and thereby recuperate the whole. Let architecture be meditation once again, and heal and make whole again.

Notes

1   Aldo van Eyck (1962) *The Child, The City and the Artist: An Essay on Architecture, the In-between realm*, SUN (no publication details given), p. 50.

2   Ibid., pp. 24, 56; Christopher Alexander (1979) *The Timeless Way of Building*, New York: Oxford University Press, p. 39.

3   Aldo van Eyck, *The Child, The City and the Artist*, p. 12.

4   See Shonaleeka Kaul edited (2014) *Cultural History of Early South Asia: A Reader*, Delhi: Orient BlackSwan.

5   The *Taittiriya Upanishad* is quoted in Bettina Bäumer, 'From Guha to Akash: The Mystical Cave in the Vedic and Saiva Traditions' in Kapila Vatsyayan edited (1991) *Concepts of Space, Ancient and Modern,* Delhi: Indira Gandhi National Centre for the Arts, p.107.

6   The *Chhandogya Upanishad* is cited in Stella Kramrisch, 'Space in Indian Cosmogony and in Architecture' in Kapila Vatsyayan edited (1991) *Concepts of Space, Ancient and Modern*, Delhi: Indira Gandhi

National Centre for the Arts, p. 102.

7   Aldo van Eyck, *The Child, The City and the Artist,* p. 49.

8   Michael Meister 'The Hindu Temple: Axis of Access' in Kapila Vatsyayan edited (1991) *Concepts of Space, Ancient and Modern,* Delhi: Indira Gandhi National Centre for the Arts, p. 269.

9   R Nagaswamy 'The Brihadisvara as Paramakasa' in Kapila Vatsyayan edited (1991) *Concepts of Space,* p. 299.

10 J McKim Malville 'Astrophysics, Cosmology, and the Interior Space of Indian Myths and Temples' in Kapila Vatsyayan edited (1991) *Concepts of Space,* p. 128.

11 *Katha Upanishad* cited in Kapila Vatsyayan edited (1991) *Concepts of Space,* p.

12 J McKim Malville 'Astrophysics, Cosmology, and the Interior Space of Indian Myths and Temples', p. 128.

Sanskrit and Society: Beyond the Politics of Language

It may be fair to say that ours is a country where an incredibly rich linguistic heritage, far from occasioning anything more than rhetorical pride, becomes often the pretext for politics. Even as most of them struggle for patronage and survival, Indian languages, classical or vernacular, ancient or medieval, are found routinely reduced in public discourse to little more than instruments of power and conflict. A case in point is Sanskrit.

In ironic contrast to the enormous prestige Sanskrit enjoyed as a language of all learning and culture throughout her millennia-long premodern career across South, Central and South-East Asia, today this prolific tongue has come to be understood in its own land as merely an instrument of ritual and repression. Therefore it is regarded by some as redundant, if not abhorrent, to the secular and emancipated sensibilities of the modern age. This is, however, a woefully inadequate understanding of the vast and variegated repertoire of Sanskrit and the many voices and visions it entails.

Name any knowledge system in the world and you will find a Sanskrit text or entire genre devoted to it. From metaphysics to erotics, logic to poetics, statecraft to medicine including veterinary science, from maths and astronomy to painting and architecture, history, law, linguistics, music, ethics, food, some say even theft (!)…the list is endless. Not many know this or have creative exposure and opportunities now to explore Sanskrit's extraordinary intellectual history. Hence, unfortunately, all sorts of misconceptions abound, associating an obscurantism and archaism with the tongue. Further, in today's polarised climate, if you are an Indian studying Sanskrit or writing history based on representing—and not bashing—Sanskrit texts in all their virtuosity, you are liable to earn a particular ideological sobriquet or be labelled a cultural chauvinist.

Putting aside this politics of language, it is important to understand that there is nothing inherently sectarian or hegemonising in Sanskrit, and to assume so would be highly reductive of its rich history. Languages are not mere instruments of power and politics! They are the fecund medium for the transmission and preservation of enormous flows of knowledge. And if anything, they may embody plural perspectives, critical voices and debates.

For example, Sanskrit treatises (*shastras*) on any subject typically employ a dialogic form where a *purvapaksha* and an *uttarapaksha*—or different points of view—are presented and interrogated. Plays and poetry (*kavya*), on the other hand, often expose and indict various forms of authority in early India. You only have to read a Kalidasa or a Shudraka to hear the Sanskrit litterateur speak truth to power, or a Bilhana and a Kalhana to glimpse the contempt in which they held almighty kings. Consider this verse from Bilhana's *Vikramankadevacharita*, the biography of Vikramaditya VI, the 11th century CE Western Chalukyan king of Kalyana, Karnataka:

> When their own accomplishments are few and far between
> Why ever do kings gather around them great poets?

What need, indeed, would berry-wearing forest dwellers
Have for goldsmiths-in-residence? (1.25)[1]

Given that ancient and medieval poets typically depended
on the court for patronage, caricaturing the king thus was a
brave and risky thing to do! And yet they did it.
Similarly, you have texts such as the *Chaturbhani*, a set
of hilarious, at times bawdy, highly satirical monologue plays
from the 5th century CE, or Mahendravarman's 7th century
CE *Mattavilasaprahasana*, Damodaragupta's 9th century CE
Kuttanimata or Kshemendra's *Deshopadesa* from the 11th
century CE, which lampoon and castigate social hypocrisies
generally, and pompous members of society overly conscious
of their status and purity, in particular. This capacity for self-
satire hasn't got quite the notice it deserves.

Still other texts present commentaries on unorthodox
or transgressive attitudes and behaviour, thereby sagaciously
engaging with and complicating the question of what
constituted right or wrong rather than propagating any
dogma. The *Mahabharata* and *Ramayana* are outstanding
examples. They take up questions of legitimacy at every
step in their complex plots, not exempting even Gods from
such an interrogation. Shri Rama's murder of Bali and Shri
Krishna's use of a half-truth to weaken the enemy warrior
Drona come to mind. The *Shrimad Bhagavadgita* is nothing
but an engagement with profound individual and social
dilemmas, placing them in the transcendent perspective of
universal good. The larger aim was perhaps moving towards
a more ethical order for the individual and the community
at large. Similarly, *kavya*s do not always appear committed to
reproducing hierarchies determined by wealth, gender, ritual

authority and monarchy, but instead may critique them in the interests of fairness. The concerns and vantages of some of these texts could extend to the underdog, the menial, the criminal, the rebel, even the 'feminist', etc. as I have detailed in my book *Imagining the Urban*.

Clearly, Sanskrit writers were not passive "housebirds of patricians", as D D Kosambi provocatively called them, simply

Figure 7.1 Shri Krishna Gita Upadesha, Vintage Print 1830. Courtesy: The Tallenge Store.

mouthing what the ruling class of the day may have wanted to hear and complicitly furthering ideologies of domination.[2] The narratives in Sanskrit literature are far more complex and profound than that and present a polyphony of worldviews—if only we are willing to listen. But modern intellectuals, while arrogating to themselves the quality of enlightened radicalism, are loathe to extend any such possibility to their forebears. The tendency has been instead to label Sanskrit as elitist and courtly and having little to do with the wider world. Below, let us further investigate these assumptions about Sanskrit literature and move towards a greater appreciation of its public interface.

Contrary to misconceptions in certain circles today associating a narrow obscurantism with Sanskrit, this essay is a reminder of the vast and variegated repertoire of this prodigious language. This repertoire has included not only virtually all knowledge systems known to humankind, but a multiplicity of voices and visions. Yet the tendency in modern scholarship has been to label Sanskrit literary culture elitist and rarefied, having little to do with the wider world. Going forward, we interrogate this assumption vis-a-vis Sanskrit drama (*natya*, a sub-genre of *kavya*), with a view to moving towards a greater appreciation of its social reach. Some of the greatest Sanskrit plays were written by luminaries such as Bhasa, Shudraka, Kalidasa, Harsha, Vishakhadatta and Bhavabhuti among many others.

We saw how Sanskrit poets were not passive "housebirds of patricians" but exercised considerable critical agency in representing figures of power and authority of their time. They also pointed to unorthodox social attitudes and behaviour, thereby sagaciously engaging with and complicating the question of right and wrong. But who was Sanskrit literature composed for?

There is no doubt that any literature that requires a great degree of learning and leisure to compose would have been patronised or cultivated by affluent individuals. This would mean the king or ministers on the one hand and wealthy magnates on the other. We must beware, however, of confusing patron and audience. This is because, as the *Natyashastra* (henceforth *NS*)—India's earliest work of dramaturgy, composed approximately in the 2nd century CE—tells us, Sanskrit plays were performed at festivals, among other occasions, in public places such as temples and city squares (*NS* IV. 269).

Indeed, Bhavabhuti's 9th century CE play *Malatimadhava* (I. prologue, p. 2) spells it out thus: "A large conclave of men (*mahajanasamaja*) residing in different quarters has gathered here in connection with the festival of Lord Kalapriyanatha and I am ordered by the assembly of the learned (*vidvajjanaparishada*) to entertain them by the performance of some new play". Note that audience and sponsors are clearly distinguished from each other. Similarly, Vijaya's 8th century CE *Kaumudimahotsava* (I. prologue, p. 3) alludes to the autumn "public festival" (*sarvajanasamanyamahotsava*) as the occasion on which it is performed, while Kalidasa's 4th century CE *Malavikagnimitra* (I. prologue, p. 3) refers to the "spring festival" in the same way. Interestingly, Bana's 7th century CE *Harshacharita* (IV. 142–8) (a biography, not a play) has also vividly described festivals as occasions when the 'high' and 'low' mingle.

Then, types of plays such as the *vithi* ('street play'), *bhana* (erotico-comic monologue) and *prahasana* (farce), with their lively, irreverent, often bawdy content, are suggestive of general lay audiences. Moreover, the *NS* (I.12) explicitly describes drama as "the fifth Veda for *all* classes of society (*panchamam sarvavarnikam vedam*)". Far from envisaging, as it is often claimed it does, a purely connoisseurial audience, this text speaks of the presence of various categories of viewers across a spectrum: the superior, the inferior and the middling (*uttamadhamamadhya*). In fact there is explicitly a reference to fools (*murkha*) and children in the theatre! (*NS* XXVII.57; XXVI.126; XXVII.61).

It is true that the *NS* first prescribes a long list of qualities such as high birth, good character, learning, a sensitive nature, etc., for a viewer. But this is clearly only an ideal, as the text goes on to realistically observe that "all these various qualities are not known to exist in any single spectator"! In fact it admonishes that a play should "contain no obscure and difficult word (*gudhashabdarthahina*) and be intelligible to country people" (*NS* XVII.121).[3]

The *NS*'s final take on the matter of audience is that "different are the dispositions of women and men, young and old, who may be of the superior, middling and inferior type, and on such dispositions (the success of) drama rests" (*NS* XXVII.59, XXVI.126). Or, as Kalidasa put it, again, in his *Malavikagnimitra* (I.4, p. 11): "Drama is entertainment for a variety of people with very different tastes" (*natyam bhinnarucerjanasya bahudhapyekam samaradhanam*). Clearly, we need to rethink Sanskrit as a rarefied language of little reach or relevance.

In fact the audience (and therefore the materialising

context) for Sanskrit drama need not necessarily have been literary or even literate. This is because of the highly visual component of theatre, where dialogue (*vachika*) was only one out of four modes of histrionic representation. The other three were gestural (*angika*: movements of the face, limbs and body); sartorial and make-up (*aharya*); and significatory (*sattvika*: tears, horripilation, etc) (*NS* VI.23; XXIV.3).

Words were to be sung or recited to a variety of metres accompanied by dance motions. Altogether then, there was a large element of pantomime and spectacle: not for nothing was drama known as *drishyakavya* (visual literature). So learning was not a prerequisite for the consumption of this kind of literature, even if it was for its creation. What's more, the actors and actresses (*nata*, *nati*) performing the plays traditionally belonged to low class and caste. That they still did justice to these plays and presumably to the laborious instructions of the *NS* suggests the popular character of the theatrical enterprise in early India.

The often non-elite venue, heterogenous audience, and pantomimic nature of Sanskrit drama thus suggest that it was not confined to aristocratic circles. And this would definitely have shaped the reception of the ideas and representations in plays, especially ones that were critical of wrongdoing authority or orthodoxy. Note that *kavya*'s functions included not just entertainment but mimesis of the ways of society (*lokasya anukarana*), followed by ethical instruction (*upadesha*) in *dharma* (piety), *artha* (power) and *kama* (pleasure) (NS 1.109–10). These reiterate the socially engaged and didactic goals of Sanskrit drama for the welfare of the world at large.

We saw how the tendency in modern scholarship has been to label Sanskrit literary culture elitist and insular, having little to do with the wider world. We interrogated this assumption vis-a-vis Sanskrit drama (*natya*, a sub-genre of *kavya*), discovering its considerable public interface. Now, let us extend that enquiry to the question of language use in early India and the myths surrounding it.

While intriguingly little is known for sure about speech practice in antiquity, there have nonetheless developed several well-established views about the ideology of languages such as Sanskrit. It is believed to have been not a spoken tongue but an esoteric language of learning, "particularly of the brahmin caste and of its religion", as Thomas Burrow put it, while Prakrit is deemed a popular tongue, "the language of the masses".[4] Relatedly, there exists the influential theory among scholars that in the plays and indeed in early Indian society, Sanskrit was spoken only by high status men while lowly characters and women spoke Prakrit.[5] In other words, a linguistic hierarchy is assumed to exist in the way Sanskrit and Prakrit are mutually deployed in literature, and this is believed to correspond to socio-economic hierarchy.

This is such a neat and persuasive interpretation that the fact that there are telling exceptions drops quite from view. The *vidushaka*, for example, the jester and hero's companion, is consciously a brahmana but always speaks in Prakrit. Merchants and courtiers are also required to do so. On the other hand, *parivrajika*s (ascetics) are women but use Sanskrit even though queens usually do not and courtesans may. Children, even when male and high-caste, speak only Prakrit.

In fact, the section on languages in the *NS* (XVIII) attests other characters and situations that do not conform to the simplistic socio-economic theory. It clarifies the actual grounds for allocating tongues in drama, from characterisation, ethnicity and vocation of protagonists, to regional phonetic peculiarities of audiences, as well as blanket considerations such as "special times and situations." Clearly, *kavya*'s understanding of language use was a self-conscious one, and so too its choice to be bilingual in the first place, but the logic was not as stock as baldly reflecting social status.

This is reinforced by the fact that Prakrit, or rather the eight Prakrits as they have come down to us, are very much literary, not colloquial, dialects—as cultivated and standardised as Sanskrit. The 8th century CE *Kavyadarsha* (I.32, 33) an influential treatise on *kavya* composition, refers to both as *shishta* (grammatically disciplined/systematised) and regards both as tongues fit for poetic composition, so that no literary privilege is really inherent in one or the other. Some famous *kavya*s in Prakrit are Hala's 2nd century CE *Gathasattasai*, Pravarasena's 5th century CE *Setubandha* and the 8th century CE *Gaudavaho* by Vakapatiraja. Scholars also now suspect that the Prakrits used in the earliest inscriptions, the 3rd century BCE Ashokan edicts, were read aloud by state officials to the populace at large rather than being directly legible by the latter.

The *Kavyadarsha* (I. 33) does describe Sanskrit as *daivi vak* (divine speech), but this seems to have been on account of it being *perfected* speech "worked out by the sages" (*anvakhyata rishibhih*). This perfection and precision indeed explain why it is today deemed the ideal choice for computer programming and artificial intelligence by some. At the same time, the term that ancient grammarians used for Sanskrit, namely, *bhasha* ('that which is spoken'), suggests that its knowledge may have been more commonplace than we imagine, though its correct or eloquent application would have been confined to the learned, as with all languages. We are reminded here of the *NS*' admonition that a Sanskrit play "should contain no obscure and difficult word and be intelligible to country people".

Moreover, the fact that they were employed in the same play shows that Sanskrit and Prakrit belonged to a common speech community. A mutual intelligibility for the two on the part of the heterogenous audiences—which, as we saw, gathered at street crossings and temple courtyards no less than in royal assemblies to watch these performances—must be assumed. In fact, some scholars argue that Sanskrit and Prakrit may have been not different languages as much as different registers of speech in a diglossic situation. The *NS* (XVIII. 30) does speak of them as the "two ways (*dvividham)* of recitation in the common language which relates to the four castes (*jatibhashashrayam caturvarnya samashrayam)*".[6]

Though this is hardly a comprehensive survey of the matter, it suffices to question rigid notions about India's earliest languages. Seen together, there is clearly a need to not only review the supposed subalternity of Prakrits but rethink Sanskrit as a rarefied language and literary culture of little reach or relevance to society. At the heart of Sanskrit literature was a deep engagement with the social in ways that defy modern-day presuppositions.

Notes

1   Yigal Bronner, 'The Poetics of Ambivalence' in Y Bronner et al. edited (2014) *Innovations and Turning Points: Toward a History of Kavya Literature,* Delhi: Oxford University Press, p. 500.

2   D D Kosambi and V V Gokhale edited (1957) *The Subhaṣitaratnakoṣa,* vol. II, Harvard Oriental Series vol. 42, Harvard: Harvard University Press, p. xlvi.

3   References in this essay are to the following text editions: *The Nāṭyaśastra Ascribed to Bharata Muni,* vol. I–II (1967) translated by Manmohan Ghosh, Calcutta: Manisha Granthalaya; *Bhavabhuti's Malatimadhava* (1967) text and translation by M R Kale, Delhi: Motilal Banarsidass; *Kaumudi-Mahotsava Nataka* (1953) text and translation (into Hindi) by Devadatt Shastri, Delhi: Sahni Prakashan; *Works of Kalidasa,* vol. I (2002) edited and translated by C R Devadhar, Delhi: Motilal Banarsidass; *The Harṣa-carita of Bāṇa* (1968) translated by E B Cowell and F W Thomas, Delhi: Motilal Banarsidass; *Kavyadarsa,* Parichheda 1&2 (1936) edited by S Vishwanathan and C Sankara Rama Sastri, Madras: Balmanorama series no. 36.

4   Thomas Burrow 'Ancient and Modern Languages' in AL Basham edited (1975) *A Cultural History of India,* New Delhi: Oxford University Press, p. 162.

5   Ibid., p. 165; Romila Thapar (1999) *Sakuntala: Texts, Readings, Histories,* New Delhi: Kali for Women, p. 78; Hans Henrich Hock and Rajeshwari Pandharipande cited in Jan E M Houben edited (1996) *Status and Ideology of Sanskrit,* Leiden/New York: E J Brill, p. 160 ; Daud Ali (2006) *Courtly Culture and Political Life in Early Medieval India,* New Delhi: Foundation Books, p. 81.

6   For a discussion of diglossia in early India, see Shonaleeka Kaul (2010) *Imagining the Urban: Sanskrit and the City in Early India,* Delhi: Permanent Black, p. 27–29.

Bridging Gaps, Creating Divides: Sanskrit Texts, Europe and the Problem of Translation

Perhaps nothing better captures the dynamics of the civilisational interface between India and Europe as the practice of translation of classical Sanskrit texts into European languages in the 19th century. It is a founding premise and 'problem' of comparative literature that translation entails not so much a transfer as a transformation of meaning, especially when the two ecumenes involved are vastly separated by time, space and worldview. This essay examines the process of translation into English of the 'first work of history in India', the celebrated Sanskrit epic *Rajatarangini* (12th century CE), to argue that it may have transformed the text in complex and crucial ways. Though traditional Sanskrit poetry replete with the aesthetic form, conventions and concerns of the *kavya* genre, the text's exegesis at the hands of European Orientalists such as Harold Hayman Wilson, Georg Buhler and Aurel Stein laid the groundwork for its reincarnation in the genre of history—with lasting, fraught results. Aspects of figuration proper to a traditional discourse such as rhetoric, myth and the ethico-didactic were dismissed, whereas empiricist qualities such as chronology, causation and objectivity were valourised, whether or not these were central to the originary Sanskrit literary culture. This essay attempts to locate this recasting of the poem's meaning and purpose in the intellectual and political trends of the 19th and 20th centuries, and to call attention to the many grave epistemic contradictions this introduced in the modern understanding of an iconic ancient Indian text. It thereby demonstrates that via translation, India was not just transferred to but transformed in post-Enlightenment Europe.

It may be fair to say that no matter the commitment to semantic fidelity or even literalism, translation seems to inevitably involve in some degree or the other a change not only in the language of discourse but, with that, in its meaning as well. The acquired or altered meaning, in the interests of intelligibility, may tend to align with the interpretive apparatus of the literary or intellectual culture into which the text is being translated, rather than that of the originating culture. This is particularly so when the two ecumenes at either end of this journey are separated by centuries and also by continents, and their conceptual categories and modes of representation, not to say concerns and worldviews, may be incommensurable and irreducible to that of each other. What may follow in such a situation is something of a shift in the characterisation and typology of the text and its evaluation, post- translation, in terms of disciplinary parameters alien to it.

In the light of these observations, this essay scrutinises the modern reinvention of the iconic *Rajatarangini*, the sprawling, twelfth-century versified account in Sanskrit of the kings of Kashmir from the earliest to the poet, Kalhana's, own time.

The first to attempt a study and partial translation of the *Rajatarangini* into English in the year 1825 was Horace Hayman Wilson, then secretary of the Royal Asiatic Society of Bengal. He also translated, during his long association with the pioneering orientalist society as well as with the East India Company College, other works in Sanskrit such as Kalidasa's *Meghadutam* and the *Vishnu Purana*. Terming it "the Hindu History of Cashmir", Wilson famously observed about Kalhana's *Rajatarangini* that it was "the only Sanskrit composition yet discovered, to which the title of History, can with any propriety be applied".[1] His reasons were simple and can be summarised as the text's deference to chronology, assigning dates for the start and end of every regime; its alleged quest for objectivity, seen in the poet's call to impartiality; and its display of causation, attributing events to explanations.

The true import of Wilson's comment can be understood against the background of the then-emerging misconception and propaganda that Indian civilisation was singularly lacking in historical sense or consciousness, a notion that came to stick. This 'lack', in turn, was believed to be on account of other stereotypes that were developing about India as the British colonial regime established itself in the early 19th century, namely, a greater proclivity of Indians to spiritual over material interests on the one hand, and a basic changelessness and stasis of Indian society itself, on the other. These together were deemed responsible for the apparent dearth of historical literature, especially as compared to an abundance of scriptures, mythologies, and aesthetic works produced in the subcontinent in the premodern period. It needs no labouring to see that, despite his lifelong sympathy to the cause of indigenous Indian languages and culture, Wilson's judgement on the *Rajatarangini* as being *the sole exception* to Sanskrit literary culture's indifference to history, both sprung from and, more importantly, fed into the notion of that culture's ahistoricity.

Perhaps the defining moment in the journey of the *Rajatarangini* was when the German paleographer and

Sanskrit scholar, Georg Buhler, a member of the Bombay branch of the Royal Asiatic Society, followed by his remarkable Hungarian-British pupil, the ethnographer-geographer Marc Aurel Stein, undertook its detailed study, an initiative that lasted many years. Stein brought out the first critical edition of the text in 1892 followed by its complete and authoritative English translation accompanied by a commentary of sorts in 1900.[2] Buhler's and Stein's separate writings on the *Rajatarangini* operated well within the Orientalist framework and reinforced Wilson's founding characterisation of the text as a unique historical narrative, qualifying it only in so far as Stein emphasised the regional character of the (historical) enterprise and its rootedness in the local geography, which he painstakingly attempted to reconstruct on the ground in Kashmir, thereby imputing to the text a defining commitment to an empirical documentation of the past.

It is worth remarking that, following from his apparent impatience for the purely poetic qualities of the text, Stein's translation, which was in any case in prose, chose to expunge several such verses as he deemed excessively rhetorical, didactic and conventionalised, and so contributing little to the 'information' the text otherwise, in his estimation, so valuably provided. Thus, as Ranjit Sitaram Pandit, a Kashmiri scholar of Sanskrit, who produced his own English translation of the poem in 1935, puts it: "[Stein's] method of translation does not give an adequate conception of the work as a literary composition ... Further, his main interest in the chronicle was archaeological and topographical and he omitted to translate verses which according to him are in the 'Kavya style.'"[3]

Though Pandit claimed to remedy this omission in his rendering that came to parallel Stein's in popularity, he nonetheless acknowledged the dichotomy of classifying the text as history or poetry.[4] (An interesting reflection of the belief in this dichotomy was also in Jawaharlal Nehru's observation in the Foreword to Pandit's translation: "It is a history and it is a poem, though the two perhaps go ill together".) The label of history for the *Rajatarangini*, thus, had come to stay.

A recent work has compared and critiqued Stein's and Pandit's translations and ideological and interpretive locations and so that need not detain us here.[5] The point to note, however, is that Stein's editorial selection or suppression, though quantitatively minor, assumes significance for what it reveals about the direction in which the text was being further pushed along at the turn of the 20th century CE by scholarly interpretation and privileging of 'objective' over 'subjective' qualities.

The classification and indeed celebration of the *Rajatarangini* as a work of history, which was inaugurated by philologists, was sealed and stamped by historians in the post-Independence era. Thus, in 1961, Kalhana was officially included in a seminal volume on *Historians of India, Pakistan and Ceylon*, where preeminent Indologist Arthur Llewellyn Basham and the nationalist historian Ramesh Chandra Majumdar, using Stein's edition as authoritative, essentially repeated the earlier points in praise of the text.

See for example this representative statement from Basham: "The work is unique as the only attempt at true history in the whole of surviving Sanskrit literature ...".[6] Or this from Majumdar: "Even a modern historian should have little hesitation in ranking Kalhana as a great historian.... [for his] correct appreciation of *the true ideals and methods of history*" [emphasis added].[7] Their definitive statements became the bible for future generations of scholars and continue to be taught in Indian universities till today.

There was, however, one major problem in this glowing cumulative appraisal. All these translators and interpreters of the *Rajatarangini* were deeply disturbed by *other* aspects of the text that did *not* fit their rather positivist idea of what history should be—aspects which they then had to disown and describe as "failings" and "imperfections". Thus, as we have seen, Stein thought the rhetorical and didactic parts of the *Rajatarangini* were redundant to the narrative proper, which was historical, while Buhler condemned the resort to myth as rendering the chronology of a large part of the text "valueless" and the author suspect. Indeed the latter even translated a famous verse from Kalhana's preamble in such a fashion as to provocatively imply that the poet had no qualms in doctoring—lengthening or shortening—the dates and durations of the reign of different kings to fit the needs of his composition. The verse in question bears quoting to illustrate what Pandit called "the gravity and nature of the errors occasionally committed by learned European scholars":[8]

Iyam nripanam ullase hrase va deshakalayoh |
Bhaishajya bhutasamvadi katha yuktopayujyate || (*RT* I. 21)

The above verse can much more readily and comprehensibly be translated as philosophically presenting the *Rajatarangini* as a medicine or remedy (*bhaishajya*) prescribed for kings in a state of ascendance or decline in their realms and reigns (*ullase hrase va deshakalayoh*). Indeed, Buhler's far-fetched and unsupported translation was shown by S P Pandit (Ranjit Sitaram Pandit's uncle and, like his nephew, a scholar of Sanskrit and Prakrit) and even Stein to be completely flawed, but what it points to for our purpose is the lingering instinctive mistrust that accompanied the conferring of the title of history on this traditional Sanskrit text.

The contradictions involved in imposing this category of objectivist history become still more acute in Majumdar. Despite christening Kalhana "a great historian," Majumdar enumerated a long list of "failings" and spoke of his "very defective" method consisting in the inclusion of mythical or legendary kings, the assigning of "absurd" lengths of rule to some out of "a blind faith in the Epics and Puranas", a belief in witchcraft and magic, explanation of events as due to the influence of fate "rather than to any rational cause", a didactic tendency inspired by Hindu views of karma and treating historical events "merely as backgrounds for display of poetical and rhetorical skill".[9] Based on this vantage, both he and Basham maintained that the first three *tarangas* or books of the *Rajatarangini* were less credible than the last five. Influentially, following their lead, Romila Thapar in 1983, again as part of a volume on *Historians of Medieval India*, suggested a separation between "earlier books", where supernatural causes and fate were important, and "later" ones, that reflected, we are told, "the maturity of Kalhana's historical thinking." She also dismissed Kalhana's moralism and didacticism.[10]

❧ ❧

The *Rajatarangini* thus ended up splintered, obfuscating in complex ways the nature of the original text as a whole. Especially damaging was that all aspects of figuration proper to a poetic discourse were deemed redundant, extraneous and detrimental to the essentially "historical" substance and intent of Kalhana's enterprise. It is significant that though derived from modern objectivist notions of history in the West, rather than from any indigenous or ancient approaches to treating the past, the underlying belief in the opposition of "factual" (true) history and "fictive" (false) literature was new even to 19th century CE Europe.[11] The Rankean or positivist turn in European historiography, with its stress on facticity, objectivity and scientific method, merged with imperialism through the agency of the likes of James Mill who, as early as 1817, in his notorious *The History of British India*, had launched a diatribe against "backward" Indian culture that did not match up to the Graeco-Roman or Judaeo-Christian civilisations. The result was a downgrading and delegitimising of indigenous Indian narratives of the past.[12] Relatedly, in being isolated as a flawed exception in all of Sanskrit literature, the *Rajatarangini* as history was both the creation and the victim of an intellectual approach that sought to simultaneously appropriate and undermine a traditional Sanskrit text. In the remainder of this essay, I shall focus on three of the major errors of category executed by modern translations of the *Rajatarangini* with respect to chronology, myth and causality, and objectivity.

Let us first take up the merit of assigning dates and sequence. While there is no doubt that Kalhana's punctilious dating of reigns is remarkable, it was not the first time that such an exercise was undertaken in early India, since *vamshavalis* or traditional royal genealogies in Sanskrit and other languages in the early medieval period, not to mention the genealogies in the 18 major Puranas, did much the same in what was obviously a long-standing documenting practice.[13] This traditional character and functional trait of the *Rajatarangini* is entirely missed by stressing its uniqueness on account of sequential dating. That apart, the scholarly valourising of linear dating of events ignores the fact that while all narratives necessarily manipulate time by rearranging it to configure a meaningful pattern, there could be different modes of configuring temporality in different times and cultures, and even within a single culture, including distinctly non-linear modes.

Thus, you have the cyclical concept of *chaturyuga*—the four, recurring mega-periods of moral ascent and decline (*krita, treta, dvapara* and *kali*)—which constitutes the understanding of time deployed across centuries by seminal texts of the Indic tradition like the *Purana*s, the *Mahabharata* and the *Ramayana*. As such, the *yuga*s may be regarded as a culturally popular choice for rendering time and so it is no surprise that Kalhana himself uses the *kaliyuga* as the basis of the dates he ascribes to the early kings of Kashmir.

In other words, there may be nothing inherently virtuous in a 12th century CE Sanskrit composition providing a linear chronology to its narrative, nor, in principle, anything objectionable in its resort to the cyclical *chaturyuga*. Yet the latter was regarded as unacceptable in the *Rajatarangini*, as we have seen, a show of "blind faith in Epics and Puranas" (Majumdar) and a reliance on "legendary and fictive events" (Buhler), such as the *Mahabharata* war which is traditionally believed to separate the *dvapara* from the *kali*. So, even as deference to chronology was a good thing, the choice of a culturally specific, if mythical, system of dating was not!

One of the things this conflicted evaluation of the *Rajatarangini* exposed was that as per the empiricist understanding of the mythical, much like of the poetic, myth was regarded as always fictive and false. In other words, myths and legends in the *Rajatarangini* evoked distrust, even dismissal, because modern scholars, forever measuring literary truth by its veracity rather than its epistemic function, treated them as incapable of capturing meanings and values imputed to the past.

Indeed, the disappointment all modern translators of the text expressed with mythical aspects of the *Rajatarangini* may have had more to do with the particular, *a priori* nature of historic truth they were searching for than with the kind of truth the text deploying myth was interested in conveying. For instance, as has been postulated for ancient Greek mythology, myth need not be about the 'real' as truth, but about *what was noble as truth*.[14] Indeed, myths in the *Rajatarangini* (*RT* I.25–27, 240–72) about unrighteous kings and their cities that were destroyed by the anger of tutelary deities (*nagas*), or about the origins of the land in an act of the great gods, display precisely such a meaning and function in Kalhana's ethicised political commentary. This would, however, be apparent only if the didacticism of the text is recognised as essential to the text's scheme of things, as I argue, rather than as external and superfluous to it, as most other scholars have maintained.

The other quality rather ardently ascribed to Kalhana, that of objectivity or impartiality, may also be based on an interpretive presumption. The verse typically cited in support of this quality is the seventh in the preamble of the poem. There, in Kalhana's description of the poet's speech being rid of liking or hatred when speaking of past matters (*ragadveshabahishkrita bhutarthakathane*), modern historians have read a manifesto for the ideal historian. This is premised, however, on a circular assumption that Kalhana is referring to a historian at work; Majumdar explicitly says so.[15]

In fact, however, the verse must be read together with the verses preceding and following it, all of which refer only to the talented poet (*gunavan, kavi*); there is no other term even remotely resembling 'historian'. Indeed, a Sanskritist has recently argued that this verse ought to be translated instead in consonance with a *kavya*'s typical agenda, namely, the evocation of a *rasa* or abstracted aesthetic state. In Kalhana's case, this was his stated project of generating a state of equipoise (*shanta rasa)* though his composition (*RT* I. 23). As stipulated by the leading *kavya* theoreticians of the time such as Anandavardhana and Abhinavagupta, the composing in the *shanta rasa* required the experiencing of a similar calm and detachment (*vairagya*), not impartiality, by the poet himself.[16]

In any case, we now know that objectivity—"*the truth out there as it was*"—as the foundation of the historian's enterprise is open to questioning, even a "preposterous fallacy", as E H Carr called it, given the central role of subjective and variable inference and interpretation in the reconstruction of an essentially unobservable past.[17] Moreover, ironically contradicting his stated aesthetic dispassion, detached and impartial are the last things Kalhana is when narrating the good or evil deeds of Kashmiris. His deep personal involvement in the events he narrates and moralises over is stark. Indeed, there are verses where Kalhana is clearly choosing to be the partisan of the good and the virtuous, and to be contemptuous and denunciatory towards dubious and evil characters, even adopting obscene or scatological language in the latter case, which is highly unusual in Sanskrit poetry (for example, *RT* V.392, VI.157–58, VII.283). At such moments, significantly, ethics seem to have weighed more with Kalhana than aesthetics.

The final trait I take up for discussion that the early translators of the *Rajatarangini* chose to highlight was its tendency to supply causes for most occurrences. Implicit in this favourable valuation of causation was the faith that it displayed in rationality. Such an expectation of rationality is, however, immediately demolished via the common criticism, from the same scholars, that Kalhana frequently cited fate and other supernatural forces. In other words, it was not just commitment to causality that was expected of Kalhana, but a particular brand of empirical rationality, failing which this supposedly historical trait would lose meaning.

Such an understanding of historical causality, however, overlooks the complexity of a traditional causal vision. Fate (*bhagya*) in the *Rajatarangini* is deployed in multiple contexts, in "earlier" and "later" *tarangas* alike. Thus, inscrutable providence shows up as a poetic device in situations of inexplicability such as King Jayapida's sudden change of character from an enlightened ruler to an oppressive one, which brings forth an exclamation from Kalhana invoking fate (*RT* IV.620).

Most of all, as the fruits of *karma* in a past life, *bhagya* is used as a didactic device, a source of blessing or punishment according to good or bad deeds of individuals or Kashmiri society as a whole. Thus the death of the cruel and tyrannical king, Mihirakula, is said to be "owing to the dawn of the subjects' merit" (*prajapunyodayaih*), while the plunder of Kashmir under officials of Queen Didda is regarded as "the result of its accumulated evil actions (*dushkritaih*)" (*RT* I.325, VI. 288). The main point is that *karma* and fate serve as an opportunity for Kalhana to, once again, insert an ethical perspective, which, I believe, is his chief interest throughout the text. On another plane, beyond the boundaries of empiricism and verifiability, fate may be construed as a particularly suitable literary device for a tale of time, since it resonates with a connectedness of the past and the present, and as such is profoundly causal, if not apparently so.

This essay thus argues that the recasting of the *Rajatarangini* as objectivist history, credited with modern qualities neither unique nor central to the concerns of the text, but shorn of all features and recurrent tendencies (such as rhetoric, myth and didacticism) true to the traditional Sanskrit poetry that it was, spawned an understanding of the text that was divorced from its literary culture and logic, and was collapsible under its own contradictions. While there is a strong case therefore for revisiting this troubled translation of the text, it remains to be asked whether this means that the *Rajatarangini* was entirely bereft of historicality. Or that whether we are returning in effect to the very opposition of history and literature that we have been critiquing. The answer to both questions is no, and that it is possible and desirable to restore the *Rajatarangini* to a more integral notion of historicality that is sensitive to the literary.

In *The Making of Early Kashmir*, and also in Chapter 9 in this book, I have proposed the need to focus on the metapoetics of the *Rajatarangini*'s parent genre, Sanskrit *kavya*— something that seems to have been scarcely deferred to by the European translators of the text.[18] I emphasise that both *kavya* generally and the *Rajatarangini* in particular staked claim to a privileged epistemic insight that extended to matters past. This was no empty boast; alongside a meticulously referential documentation of umpteen figures and events from Kashmir's history, Kalhana's representation of the past was also deeply imbued with the ethical principles of *dharma* and *karma*, which I translate as critical idealism and call to action. These constituted, according to him, true knowledge of time and human behaviour and were the principles around which he wove his entire narrative. Thus, as true to a *kavya*, the primary enterprise of the *Rajatarangini* was the representation of Kashmir as a discursive political space mediated by an ethical paradigm.

In sum, such a translation alone that does justice to the injunctive-ethical ideals and framework of the *Rajatarangini* can perhaps do justice to its literary and historical vision. And such an approach alone that reads and respects Sanskrit literature on its own terms can perhaps challenge persistent errors in colonial Indology.

Notes

1   Horace H Wilson (1825) 'An Essay on the Hindu History of Cashmir,' *Asiatick Researches*, XV, pp. 1–119.

2   Kalhana's *Rajatarangini or Chronicle of the Kings of Kashmir*, vol. I, M A Stein edited (1960) [1892] Delhi: Munshiram Manoharlal.

3   Ranjit Sitaram Pandit (2004) [1935] *River of Kings: Rajatarangini, The Saga of the Kings of Kashmir,* New Delhi: Sahitya Akademi, p. xv.

4   Ibid., Translator's note, xiii to xvii.

5   Chitralekha Zutshi (2011) 'Translating the Past: Rethinking Rajatarangini Narratives in Colonial India', *The Journal of Asian Studies*, 70, 1, pp. 5–27.

6   A L Basham 'The Kashmir Chronicle' in C H Philips edited (1961) *Historians of India, Pakistan and Ceylon*, London: Oxford University Press, p. 58.

7   R C Majumdar 'Ideas of History in Sanskrit Literature' in C H Philips edited (1961) *Historians of India, Pakistan and Ceylon*, pp. 14, 25.

8   Quoted by Pandit, *The River of Kings*, p. xv, 8, fn 21.

9   Majumdar, 'Ideas of History,' pp. 22–24.

10   Romila Thapar 'Kalhana' in Mohibul Hasan edited (1983) *Historians of Medieval India*, New Delhi: Meenakshi Prakashan, pp. 52–62.

11   19th century Europe also saw exceptions to the Rankean school in the form of Hegel, Droysen, Nietzsche and Croce who stressed the inventive aspect of the historian's putative enquiry, and that "facts" were not apodictically provided but constituted by the historian's own agency. Hayden White argues that all of them sought to ground historical insights into reality in a poetic intuition. See Hayden White (1978) *Tropics of Discourse: Essays in Cultural Criticism*, Baltimore and London: Johns Hopkins University Press, pp. 53–54. It was undoubtedly Ranke's work, however, that came to have a defining influence on modern historiography.

12   See Rama Mantena (2007) 'The Question of History in Precolonial India,' *History and Theory*, 46, 3, pp. 396–408.

13   See Michael Witzel (1990) 'On Indian Historical Writing: The Role of *Vamshavalis*', *Journal of the Japanese Association of South Asian Studies*, 2, pp. 1–57.

14   Paul Veyne (1988) *Did the Greeks believe in their Myths?* Trans. Paula Wissing, Chicago: Chicago University Press.

15   Majumdar, 'Ideas of History,' pp. 21–22.

16   See Slaje, 'In the Guise of Poetry–Kalhana Reconsidered', pp. 224–26.

17   E H Carr (1961) *What is History?* Cambridge: Cambridge University Press, p. 12. Leon Goldstein has best theorised this critique by

pointing out that historical knowledge is necessarily inferential, since "the past as such" is an absent object of enquiry. History therefore cannot have truth correspondence with the past in ways traditionally seen as mimetic or empirical. For a lucid discussion, see B. Surendra Rao (2010) *History as Historiography,* Bangalore: Indian Council of Historical Research, pp. 9–10.

18 Shonaleeka Kaul (2018) *The Making of Early Kashmir: Landscape and Identity in the Rajatarangini*, Delhi: Oxford University Press.

Early Indic Visions of History

9

In 1825, Horace Hayman Wilson, Member of the Royal Asiatic Society of Bengal and translator of gems of Sanskrit literature such as Kalidasa's *Meghaduta* and the *Vishnu Purana*, translated parts of Kalhaṇa's *Rajatarangini*, the 12th century CE "Hindu History of Cashmir", as he called it. Wilson famously observed about the *Rajatarangini* that it was "the only Sanskrit composition yet discovered, to which the title of History, can with any propriety be applied".[1]

Read closely, Wilson's apparent adulation for the text's historical qualities was in fact indictment of an entire literary culture and civilisation for its lack thereof. Just a few years before him, the imperialist historian James Mill, in his notorious *The History of British India* (1817), had launched a diatribe against 'backward' Indian literary and cultural traditions for not matching up to their Graeco-Roman or Judaeo-Christian counterparts, which were celebrated for their historicity. The culmination of such assessments was a downgrading and delegitimising of indigenous Indian narratives of, and approaches to, the past.

As we saw in Chapter 8, comments such as those of Mill and Wilson can be understood as both illustrative of and foundational in the then-emerging misconception and propaganda that Indic civilisation, and particularly Sanskrit traditions, were singularly lacking in historical sense, a notion that came to endure and enjoyed great currency ever since. This 'lack', in turn, was believed to be on account of other Orientalist stereotypes that were developing about India as the British colonial regime established itself in the early 19th century, namely, a greater proclivity of Indians to spiritual over material interests, and a changelessness and stasis of Indian society itself. These together were deemed responsible for the apparent dearth of historical literature in India, especially as compared to the abundance of scriptures, mythology and aesthetic works.

Against this entrenched colonial bias of two hundred years, documenting and understanding early Indic visions and methods of history on their own terms assumes considerable significance. We will do so by: (a) surveying the range of evidence available of early Indian societies displaying a distinct regard for time and time-keeping and preserving and chronicling events for posterity, and (b) questioning the Positivist Eurocentric basis on which the modern discipline of history has come to exclude traditional Indic modes of narrating the past such as myth and ethical instruction.

Time and chronology are regarded as perhaps the single most important element of historical consciousness. Early India deployed both linear and non-linear systems of reckoning time. Among the former were a number of eras or calendars (*samvat, kala)* that were evolved and used over centuries. The most famous of these would be the Vikram *samvat* dating to 57 BCE and the Shaka *samvat* inaugurated in 78 CE. (The latter was adopted as the official calendar of Government of India.) Some other calendars were the Gupta *kala* (319 CE), the Kalachuri-Chedi era (248 CE) and the Harsha era (606 CE). Though occurring also in texts, the use of these *samvats* is most prominently seen in thousands of inscriptions.

Epigraphs from the 3rd century BCE onwards display a striking sense of history in so far as their scribes were, by and large, punctilious about recording the date of their being inscribed as also of the event they were recording or commemorating, or of the king during whose reign the inscription was instituted. Later, more elaborate inscriptions, especially from south and central India, called copper plate land grant charters, included a detailed genealogy of the ruling king and his entire dynasty. They tended to give highly precise and complex dates starting with the era (*samvat*), year (*varsha*), month (*masa*), lunar fortnight (*paksha*), week (*saptah*), date (*tithi*), down to the day (*divasa*) and hour (*muhurta*) of the day!

However, Indic conceptions of time were not confined to anthropic and quotidian time; Indians were as conscious of vast cycles of cosmic time, against which also they thought it important to situate human history. Thus the concept of *chaturyuga* ('four eras') arose, to be found primarily in that vast corpus of texts called the *puranas*. One *yuga* followed another in a cycle characterised by declining moral values and general lawlessness, which, however, was followed by another cycle of regeneration.

The four *yugas* were *krita* (the golden age), *treta*, *dvapara* and *kali* (the dark or polluted age). Together they constituted a *mahayuga*, and one thousand *mahayugas* formed a *kalpa*, which was equal to 4.32 billion (human) years! Each *kalpa* was divided into 14 intervals known as *manvantaras*. The end of every *kalpa* was marked by deluge and annihilation of the world—till the next cycle of creation began. All these were exponentially widening divisions of time. Our present time is believed to be in the middle of the *kaliyuga*, which clocks a total of 4,32,000 years.

Rather than see *yuga*s and *kalpa*s or cyclical time as mythic time, their sheer enormity and scale can be read as a statement on the unreckonable nature and vastness of time when seen from the very beginnings of creation. This may be perhaps among the earliest expressions of the recent fields of 'deep history' or 'big history', which also seek to look back to the origins of the earth and the solar system. Further, the placing of moral order at the centre of time suggests a deeply ethical worldview. And the cyclicity of moral ascendance and decline, where history and human behaviour repeat themselves over and over again across the millennia, suggests a historical vision crucially invested with cultural memory.

❧

To recap: Thus what we have are Indic concepts of time which reflected an idea of history that spanned anthropic specificity or precision on the one hand and cosmic vastness or unreckonability on the other. These were infused with ethics and cultural memory to boot. Of these, the exponentially widening notion of time denoted by *yuga*s is best articulated in a corpus of texts known as *purana*s, literally 'ancient narratives on the past', as we saw. Eighteen pan-Indic *mahapurana*s have come down to us such as the *Vishnu Purana*, *Shiva Purana* and *Shrimadbhagavata Purana*, which were composed between the 3rd and 9th centuries CE; and many more subsidiary ones, *upapuranas*, such as *Kalika Purana* and *Vishnudharmottara Purana*; and still other local or *sthalapuranas*, including the *Nilamata Purana* and *Devanga Purana*.

The *puranas* are essentially sectarian, encyclopaedic texts in Sanskrit that claim to cover five themes (*panchalakshana*) (though they actually contain much more material): *sarga* (creation), *pratisarga* (re-creation), *manvantara* (epochal intervals), *vamsha* (genealogy) and *vamshanucarita* (biographies). So, it will be clear that apart from cosmology and theology, *puranas* also document vital information on ruling families as well as great sages, and their entire lineages and life-histories, many of these being historical. Therefore, these *vamshavalis* are an invaluable record of the political history of early India, including important dynasties such as the Barhadrathas, Haryankas, Shaishunagas, Nandas, Mauryas (founders of the first empire in Indian history), Shungas, Kanvas, Satavahanas and so on down till the Gupta kings. The *puranas* are also of course a treasure trove of geographical and cultural history of the entire country.

A companion genre to *purana* is *itihasa*—literally 'thus it was', thereby attesting an explicit engagement with the past. Tradition defines *itihasa* as:

> *dharmarthakamamokshanam upadeshasamanvitam*
> *kathayuktam puravrittam itihasam prachakshate.*

(Tales of the past, rendered in a narrative style, containing instruction in the four goals of life—piety, power, pleasure and liberation—is known as history.)[2]

This offers one of the earliest explicit definitions of history, which shows that a literary and socio-ethical pedagogy may have been at the heart of the Indic vision of the discipline.

Specifically, however, *itihasa* refers to the Sanskrit epics,

Mahabharata of Vyasa (400 BCE–400 CE) and *Ramayana* of Valmiki (500 BCE–500 CE) which record in detailed, continuous narrative form the stories surrounding important events in the lives of kings and kingdoms of early historic India such as the Kuru-Panchalas of Hastinapura and Ikshavakus of Ayodhya, along with a host of other allied dynasties said to be ruling over a large part of the subcontinent.

However, the presence of myths in the Epics has, among other reasons, led historians to deny them the status of history, thereby defying the tradition's self-understanding. Or, they have only grudgingly accorded them the defensive epithet of 'embedded history' for aspects of the past incidentally captured in them. But it needs to be remembered that both Epics deal centrally with issues of royal succession and war, thereby reflecting on important processes of state formation in early India vis-a-vis real polities. And again, piercing through all the mythology and indeed facilitated by it, at the heart of both Epics are meta-historical questions of ethics (*dharma*) and socio-political legitimacy, which merge with the divinity of the two central protagonists, Shri Krishna and Shri Rama.

Traces, however, of a society self-consciously recording and preserving for posterity the names and feats of significant individuals go still further back to the Vedas themselves, the most ancient literature of India dated (most conservatively) to 1500 BCE. Categories of Vedic verses titled *Danastuti* ('praise of charity'), *Narashamsi* ('praise of men') and *Gatha* ('stories') provide accounts of meritorious or heroic individuals and their social altruism.

In a sense, the same impulse is seen in mature and expanded form a millennium later in the independent poetic genre of *charita,* which are biographies chronicling, eulogising and also at times critiquing the lives of important personages, mostly kings and seers. Among the earliest *charita*s we get are the life stories of Gautama Buddha, such as Ashvaghosha's *Buddhacharita* (2nd century CE), and of King Ashoka, namely the *Ashokavadana* (6th century CE) which was composed in Sri Lanka.

Thereafter we see a spate of political biographies composed by court poets in regional kingdoms across the subcontinent such as Bana's *Harshacharita* (7th century CE Sthanishvara/Kanauj), Bilhana's *Vikramankadevacharita* (11th century CE Karnataka), Atula's *Mushikavamsha* (11th century CE, Kerala), Sandhyakara Nandin's *Ramapalacharita* (11th century CE Bengal), Jayanaka's *Prithvirajavijaya* (12th century CE Rajasthan) and Hemachandra's *Kumarapalacharita* (12th century CE Gujarat).

Among regional histories, the one name that towers above the rest comes from Kashmir, Kalhana's *Rajatarangini* (12th century CE), to which we will devote the concluding part of this essay. There are two reasons for this emphasis: (a) this text is generally (and mistakenly) understood to represent the only specimen of true history in all of Sanskrit literature; and (b) it provides an opportunity to illustrate traditional Indic modes of history such as rhetoric, myth, ethics and didacticism in high relief.

The *Rajatarangini* (*RT*) gives a continuous chronology for early Kashmir, using traditional Indic calendars such as *kaliyuga* and *shaka samvat,* to record the reign of every monarch of every dynasty that ruled the land. It also recounts a host of events that occurred during these regimes, and their policies, deeds and struggles, and explores a range of historical causes and explanations for them as well. Interestingly, the poet, Kalhana, claims to have consulted local land grant inscriptions (*shasana*), and older texts, to write his history, thus giving insight into the sources and techniques of the practice.

One of the outstanding features of the *RT* is that it begins with a prolegomenon clearly stating its purpose (*prayojana*) and philosophy. Kalhana states that 'shedding both attachment and aversion, the voice of the poet should be unwavering when recounting matters of the past' (I.7). Modern scholars have read this as a statement recognising objectivity as a virtue in a historian. It is worth noting, however, that Kalhana presents this as a poetic virtue and it may refer to the state of equipoise (*shanta rasa*) that Sanskrit poetics of the time recommended and which Kalhana adopted.

While most scholarship on the *RT* has valourised its empiricist qualities such as deference to chronology, 'objectivity', and causality (see Chapter 8), in my book *The Making of Early Kashmir* I have drawn attention to its poetic and figurative aspects as enunciating a historicality deeply charged with culturally specific meanings. The *RT* was, after all, classic epic poetry (*mahakavya* or *prabandha*), and according to tradition, the poet (*kavi*) was a seer (*rishi*) who possessed omniscience and divine sight (*divyadrishti*). With these powers, which arose from intuition (*pratibha*), *kavis* could gauge the real nature of things and even apprehend different dimensions of time.

Thus Kalhana says: 'Who else is capable of making visible (*pratyakshatam*) bygone times except the poet-creator who can make delightful productions (*ramyanirmana*)?' (I.4).

Here is an explicit Indic belief in the poet's creative ability to make the unobservable past perceptible—the quintessentially historical function. This claim to epistemic authority, however conventional, rendered such poetry the lamp that illuminates past realities (*kavyadipam bhutavastuprakashakam*).[3]

Significantly, however, *kavya*'s vision of history was inflected by a didactic mandate to provide instruction (*upadesha*) on a range of human affairs such as *dharma* (piety), *artha* (power), and *kama* (pleasure). For the *RT*, the area of instruction was specifically political morality (*rajadharma*), with the aim of ensuring social order and people's welfare (*prajanupalanam*). Accordingly, the primary enterprise of the *RT* was not merely penning a factual record of Kashmir's past, but representing Kashmir as a discursive political space infused by ethics.

Thus, kingship in the RT is evaluated according to certain principles: Good conduct (*sat*), righteousness, generosity/liberality (*dakshinya*), discriminating intellect (*sarasaraviveka*) which encouraged men of merit, character and learning, and the will to enforce justice (*dharma*) and ensure absence of fear (*abhaya*) among subjects. These constituted the personal and political values to which the sovereign's commitment was expected in the early Indic vision.

Then, these values were plotted through a series of exemplars that Kalhana identified in Kashmir's kings, clubbing them in pairs elucidating their comparative morality (good versus bad rulers). Thus, the entire *River of Kings* can be understood as a flow of ethical figures, in which didactic and historical functions coalesced. This in turn meant that truths in the *RT* were both transcendent, in invoking higher ethical ends, and contingent in so far as they were located in a real historical past.

What's more, myth and popular memory were used

to further this ethico-political vision of history. Modern historians have tended to regard myth with consternation, believing the mythic to be always fictive and false rather than a society's meaningful rendition of truth claims. However, as Paul Veyne observed, myth is not about the 'real' as truth, but about what was noble as truth.[4] Indeed, myths in the *RT* (*RT* I.25–27, 240–72) based on local Kashmiri legends about wrongdoer kings and their cities catastrophically destroyed by the anger of tutelary deities (*naga*s), or about the origins of the land of Kashmir in an act of the great gods—display such a meaning and function in this ethicised commentary.

Far from being a lapse in critical judgment, then, the inclusion of myths was critical in the text's scheme of things. By sanctifying the land and warning unrighteous social actors about the consequences of their actions, it provided the synergistic background for the unveiling of ethical governance, which seems to have been the larger purpose of composing the *RT*.

❦

Thus our ancient historical traditions span a wide variety, from the highly precise and factual such as the public epigraphs, to the ethical and didactic such as the literary representations of human history as a laboratory of idealism and a call to action (*dharma* and *karma*). The sacred and the profane, the transcendent and the contingent, were intertwined in this understanding. Rather than inflict inapt colonial parameters on it, it is best to grasp Indic history-writing in this larger sense, sensitive to the culturally specific functions this civilisation assigned the genre.

Notes

1   Horace H Wilson (1825) 'An Essay on the Hindu History of Cashmir,' *Asiatick Researches*, XV, pp. 1–119.

2   This is the most widely quoted version cited by V S Apte under the head of itihasa in his The Practical Sanskrit-English Dictionary, p. 276. A slightly different version that occurs in *Vishnu Dharmottara Purana* 3, 15, 1–2 says: *purvairacaritam siddhidharmarthakamasadhakam mokshasya yatropanyasa itihasa sa ucyate.*

3   *Rājataraṅgiṇi of Śrīvara and Śuka*, I. 1, 4. For more on the theme of *kavya* as history, see Shonaleeka Kaul (2023) 'The Lamp that Illumines the Past: Sanskrit Kavya and the Writing of History in Early India', *Indian Historical Review*, 50, 2, pp. 1–15.

4   Paul Veyne (1988) *Did the Greeks believe in their Myths?* Trans. Paula Wissing, Chicago: Chicago University Press.

The Politics of Time: Reclaiming Poetry

10

What is time? Reams of scholarship have long concluded that time, like one's shadow, may be that which most eludes the grasp of comprehension the more one tries to capture it. It cannot be known by either its affirmation (time *is* this) or its negation (time is *not* this). It is a point but also a duration. It is measurable but measureless. It finishes but does not end. It is absolute but relative. Objective but subjective. One could go on.[1]

Something so elusive has also, however, along with space, attained the status of a fundamental dimension of existence—a measure and frame of all action and inaction, of change and of movement, of progress and growth, and thereby of life and vitality itself. A first principle, if ever there was one.

And yet, is time even real? Unlike space, does it have an existence in itself, independent of experience or even apprehendible through the five senses? It may be reasonable to assert that it does not. In other words, there is no clarity about the ontological status of time. And this, together with the large number of paradoxes about it, only some of which are listed above, suggests that it is highly likely that time has been little more than a human construct.

Of course we are not speaking of natural cycles and rhythms here. Time, as a human construct, may well be as Norbert Elias put it, "first and foremost the medium of orientation for the social world, regulating it in relation to human life".[2] But which social world do we speak of? In answer, it may be useful to think about time through its functions, its fields of operation, or its contexts, and thereby through its multiplicity. As my book *Retelling Time: Alternative Temporalities from Premodern South Asia* elaborates, ancient and medieval India engaged in deep and prolific ways with the many faces and functions of time.

So, why does time need to be retold? This is an academic question but also a political one, a question of physics and metaphysics but also an ethical one. This is because, as Francois Hartog, Aleida Assman and other scholars have shown, the "regime of time" that has been ordering our lives, and which we have been inhabiting unquestioningly as global time for the last two to three centuries, is only the creation of western modernity. The metaphor of regime implies an ordering nexus of powers, a dominion in and through which historical actors seek to control space by mastering time.[3] Likewise, the modern regime of temporality was a mode of governing time and thereby peoples who were brought, or in other ways came, under its sway.

Thus, western modernity, as I have argued in the book, was experienced as colonial modernity, a project of Empire, in large parts of the non-West, including India after it came under British rule. Emerging out of 18th century Western Europe, the modern regime of temporality, also known as Hegelian or Newtonian time, was characterised by proclamations of the homogeneity, discreteness, linearity, directionality (progress to the future), immanence and absoluteness of time. The invention and imposition all over the world of this single, universal, linear standard of time was operationalised through mechanisms such as the Greenwich Mean Time (1884), the Gregorian Calendar (spread between 1582 and 1882) and the Before Christ/ Anno Domini mode of chronology-marking, to give but a few examples. So whether it was quotidian time we are speaking of or historical time, there was—and still is—but one, uniform measure applied across the entire modern world. In homes and in factories, in classrooms and in offices, in the field and in the marketplace, the time of modernity came to rule.

This ordering of time effectively elided from view a host of alternative visions and practices of time that had in fact obtained throughout the non-West for millennia. Denied their own temporalities, the possibility of genuinely diverse regional histories was foreclosed. Thus this global regime of time was experienced by much of the non-European world as a project of colonialism, complete with its irruptive political violence that was predicated on the delegitimation and destruction of the premodern past and the construction of a victorious 'present' which, given the apogee of human historical development that the modern stood for, brooked no alternatives. This was the modern dominant narrative of 'rupture and progress'. As Aleida Assman writes:

> Unlike previous cultural time regimes, which aimed to ensure continuity, modernity provided concepts indicating a new beginning, the creative destruction of the past, the invention of the 'historical' as engagement with a past that is no longer present, as well as a logic of accelerated change, which, in contrast with the slow life of traditions, identified the modern with a temporality of the break.[4]

The politics underwriting this modern regime of time and its close fit with the ends of Empire should thus be evident.

As Helge Jordheim reminds us, it birthed an entire vocabulary of delays, lags and accelerations, as evidenced in terms such as the 'first world' and 'third world', 'developed' and 'developing' countries, and so on, used consistently right into our times to signal global orders and disorders.[5] The colonial juxtaposition of temporal difference onto cultural difference achieved the inferiorisation of local life-worlds as compared to the European standard.

꧁ ꧂

In this context, it begs stating that history as a discipline, which is another product of post-Enlightenment modernity, has been a crucial agent of Empire. It has been instrumental in constructing and valourising a colonial epistemology at the cost of local historical modes. This is especially and amply demonstrable in India (see Chapters 8 and 9). What's more, the project of history has outlasted Empire itself by enshrining a deeply empiricist and exclusionary self-definition which is hegemonic in academia across the world till today. This definition papers over and brackets out the multiple visions and purposes of representing the past that flourished in premodern India, with their emphasis on the didactic and the ethical, for example, and the use of figurative and mythical registers, over and above the documentary function of history. Instead, the modern 'global' discipline of history set up the tyranny of the 'fact', of scientific method, chronology (dates and precedence!), objectivity and rational causality—prime but fraught emblems of a 'modern/Western' intellect—whether or not these were material to the logic of the intellectual cultures on which these were imposed. In classic circularity, these non-European, premodern cultures and their texts ended up being heavily misinterpreted in the process, furthering the production of the colonial Other.

꧁꧂

All in all, it is appropriate that we now challenge precisely this hegemony of colonial modernity over ways in which we think about something as fundamental to existence and cognition as time. And reclaim a bouquet of alternative practices of time from premodern India, which stem from multiple world-views that have been marginalised, representing multiple languages—Sanskrit, Persian, Pali, Prakrit, Awadhi, Malayalam, Kannada and Bengali—and multiple knowledge traditions viz. Hindu, Jaina, Buddhist and Sufi Islam to logic, yoga, tantra, theatre and poetics.

In the process, it is possible to question the modern Eurocentric belief in an empty, homogenous, abbreviated, secular and irreversible time. And to propose, instead, that premodern India invested time with cultural function and value, which ranged from the contingent to the transcendent, the quotidian to the cosmic, the fleeting to the eternal, and the social to the spiritual. Accordingly, time was reworked—it could be stretched, melded, collapsed, recursed, rolled over, and even extinguished. To reclaim these alternative, plural understandings of time is to attempt to decolonise our ways of knowing and being. This is a project of the intellectual Global South.

What does that mean? The way we figure time figures us,[6] and further, assumptions and habits about time may shape entire fields of knowledge. Hence, time helps formulate a political challenge which engages the hegemony of the time of colonial modernity and its concomitant worldview. The challenge posed by alternative Indic notions of time is collective: to "deoccidentalise" yet again, and desync from modernity, our ways of seeing and knowing the world and our place in it, for which the diagnostic of time offers a fundamental opportunity. Given that time is crucial to how societies understand their pasts and themselves—their genealogies—the import of the clash between these alternative temporalities, it bears repetition, runs deeper than a concern for mere chronology; it represents alternative epistemologies and ontologies—and a multiplicity of them.

One hastens to add, however, that this is not a resort to the familiar, if inaccurate, binaries of physics versus metaphysics, or materialism versus spiritualism, which replay the Orientalist stereotypes about the West and the East. Such binaries would be highly reductive of the diversity of treatments of time and their multifarious contexts. Similarly, it must not be assumed that premodern time was essentially 'religious' time. Not only is the Judaeo-Christian category of 'religion' inapt for early India; it would also misleadingly conflate discrete modes of Indic belief and practice, such as devotionalism on the one hand and monism and gnosis, on the other, with different brands of atheism and rejection of the soul in between. Moreover, tracing a fixed line between the sacred and the profane may not be a worthwhile pursuit either. It would overlook both the interpermeability of the two in premodern India and their mutual autonomy. Similarly, early Indian notions of time were not primarily about historical time any more than they were exclusively about sacred time. Time appears instead as naturally both social and spiritual, both quotidian and cosmic. In contrast to what Walter Benjamin called the "homogenous empty time" of modernity, Indic expressions of time *served certain functions*—sometimes specific to their contexts and sometimes transcendental, but *always foregrounding values*.

To reimagine time, and allow for Indian varieties of it, is to open a window to reimagining India itself. It is also, as we saw, to challenge colonial epistemic hierarchies, which remain firmly entrenched in pedagogic practice in mainstream Indian academies, however much they may have been indicted in theory and rhetoric.

❦

Let us now look at alternative temporalities in Sanskrit poetics, beginning with this verse:

Shaktyatmadevatapakshair bhinnam kalasya darshanam/
Prathamam tad avidyayam yad vidyayam na vidyate//
(*Kalasamuddesha*, 62)[7]
(In a state of ignorance, time is the first to manifest itself in different forms—power, soul, or God they say; in a state of wisdom but, it disappears.) (translated by author)

This Sanskrit verse from the 5th century CE poet-philosopher Bhartrhari is an excellent introduction to all the many difficulties in talking about time. The biggest is the contradiction or aporia that while time is such an inescapable and ubiquitous existential dimension, it is essentially ungraspable, and we can resort at best only to representations of it in order to grapple with its opacity. The poet refers to three such representations or manifestations of time (*kalasya darshanam*) which can broadly translate into historic time, cosmic time and inner time of consciousness, if you will.

However, while the modern academic response to temporal aporia has been perhaps to give up on it and settle for engaging with these mere representations, early Sanskrit poets and thinkers showed no such fear or confusion when confronting time. What Bhartrhari does, in fact, is to take us beyond the aporia to its resolution. He first shatters the apparent uniformity of time, indicating its different possible spheres of experience; but then goes on to expose that very multiplicity as being in fact superficial in the face of an underlying implacable indivisibility of time which is knowable only on transcending it. He calls that transcendent state *vidya*.

In other words, in Sanskrit thought (to use a very sweeping category), there is a comfortable acceptance of the fundamentally correlative nature of time. To put that differently, it is believed that the key to understanding time lies not in its representations but in its functions. Functions in turn could relate to the finite or the infinite. I will argue that Sanskrit poetics (*alamkara*) showed a predilection for functions of infinitude—representing not only historically contingent truths but also transhistorical dynamics that were unending and repeated incessantly, in the nature of transcendent truths.

Now, this is not an entirely new observation. Western scholarship has long misread this predilection for the infinite as traditional Sanskrit literature's lack of a sense of time and history, and its espousal of timelessness instead. This in turn was believed to derive from other stereotypes developed by the establishing colonial state in early 19th century India: namely, Indian society's stasis on the one hand, and her proclivity to spiritual over material interests, on the other, both of which, it was suspected by the likes of James Mill, who wrote the infamous *History of British India* in 1817, rendered the tracking of worldly, linear time redundant to Indians.

This colonial construction of India as a timeless society was closely tied up with their construction of India as an ahistorical society as well. As I have argued elsewhere,[8] this directly led to Orientalist scholars such as Harold Wilson in 1825 isolating and valourising a work of epic poetry such as Kalhana's *Rajatarangini* from Kashmir as the only work of true history in all of Sanskrit literature for, among other things, its deference to chronology in dating the kings and dynasties that it named. So the celebration of one text stood on the back of the indictment of the entire literary culture to which it in fact belonged, but from which it was segregated hereby on the ground of time-keeping.

More recently, scholars such as Sheldon Pollock have shown perhaps a greater sympathy to Sanskrit literature's mechanisms. Pollock influentially suggested that Sanskrit's apparent indifference to history and time was really an eccentric cultural indifference to transience—something temporary—in favour of an eternalising discourse informed by the immutability of Vedic scriptures.[9] One notes the fundamental validity of the observation that some Sanskrit genres, including classical poetry or *kavya*, as I too have argued elsewhere,[10] do appear to try to escape limits of time and place, and we will see later why they may have done so.

However, whatever the merits of this argument, it will be clear that in attempting to explain Sanskrit's purported ahistoricity thus, this theory essentially restated it. Here, I will explore some prominent strands of *alamkara/kavya-shastra* from circa 1st millennium CE, to argue that what has been projected as an aberrant, civilisational ahistoricity was in fact a cultivated and purposive transhistoricity—not indifference to time, but a self-reflexive reworking of it to serve functions and foreground values far removed from what Eurocentric modernity allows. Moreover, these values and functions of time were not necessarily sacred or scriptural—phenomena deemed to stand outside of time—but often firmly located in, and oriented towards, the social. Of course I make this distinction between the spiritual and the social or aesthetic in a qualified and entirely provisional sense, since Sanskritic traditions do not uphold it in any absolutist way, preferring perhaps a more integrated idea of life goals. The point here is merely to emphasise values and functions of time within a discourse such as *kavya* that was not primarily sacred.

Alamkarashastra is the theory of the composition of Sanskrit *kavya,* that is, highly aesthetic poetry, prose and drama, composed chiefly in Sanskrit all across India during the first millennium CE and after. The composer of *kavya* was the *kavi,* the quintessential poet. It is important to note the *kavi's* claim to epistemic insight, which was believed to provide, among other things, a unique access to and knowledge of time. The earliest work on Sanskrit etymology, the *Nirukta* by Yaska, circa 5th century BCE, gives the meaning of *kavi: kavih krantadarshano bhavati,* or the poet is the true seer (*Nirukta* 12.13). Remarkably, this remained the understanding over the next 1500 years or more, as seen in the works of poeticians such as Rajashekhara (10th century CE), who said: "Poets explore with their words that which *yogin*s see through the power of their spiritual accomplishments" (*Kavyamimamsa* 12.62–63; see also 1.17–21).[11] This omniscience of the *kavi* empowered him to speak of all past realities (*bhutarthakathanam*), as Kalhana averred in the 12th century CE.

However, the Sanskrit poet is understood to be not just the "knower" but even the "creator" of the past: *kavi-prajapati* or *kavi-vedhas*. Thus Kalhana writes: "Who else is capable of making visible (*pratyakshatam*) bygone times (*kalamatikrantam*) except the poet-creator who can make delightful productions (*ramyanirmana*)?" (*Rajatarangini* I.4). Here again, then, is Sanskrit *kavya's* belief in the poet's creative ability to make elusive, ungraspable time perceptible and indeed a statement on time itself so rendered as a construction or production (*nirmana*).

From the practitioner to the praxis: The poet did not only construct time in this fashion—specifically past time; they could rework time in other ways as well. Let us look at two examples.

The first example I take up relates to the centrepiece of Sanskrit aesthetic theory to which all *kavya*—poetry, prose or drama—was directed. This was *rasa*, literally juice or flavour, which referred to the savouring of essentialised emotions (*bhava*) rendered as aesthetic experience. If there was one purpose of *kavya*, it was the generation and enjoyment of *rasa*. Thus from its first statement in Bharata's *Natyashastra*, circa second century CE, there were eight *rasa*s to which a ninth was added a few centuries later. These *rasa*s are: *shringara*, translated as the erotic and the beautiful more generally; *hasya* or comic and entertaining; *karuna* or the piteous and the compassionate; *raudra* or the angry and violent; *virya* or the heroic and the noble; *bhayanaka* or the fearful; *bibhatsa* or the macabre; *adbhuta* or the wondrous or amazing; and *shanta* or the equanimous or the quiescent.

These choices were not randomly arrived at; the nine *rasa*s were the distillate of a much larger, carefully collated list of nearly 50 emotions and emotion-like situations (*NS* 342.8).[12] Some examples are beauty, despair, fatigue, determination, languor, resentment, shame, intoxication, joy, madness and perplexity. These categories of feeling were meant to cover a very wide, if not comprehensive, range of common human sentiments and behaviour that cut across ages and even social groups. *Kavya* was, after all, *sarvavarnikam* (for all varnas), as Bharata tells us (*NS* I.12). At its basics, Bharata simply says: "That subject matter with which the heart concurs is the source of *rasa*" (*yoartho hrdayasamvadi tasya bhavo rasodbhavah*) (*NS* 7.7). Thus rendering emotions as universals, the *rasa* theory argues against the historical contingency of human affect. Feelings were not bound by time, according to *alamkarashastra*. *Rasa* collapses time instead and instates emotions as a deeply humanising, and hence inherently transtemporal, reality.

Not only the generation of *rasa*/aesthetic pleasure, but its reception too was understood by *alamkarashastra* as a fundamentally transtemporal process. This is because the only way readers, who were potentially separated by many centuries from the composition of a literary work and the protagonists in it, say, Rama and Sita or Chanakya and Chandragupta, could still experience the emotions of these protagonists was precisely because of the literary force of *rasa*. The poetician Bhatta Nayaka in his 10th century CE *Hrdayadarpana* called this literary effect *sadharanikarana* or the commonisation of aesthetic experience that facilitated its recovery or enjoyment (*bhogikarana*) across time and space.[13] The result: "…a unique mode of aesthetic knowledge that replaces an empirical imaginary of time with a figural one".[14] In this, the literary experience was indeed akin to the spiritual experience, for *rasa* emerged quite like an experience of consciousness itself, rid of the dross of everyday life by ridding itself of the very element of time and the change it would entail.

❧

And now let us turn to the second example of the reworking of time in *kavya*'s vision. It can be argued that at the heart of all this investment in emotion that the *rasa* theory stands for is a concern for the social—so, not only for the spiritual, but also a concern for representing a broad gamut of social and therefore emotional situations and experiences. Extending this concern was another momentous and complementary strand of *alamkara*, namely, an insistent theory of *kavya* as social and ethical pedagogy.

Though, till recently, scholars such as Pollock believed the didactic function to be entirely subordinate to *kavya*'s aesthetic aims,[15] I have argued that faith in literature's capacity for refining our ethical imagination—*kavya* as *upadesha* or instruction—resonates from as early as Bharata in the 2nd century CE, through Bhamaha in the 5th century CE, who used the term *vaicakshanya* (insight/expertise), up till Bhoja in the 11th century CE, who coined the term *adhyeyam* (lesson/learning) for one of the main goals of composing and consuming *kavya*.[16]

But instruction and insight and learning in what? In the entire spectrum of human goals and activities, perhaps, captured in the concept of *purushartha*: *dharma* (piety/duty), *artha* (power/domination), *kama* (pleasure/desire) and *moksha* (liberation). The point is most directly made by Abhinavagupta in his 11th century CE commentary on the *Natyashastra*, the *Abhinavabharati*. He writes in no uncertain terms that the end-result of the savouring of *rasa* is instruction in *dharma* and the other ends of man.[17] Now, I am not going into Abhinava's prodigious exposition on the aestheticisation of metaphysics—aesthetics as a form and mode of transcendent consciousness. According to this theory, in fact, time emerges as the external manifestation and doing of pure consciousness, something he develops also in his *Tantraloka,* as a unified project of soteriology and poetics. Here, however, we are speaking only of the social dimension.

Sanskrit k*avya*'s predisposition to ethical instruction should thus be more than evident. I suggest that under the influence of this ethical-injunctive understanding of its own project, *kavya* conceived of time as a laboratory where overarching ethical principles governing social behaviour (*dharma, karma*) played out. An excellent example of this is in fact the same 12th century CE *mahakavya*, Kalhana's *Rajatarangini*, the history of the kings of Kashmir over two millennia, to which we must keep returning.

As I have argued in Chapter 9, the organising principle of time in Kalhana's narrative is a set of prescriptive ethical values—good conduct (*sadacara*), liberality (*dakshinya*), discriminating intellect (*sarasaravicara)*, and love for ensuring justice and fearlessness in the subjects (*dharma, abhaya*)—according to which he classifies the ancient kings of Kashmir into pairs of ethical models. Again and again there came kings such as Mihirakula, Jayapida, Kalasha and Harsha, who were greedy, tyrannical or degenerate, and again and again there were kings such as Lalitaditya, Chandrapida, Avantivarman and Uccala, who were high-minded, just, and dedicated to people's welfare (*prajanupalanam*).

Kalhana self-reflexively clubs these disparate kings into two groups, collapsing the gulf of centuries of time that actually separated them from each other. Ethics then, more than chronology, seems to determine the larger poetic order after all. In fact, I argue that the title of the poem, *Rajatarangini*, which means River of Kings, makes of history precisely this endless flow of ethical exemplars through time, thereby endowing time with culturally sanctioned meanings.

At one point in this *mahakavya*, attesting the internal memory of the massive text spanning two thousand years and more, Kalhana zigzags through the centuries in eleven verses, wherever his quest for the ethical takes him. With the principle of royal greed (*lobha*) as the thread, he concludes by bunching together half a dozen exploitative kings and another half a dozen virtuous ones and says of them respectively: "The wealth of kings acquired by persecution of the commonalty went either to their rivals in love, or to their enemies, or to the flames. [But] those who unflinchingly upheld dharma, their justly acquired treasure never found an indecent end" (*RT* VIII.1951– 61).

At other places too in the text, the poet collapses time as it were. To give just one more instance, when noting the "transient nature of existence" (*asthayinim sthitim*), which is a major concern in the poem, the poet speaks of how "on the same path of death is every individual plunging headlong. I am the slayer and he the slain—the notion of a difference [between the two] lasts but a short while…He who but yesterday exults while slaying his foe, at the end sees an enemy gloating over him when he is himself about to be killed" (*RT* VIII.358–59).

Thus time in *kavya* 'returned' relentlessly, mirroring persistent patterns of human thought, action and experience. It looped around deeply ethical moments or ruptures in history, which connected with other such moments otherwise far apart in time from one another. Hence, Sanskrit poetry's preference is not for linearity or diachronicity alone, but for recursivity and synchronicity of a fashion alongside.

Returning to Bhartrhari then, and to functions of infinitude, I would submit that not only spiritual knowledge but also aesthetic and socio-ethical knowledge seemed to render divisions of time as we know them peripheral. Time stretched and melded to produce or capture a simultaneity in difference. Time persisted—because perhaps so did human affect and ethics. Indeed, more than any other Sanskrit genre, *kavya* instated emotions and ethics as deeply humanising, and hence inherently transtemporal, not ahistorical, realities. And this speaks to a fundamentally non-teleological view of time, since the telos or ethically imbued cultural purpose was not out there in the future but 'already-always'.

Notes

1   This essay draws on the study first published as 'Of Rasa and Recursivity: Ethics and Aesthetics of Time in Sanskrit Poetics (Alamkarasastra)' in Shonaleeka Kaul edited (2021) *Retelling Time: Alternative Temporalities from Premodern South Asia,* London: Routledge, pp. 89–96. Reused here with permission.

2   Norbert Elias (1988) Über die Zeit, Frankfurt am Main: Suhrkamp,
     p. xix.

3   Alexandra Lianeri (2014) 'Resisting Modern Temporalities: Toward a
     Critical History of Breaks in Time', *History and Theory*, 53, 4, p. 605.

4   Aleida Assman paraphrased by Alexandra Lianeri, 'Resisting Modern
     Temporalities', p. 606.

5   Helge Jordheim (2014) 'Multiple Times and the Work of
     Synchronization', *History and Theory*, 53, 4, p. 513.

6   Richard Terdiman (2008) 'Taking Time: Temporal Representations
     and Cultural Politics' in Tyrus Miller edited *Given World and Time:
     Temporalities in Context*, Budapest: CEU Press, p. 142.

7   *The Kalasamuddesa of Bhartṛhari's Vakyapadiya* (1972) translated by
     Peri Sarveswara Sharma, Delhi: Motilal Banarsidass.

8   Shonaleeka Kaul (2018) *The Making of Early Kashmir: Landscape and
     Identity in the Rajatarangini*, Delhi: Oxford University Press.

9   Sheldon Pollock (1989) 'Mīmaṁsa and the Problem of History in
     Traditional India', *Journal of American Oriental Society*, 109, no. 4,
     pp. 603–10.

10   Shonaleeka Kaul (2010) *Imagining the Urban: Sanskrit and the City in
     Early India*, Delhi: Permanent Black/New York: Seagull Books.

11   Phyllis Granoff (1995) 'Sarasvati's Sons: Biographies of Poets in
     Medieval India', *Asiatische Studien/ Études Asiatiques* 49, 2, p. 364.

12   Cited in Sheldon Pollock (2017) *A Rasa Reader: Classical Indian
     Aesthetics*, New York: Columbia University Press, p. 54.

13   Cited in Ibid., p. 24.

14   Ibid.

15   Sheldon Pollock 'Sanskrit Literary Culture from the Inside Out',
     in Sheldon Pollock edited (2004) *Literary Cultures in History:*

Reconstructions from South Asia, New Delhi: Oxford University Press, pp. 49–50.

16 Shonaleeka Kaul, *Imagining the Urban*, p. 20.

17 *Abhinavabharati* 1.261 and also 1.36, 1.292.20 and 1.276. Cited and translated by Sheldon Pollock *A Rasa Reader*, p. 33.

The Politics of Place: Reclaiming Myth

11

The fascination that mythology traditionally holds for people at large in this country is often in direct contrast to the suspicion with which it is regarded by historians. Caught between a colonial high history that has disowned it and a popular fiction that has assimilated it to figment in recent times, myth's recovery as a historical vector and epistemic mode in its own right has been imperilled. The essay that follows is a deemed response to this situation. It arises from two decades of my being in and thinking about the discipline of history and also pondering over the cultural and emotional significance of places and what Robert Goldman called the 'realities of fantasy' that were often more keenly felt than those of history and geography. Myths are effective in so far as they are affective, as Ernest Renan once said, yet they had been considerably stripped bare of this content in academia to serve a philosophy of history that preferred value judgments and reduction of all cultural forms to power.

Dubbed irrational, primitive, superstitious, un-dateable and untrue, myth has often been discredited either as relaying an unhistorical obscure past of little value or relevance today or as mediating relationships of inequity between and within communities in history. It has tended to be seen not as the self-expression of a people, but typically as a veiled, ulterior project—a result perhaps of the modern historian's 'perturbation at their own inheritance'. I believe it is time to confidently depart from these interpretations and rehabilitate myth, not as history's primeval Other, nor as an instrument of power and acculturation, but as communitarian mechanisms by which societies made sense of themselves and their world: local self-understandings recoverable from mythicised narratives of landscapes. Such an approach would help redress the discipline of history's cultivated disconnect from a cultural construct that was—and is—obviously central to the beliefs and practices, the imagination and lived lives, of diverse groups of Indians across space and time.[1]

The Native American poet and literary critic Paula Gunn Allen once asked: "Is it we who invent the stories and thus inform the land? Or does the land give us the stories, thus inventing us?"[2] Substitute 'myths' for 'stories', and this is precisely the dialogic, disentanglable relationship that exists between myths and places.

Myth may be broadly defined as the stories told by a specific cultural group to comprehend and articulate their experience of the world they inhabit. From the ancient Greek 'mythos', meaning 'story' or 'plot', the word was originally applied, at some variance from its modern connotations, to narratives both sacred and profane, both imaginary and true. Again, contrary to the primitivist associations lent to mythology by the rationalist anxieties of modernity, historically all cultures— not only 'traditional' or non-literate or 'socially naïve' ones given over to superstition—gave rise to myths. Myth-making was (and is) a crucial heuristic process of meaning-making for any society.

Ironically, this would apply even to the contemporary modern era which sports what Jason Josephson-Storm has called the myth of disenchantment, a misplaced belief that modernity has truly shed faith in magic, mystery and wonder. This 'departure of the supernatural',[3] believed to be emblematic of modernity, has also been a prominent element of secularisation, which has gone hand in hand with modernisation based on the Western experience of the same. Here religion and the supernatural—and by extension myth—have been posited as opposed to reason and progress.

Back in premodernity, dealing centrally with nature and with accounts of the "origins", "destinies" and mysteries of humankind and the universe, myths were sometimes deeply rooted in the land and the ecology. They could, however, invoke supernatural forces as well, usually wedding the two seamlessly. Significantly, even if or when a culture no longer believed that its myths were literally true explanations, the stories often survived as receptacles of important cultural values. Myths were thus expressive, culturally accepted ways of knowing and being.

Beyond the limits of verification or refutation, myth then may often have been not about the real as true but about the noble as true, as Paul Veyne[4] perceptively observed for the ancient Greeks. Ancient Indians even asked: What is real and true? And their answer went beyond the contingent to the transcendent, that is, beyond the empirical and ephemeral to the ethical and eternal (see Chapter 10).[5] Myths were thus more than real. They were about that in which, socially speaking, "something new, strong and significant was manifested".[6]

They thereby epitomised cultural curiosity and virtuosity. Therefore the inclusion of myth in ancient Indic narratives, far from being a lapse in critical judgment, served a crucial purpose. Its function included not only making sense of their

Figure 11.1 Myth of the churning of the ocean of milk (*sagar manthana*), Bazar art print 1910s. Courtesy: Wikimedia Commons

world for a people, but also enshrining and transmitting community and ultimately civilisational paragons—a seminal aspect of identity formation for any demographic group. Here myth acted inextricably in concert with orality and collective memory, those other categories of scholarly analysis which, like myth, have until recently been confined to the margins of the conventional discipline of history.

We know that the fields of folkloristics, anthropology, and religious studies have all long invested in the study of myth as a key to understanding cultures from the inside. However, given its ambiguous, often symbolic and subjective rather than literal relationship with 'facts' and empirical reality, myth has suffered an uncertain status in the field of history, especially in the manner in which the latter has been 'professionally' practised since at least the 19th century, if not earlier. Indeed myth has perhaps always been regarded as something of an antithesis and anathema, hence the loaded binary of 'historical versus mythical'. As Joseph Mali explains for the world stage:

> In the long history of historiography, the basic categories of both myth and history have always been defined antithetically, as if myth was all fabrication and pure fiction and therefore a spurious description of what merely appears to have happened, whereas history was a serious and reliable explanation of what actually happened insofar as its empirical sources and discourses were veritable. Assuming thus ... critical historians from Thucydides to Ranke as well as all their modern followers, have commonly failed to account for these archaic modes of historical comprehension and composition [myths] ... what higher metaphysical truths they served, and, ultimately, why they still persist in the collective imagination and cultural

traditions of all religions, nations and civilizations.[7]

No doubt this has a good deal to do with the fact that Rankean history (after Leopold von Ranke, a philosopher of history), or 'scientific historiography', came to be a colonial project, even an agent of Empire, in so far as it helped construct epistemologies of Otherness. Thus, we were told that there were societies that possessed history and those that had (only) mythology! Through the works of Imperialist-Orientalist scholars such as James Mill, H H Wilson and others, India was, in effect, developed as an excellent example of the latter (see Chapter 8).

What's more, as I have explained elsewhere,[8] this project of history has outlasted Empire itself by enshrining an exclusionary self-definition as hegemonic even today, one that privileges certitudes, verifiability, and linearity, underwritten, in some measure, by Semitic theologies and mensuration. This definition, complete with what Ethan Kleinberg et al.[9] have called history's "disciplinary essentialism" and "methodological fetishism", delegitimises and brackets out the alternative visions and modes of representing the past that flourished in premodern India. Instead, the modern 'global' discipline of history set up the tyranny of the 'fact', of scientific method, chronology, objectivity and rational causality—prime but fraught emblems of a 'modern/Western' intellect. In classic circularity, non-European, premodern cultures and their texts ended up being heavily misinterpreted in the process, furthering the production of the colonial Other.[10]

To repeat, while the mythological occupied a discrete place in ancient and medieval worlds and was understood to perform certain central social functions, the post-

Enlightenment obsession with rationalism and scientifism[11] as against more humanistic orders of imagination, and its concomitant, resilient hold over professional history-writing, brought about for the modern historian the instant and overwhelming delegitimation of any cultural form that did not pass the test of objectivity and fact. Myth, especially in 'traditional' non-Western societies, did not just fall from grace in the process; it also came to be exoticised as the practice of primitive people who became objects of the colonial gaze.

❧

In India, a case in point would be some of the older readings of myth found in texts such as the Vedas and Puranas, by Orientalists such as W J Wilkins of the London Missionary Society (1882, 1900) and A B Keith of the Asiatic Society (1916). While these tended to document in the abstract mostly Hindu but also Buddhist and Jaina myths, they clearly struggled with what was for them the alien character of the Indic mythological enterprise. The result was stereotyping assessments and pejorative, comparative comments such as the following:

> Gods and demons were very present to the mind of the Indian then as they are today . . . [there exists] the essential vagueness of many of the figures of Indian mythology: the mysticism of Indian conception tends ever to a pantheism alien to the clear-cut creations of the Hellenic imagination.[12]

And:

> I feel that a mere statement of much that was written in books professedly inspired by God, carried its own

condemnation. And at the same time ... amid much evil, there was also much good. The sages of India were not in complete darkness.... [But] As we examine the earlier writings ... instructive to note the marked deterioration in the quality of the teaching [later].[13]

After Independence, as scientific temper and modernisation became something of a patriotic duty in a nation whose 'soul, long suppressed, had now found utterance', scholars such as the Marxist mathematician-historian D D Kosambi (1962) and the archaeologist H D Sankalia (1973) creatively engaged with the question of whether myths were truly divorced from reality or somehow connected with it.[14] Kosambi's work also explored cultural continuities from the past to the present through the medium of living myths. The enquiry into the relationship between myth and reality is in fact essentially the question that has consumed scholars of the two Indian epics, the *Ramayana* and the *Mahabharata*, as well as the *Puranas*, in their search for historicity in a genre which, ironically, in its self-understanding, had no doubts about its own historical nature and function.

Of course, it is another question—fundamental yet moot—whether these master texts of Indic civilisation, which call themselves *itihasa-purana*, or ancient narratives on the past/history (literally 'thus it was'), should be classed as mythology in the first place. However, as materialist historiography in India took over from more culturally embedded approaches to indigenous narratives, it found itself embracing and reproducing colonial perspectives in strange ways. Thus myth journeyed from being a victim of colonial power to being regarded as an instrument of the propagation of power within Indian society itself. Such a position also seemed to mirror in the 1970s the post-structuralist explication of a knowledge/power nexus. Myth came to be treated by this school of thought as an agent of acculturation and hegemonisation by postulated superior, expanding social groups over other native groups deemed to be less advanced materially and culturally.

A powerful example of this approach is Romila Thapar's study of the *Ramayana* which appeared under the auspices of The Mythic Society.[15] Thapar argued that the men of Ayodhya and the demons of Lanka, together with the monkeys of Kishkindha, all represented contrasting human social groups in conflict, namely, agrarian 'Aryans' aggressing against forest-dwelling non-Aryan 'tribals' respectively. Similarly, Vijay Nath argued that Sanskrit *Purana*s were an acculturative instrument for the imposition of "mainstream civilisation" and "brahmanisation" on "tribal societies" to facilitate the spread of agriculture.[16] As Christopher Minkowski put it, this is "as if brahmins were a species of beneficial, exotic plant or insect"![17] It is also worth asking how a genre (the *Purana*s) that, it is well known, was an amorphous and heterogenous compilation of free-floating oral narratives and encyclopaedic materials over centuries, if not millennia, could have played such an essentialist and instrumentalist role in a concerted manner. Yet this is how these texts are seen even today, in other influential studies of religious process in early India, as some kind of orchestrated project of power and domination, be it based on caste, ethnicity, state or gender.

However, some scholars such as the anthropologist Arjun

Appadurai have significantly called out this obsession with hierarchy in studying India and cautioned that concepts such as legitimation, acculturation and indeed Sanskritisation as the prime vehicle of such acculturation in the Indian subcontinent have become "theoretical metonyms" and surrogates for Indian civilisation as a whole, "gate-keeping concepts" thought to apply to every socio-cultural process. This approach limits the full potential for apprehending what was in fact a complicated compound of local realities.[18]

And this is why, tempting though the materialist approaches to reading Indic mythology may be, they remain speculative, running the risk of force-fitting a sociological narrative on the text, rather than tapping the semantic potential of a less literal and riven reading, aligned with the text's own didactic purpose and strategies of representation instead. For example, the Sanskritist Sheldon Pollock pointed out a needed corrective to interpretations of the *Ramayana* by reminding us of what the text itself may have been aiming at, namely, the pedagogical depiction of righteousness via Ayodhya and Lanka.[19] These two represented perhaps two different ideals and models of emotion and behaviour (disciplined and affective versus licentious and unbridled) as symbolised ethical choices before one and the same society/audience rather than a portrayal of two real and antagonistic social groups.

In fact, to remind the reader, it can be argued that ethics and didacticism lay at the heart of not just Indic mythology but Indic historical visions as well, as seen in *itihasa purana* but also other historical texts such as the *Rajatarangini*. (See Chapter 9.) These ethics inscribed cultural truth-claims. And the stories bearing and projecting these truth-claims must be understood as "not dogmatic but dramatic stories of tradition", whose social utility lay precisely in their dramatic reactivation of the community's original motivations.[20]

Similarly, R P Goldman argued for creative ways of reading myth in connection with symbolic constructions put on the city of Mathura in the Epics and the *Puranas*. Goldman significantly spoke of the "cultural and emotional significance of a place important in literature" and of the "realities of fantasy" that were "often far more keenly felt" than those of history and geography.[21] Myths were thus "effective in so far as they were affective", to borrow Ernest Renan's insightful comment about myths surrounding the French Revolution.[22]

However, these interventions, all by scholars who, tellingly, belong to disciplines other than history, have remained largely unrecognised in the historical mainstream in India, where myth has come to be considerably decontextualised in the name of being historicised, wreaking what T S Eliot may have called a "dissociation of sensibility". Joseph Mali argues that worldwide Marxist positions have aimed at "exposing and thereby opposing" historical myths and purging the historical discipline of mythological fallacies.[23] There has been little place in this binary view for the meanings that the myths concerned, which typically originated and travelled orally and in nebulous fragments, may have held for the communities themselves in their worldviews rather than for interpreting historians deeply imbricated in those of the 21st century CE. Appealing for reconciling myth and history once again, Mali coins the phrase "mythistory".

Of course, taking such a critical position today amidst the

deeply polarised politics of history in contemporary India, that too on an emotive issue such as myth relating to real and often contested places, runs the risk of getting sucked into ideological battles, which are often themselves about power in and through academia. But this is a risk that must perhaps be braved and defied; else we run the greater risk of not only acquiescing in the subjugation of history to politics, but also losing out on endogenous perspectives to recover a people's history and geography of the land.

Indeed, it is a travesty of the obviously subaltern and complex nature of so many of the mythologies that abound in Indic history that, for many historians, myth became a top-down imposition on a people rather than an element of their own daily lived lives and beliefs, intrinsically tied to their land and their being, and to which different sections of a composite society could well have subscribed and contributed. A K Ramanujan's sagacious warning[24] that when it came to cultural production, the classical and the folk, the elite and the popular, were points on a shifting continuum rather than mutually exclusive oppositions—was ignored. Instead, an imperialist prism of power and virtue signalling—rational versus irrational, modern versus traditional, progressive versus backward people—was ironically reproduced within the Indian past by the academy in the form of advanced versus inferior, 'Great' versus 'Little' Traditions, elite versus folk, Aryan versus non-Aryan, Sanskritic versus non-Sanskritic, centre versus periphery, and so on.

Of course there have been other, more productive approaches to myth in India. But it may be fair to say that due to the stature of positivist and materialist historiography in the disciplinary mainstream in India, myth has been on the back foot and more or less discredited, either as relaying an unhistorical obscure past or as mediating relationships of inequity between and within communities. It has tended to be seen not as the self-expression of a people, but typically a veiled, ulterior project—a result perhaps of the modern historian's "perturbation at their link to their own inheritance".[25] It is high time to depart from these approaches and rehabilitate myth, not as history's primeval Other, nor as an instrument of socio-religious propagation, i.e. an instrument of power and acculturation, but as communitarian mechanisms by which societies made sense of themselves and their world.

As noted before, myths were ways of knowing and being—a reminder that "historical communities ... consist in the beliefs that their members have about them[selves] ... in the stories they tell about them[selves]"[26] and indeed about the spaces they come to make their own. As Wendy Doniger put it, "a myth is a story that is sacred to and shared by a group of people who find their most important meanings in it".[27] And its importance stemmed perhaps from the fact that myth usually contained or referred to certain crucial issues in the history of the community such as common ancestry or territory or fertility or morality or fraternity or heroism—those "practical verities in which the members of the community all believe and live", which found their way into what Ernst Cassirer called "an unconscious grammar of experience".[28]

Thus myths helped communities fashion their identities and their habitat/habitus alike and were fashioned by these in turn. Studying myths within the ambit of history, but in culturally sensitive ways that do not alienate myth or reduce it to something other than itself, can provide an important route for scholars and social groups alike to reclaim regional/

local pasts and their self-understanding. For this, as I have proposed in my book *Myths and Places,* myth should be read as animating ontologies, to borrow Josephson-Storm's phrase.[29] What does that mean? It means restoring people and places to their myths and then working through those myths to understand the people and their cherished locales.

Such an approach repositions not just how historians understand myth but also place. The 'cultural geography' approach philosophically and methodologically signifies, in the main, replacing quasi-scientifism with hermeneutics—the search for meaning and not just 'facts', for truth-claims and not just 'truths', for subjectivities as much as verities.

Specifically, I champion the relatively recent paradigm of 'cultural landscape'—largely used so far in archaeology rather than in the study of literature or mythology—to now read myth for exploring the fundamental relationship between stories, peoples and places. This involves identifying the range of cultural constructions that societies cast onto the physical features of a site or region through myth and memory. To do this is to view the land as landscape, that is, to understand geography (natural and man-made) as overlaid by narrative.

To elaborate, myths invoking natural or built features—mountains, forests, rivers, pastures, cities and villages—generated a sense of place and a rootedness in the land, as Diana Eck has shown.[30] These myths could be local lore, or they could be derived subcontinentally from Epic and Puranic archetypes, weaving together gods, demigods, kings, peoples and places, as well as the past and the present. They filled out and lent tradition to the land, anchoring and orienting its people, not only to their own physical world but willy-nilly to the moral truth claims that inhered in these constructed and preserved memories. Here was myth in its classic role as a teaching tool. Indeed, in the Platonic exposition of myth ('mythos'), it is considered ethics by other means, which is needed to charm one into agreement when logic fails to do so.[31] And, as Christopher Tilley put it, "Both land and language are equally symbolic resources drawn on to foster correct social behavior and values. In narrative [texts], geographical features of the landscape act as mnemonic pegs on which moral teachings hang".[32]

In a remarkably pan-Indian pattern, mythology and geography appear as "a joint imaginative and descriptive undertaking". Geographical knowledge was "grounded in the mythical apprehension of the world's meaning and order",[33] even as myth-making itself was resonant with geographical markers of the land. Together, these generated a sense of spatial identity and ownership of a place by a community.

To put it differently, myth transforms abstract space into intimate place. And a dialectical, mutually constitutive relationship between geography and culture is revealed, mediated by myth. Further, as mentioned before, since some of these myths could be pan-Indic in character and others deeply local, myth is an excellent illustration of the interplay of the universal and the particular in India's hoary past.

What's more, the concrete relationship between myths and the locales these inhabited was not confined to the realm of religion alone. Of course, perhaps "it is the privilege of antiquity to mingle divine things with human, and so to add dignity to the beginnings...", as Livy famously pronounced.[34]

But while not missing out on exploring sacred centres all across India and the myths that inscribe and vivify them, toning down the expectation of a sacred imperative from myth in every instance may go some way towards collapsing the 'spiritual versus materialist', 'mythical versus historical' dichotomous stereotypes with which the 'Orient' has long had to contend. Indeed, as I have shown in my book *Myths and Places*, apart from religion, myth could relate to ecology, ethnicity, urbanism, mercantilism, politics, tourism, art, philosophy, and performance, and thereby intersect with ideology, identity, migration/mobility, borderlands, orality, language and the everyday.[35]

Thus, to recap, I argue for redressing the somewhat chauvinistic binary of history and myth by re-approaching history through the entry point of myth, exploring the latter as a uniquely expressive historical mode in its own right, as well as integrating both with geography in a fulsome way. Indeed, it can be argued that a sense of territorial becoming and belonging has perhaps always had less to do with objective history than with subjective traditions and associations, such as not only myths but also legends and imagery about the land and its people that gain currency often precisely through storytelling or narrativisation, textual or otherwise. Reclaiming, rather than dismissing, such modes of territorial becoming and belonging is invaluable for any society.

Notes

1   This essay is an abbreviated version of the introduction titled 'Reclaiming Myth, Emplacing History' first published in Shonaleeka Kaul edited (2023) *Myths and Places: New Perspectives in Indian Cultural Geography*, London: Routledge, pp. 3–16. Reused here with permission.

2   Paula Gunn Allen (1997) '*Cuentos de la Tierra Encantada*: Magic and realism in the southwest borderlands' *in:* D M Wrobel and M C Steiner edited *Many Wests: Place, Culture and Regional Identity*. Lawrence, KS: University Press of Kansas, p. 357.

3   J A Josephson-Storm (2017) *The Myth of Disenchantment: Magic, Modernity, and the Birth of the Human Sciences*. Chicago, IL: University of Chicago Press, p. 4.

4   Paul Veyne (1988) *Did the Greeks Believe in Their Myths? An Essay on the Constitutive Imagination* (first published 1983 in French, translated into English by P Wissing). Chicago, IL and London: Chicago University Press.

5   Shonaleeka Kaul (2018) *The Making of Early Kashmir: Landscape and Identity in the Rajatarangini*. Delhi: Oxford University Press.

6   Mircea Eliade (1963) *Myth and Reality*. New York: Harper and Row, p. 19.

7   J Mali (2003) *Mythistory: The Making of a Modern Historiography*. Chicago, IL and London: University of Chicago Press, p. xii.

8   Shonaleeka Kaul (2021) 'Temporality and its discontents or why time needs to be retold' *in:* S Kaul edited *Retelling Time: Alternative Temporalities from Premodern South Asia*. London: Routledge, pp. 1–10.

9   Ethan Kleinberg, J W Scott and G Wilder (2018) *Theses on Theory and History* in *Wild on Collective*. Available from: Theoryrevolt.com.

10   Shonaleeka Kaul, 'Temporality and its discontents', p. 3.

11   For a succinct discussion of how science itself may not be

counterposed to myth but a form of it, see J. Mali, *Mythistory*, p. 18.

12 A B Keith (1916) *Indian Mythology, Vol. 6, The Mythology of All Races* (ed. L H Gray et al.). Boston, MA: Marshall Jones Company, p. 6.

13 W J Wilkins (1900 [1880]). *Hindu Mythology: Vedic and Puranic*, reprint edition 2012. Delhi: DK Printworld, p. vii.

14 D D Kosambi (1962) *Myth and Reality: Studies in the Formation of Indian Culture*. Bombay: Popular Prakashan; H D Sankalia (1973) *Ramayana: Myth or Reality?* New Delhi: People's Publishing House.

15 Romila Thapar (1978) *Exile and the Kingdom: Some Thoughts on the Ramayana*. Bangalore: Mythic Society.

16 Vijay Nath (2001) *Purāṇas and Acculturation: A Historico-Anthropological Perspective*. Delhi: Munshiram Manoharlal.

17 C Minkowski (2001) 'The Pundit as public intellectual: The controversy over virodha or inconsistency in the astronomical sciences' in A Michaels edited *The Pundit: Traditional Sanskrit Scholarship in India*. New Delhi: Manohar, p. 94.

18 A Appadurai (1986) 'Theory in anthropology: Centre and periphery', *Comparative Studies in Society and History*, 28 (2), pp. 356–361.

19 Sheldon Pollock (1986) 'Introduction' in S Pollock edited *The Ramayana of Valmiki: An Epic of Ancient India*, Vol. 2, *Ayodhya Kaṇḍa*, Princeton, NJ: Princeton University Press, pp. 1–76; and his (1991) 'Introduction' in S Pollock edited *The Ramayana of Valmiki: An Epic of Ancient India*, Vol. 3, *Araṇya Kanda*. Princeton, NJ: Princeton University Press, 3–84.

20 Victor Turner paraphrased by Joseph Mali (2003) *Mythistory: The Making of a Modern Historiography*, Chicago, IL and London: University of Chicago Press, p. 6.

21 R Goldman (1986) 'A city of the heart: Epic Mathura and the Indian imagination', *Journal of the American Oriental Society*, 106 (3), p. 471.

22   E Renan 1939 [1882] 'What is a nation?' in M Zimmem edited *Modern Political Doctrines*. Oxford: Oxford University Press, pp. 190–203.

23   J Mali, *Mythistory*, p. 7.

24   A K Ramanujan (2013) [1990] 'Who needs folklore? The relevance of oral traditions to South Asian studies' in S. Kaul edited *Cultural History of Early South Asia: A Reader*, Delhi: Orient BlackSwan.

25   R Terdiman (1993) *Present Past: Modernity and Memory Crisis*. Ithaca, NY: Cornell University Press, pp. 3–4.

26   J Mali, *Mythistory*, p. 4.

27   W Doniger O'Flaherty (1988) *Other People's Myths: The Cave of Echoes*. New York: Macmillan, p. 27.

28   J Mali, *Mythistory*; E. Cassirer (1953) *Language and Myth*, New York: Dover Publications.

29   J A Josephson-Storm (2017) *The Myth of Disenchantment: Magic, Modernity, and the Birth of the Human Sciences*. Chicago, IL: University of Chicago Press, p. 5.

30   Diana L Eck (2012) *India: A Sacred Geography*. New York: Harmony, Random House, p. 1.

31   C Partenie (2018) 'Plato's myths' in E.N. Zalta edited *Stanford Encyclopaedia of Philosophy*. Available from: https://plato.stanford.edu/archives/fall2018/entries/plato-myths/ Last accessed 21 May 2022.

32   C Tilley (1994) *A Phenomenology of Landscape: Places, Paths and Monuments*. Oxford: Berg Publishers/Bloomsbury, p. 33.

33   Diana L Eck, *India*, p. 53.

34   Livy (1919) *History of Rome* (trans. B O Foster), Cambridge, MA: Harvard University Press, I. pref. pp. 6–9.

35   See the essays in Shonaleeka Kaul, *Myths and Places*.

Krishna in Mathura

12

While popular faith has never had any doubts about the antiquity of the association between Krishna worship and the city of his birth, Mathura, academic opinion has occasionally questioned it. Thus some scholars such as Charlotte Vaudeville influentially posited that Mathura had but a fleeting relationship with Krishna, "providing but an entrance and exit" for him, and that it was only very late, in the 16th century, that the area came to be truly a centre of Krishna worship when it was "occupied" by the devotional movements of Chaitanya and Vallabha.[1] It was argued that the early Krishnite texts, the *Harivamsha* (*HV* 1st–3rd century CE) and *Bhagavata Purana* (*BP* 9th century CE), located Krishna *outside* Mathura, in Vraja and later Dwaraka; and that images of Krishna from Mathura were scarce before the 6th century CE, with more Buddhist and Jain remains instead.

The invocation of the paucity of iconic remains would seem to overlook the finding of more than two dozen four-armed (*caturbhuj*) Krishna images and four kinship triads (joint images of Krishna, his brother Balarama and sister Ekanamsha), all from Mathura circa 1st century CE.[2] However, another theory preferred by some historians is that the 'cult' of Krishna was an engineered one, consisting of the late amalgamation of two different 'cult-heads': Krishna Gopala, the cowherd god, and Vasudeva Krishna, the Vaishnava kshatriya hero-god.[3] To them, the early images found would not count as representations of the former but of the latter. In other words it was also being suggested that Gopala was not identified with Vasudeva, nor with Vishnu, in the beginning.

In this essay, let us look at the historical evidence on the ground and in literature for what light it sheds on Krishna at Mathura.

First, was Krishna really textually absent from Mathura? And does this also translate into an absence of Krishna worship from a Buddhist/Jaina site? Paradoxically, while Buddhism and Jainism are visible in the material remains, there does not appear to have been involvement with the city in these traditions in anywhere near the same degree in which the cult of Krishna comes to relate to it and its environs. Thus in the Buddhist *Divyavadana* (2nd century CE) and Jaina *Paumacariyam* (3rd century CE), there is but a reference to Mathura as a background for Balarama and Vasudeva (enumerated as *shalakapurusha*s or 'great men'), and nowhere near a dwelling on or celebration of the city. In contrast, the *Harivamsha,* a supplement to the *Mahabharata* detailing the life of Hari, is dedicated to an expansive mapping of the sacred geography of the Mathura region, saturating the landscape with tales of the divine.

Indeed the purposive naming and charting of Vrindavana, Gokul and Govardhana as elements of this sacred terrain adjoining the city in the early *HV* deserves to be emphasised when reviewing the claim that it was the medieval Gaudiyas and Vallabhites who inaugurated these sites of veneration. Or are we saying that Mathura of *HV* or even *BP* is to be understood as merely a literary figment, with no connection to ground realities?

Let us remind ourselves of the earliest independent associations of Krishna worship with Mathura in the historical record. First is the 4th century BCE reference in Megasthenes' *Indika*, the first person account of the Greek ambassador to the Mauryan court. The *Indika* records the veneration in which Herakles was held among the people of Shoursenoi, whose major cities were Methora and Kleisbora, where the river Jobares flowed.[4]

The following are easily recognised in this testimony: Shurasenas, a branch of the Yadu dynasty to which Krishna is said to have belonged and a kingdom named in Buddhist Pali literature circa 6th century BCE as one of the first 16 states (*mahajanapadas*) of India; the river Y/Jamuna; and the urban settlement of Mathura. Moreover, scholars believe that Megasthenes mistook Krishna for the Greek god named Herakles. Interestingly, given the monster-slaying feats attributed to Herakles in Greek mythology, it is possibly the veneration of Gopala, the slayer of theriomorphic demons Arishta, Keshi, Hayagriva and Kaliya, all in the environs of Mathura, that inspired the comparison rather than that of Vasudeva, if the two ought to be distinguished at all.

And yet the association of the line of Satvata Vrishnis, to which Vasudeva is said to have belonged, with the ruling family of Mathura, has also always been clear from the *Mahabharata, Vishnu Purana* and Jaina texts. While the Vrishnis *per se* are heard of from as early as the Later Vedas, Panini in the 5th century BCE refers to the worship of Vasudeva and Arjuna (*vasudevarjunabhyam vun*) and possibly even to the images of the former being in circulation.[5]

The 1st century BCE Mora inscription from Mathura, on the doorjamb of a shrine which has not survived, also clearly establishes Bhagavat (Krishna) worship there as does the still older brick inscription (3rd–2nd century BCE) from Dwadash Aditya Tila, Vrindavana, the site associated locally with the *Kaliya daman* episode of Gopala.[6]

Note that the 2nd century BCE Ghoshundi inscription (Rajasthan) already identifies the Vrishni deity with Narayana just as the Besnagar inscription (MP), also circa 2nd century BCE, does with Vishnu. All these sites further prove that, contrary to scholarly opinion, Krishna worship was performed in stone temples long before the Gupta period. It was also widespread quite early, as seen in clear references/representations from Nasik (Maharashtra), Kondamotu (Andhra Pradesh), Chilas (Gilgit-Baltistan) and Aikhanum (Afghanistan) from around the same time.

In other words, both Krishna-Gopala and Vasudeva-Krishna were clearly esteemed in Mathura, and most probably as one, from at least the 4th century BCE onwards. The mythology is not gainfully bisected. That this happens for a date long preceding the *HV* would show that the text may have been merely articulating a phenomenon already in place in Mathura. After all, we do know from Patanjali that in the 2nd century BCE, Mathura-centric stories such as *Kamsa vadha* from this conjoint myth cycle were in currency and even the object of theatrical representation. And this Krishnite myth as well as that of *Keshi vadha* are found incorporated from the 1st century CE onwards in *kavya*s such as Ashvaghosha's *Saundarananda* and Bhasa's *Balacaritam* as well.[7]

To summarise: we survey here the historical evidence on

Krishna worship at Mathura, the antiquity of which has been questioned by some historians who trace it only to the medieval period. We noted that, though extant evidence of stone shrines dedicated to Krishna at Mathura (and indeed elsewhere) appear from at least the 2nd century BCE onwards, the earliest stone icons relating to the Krishna cult there, including 30 four-armed *chakradhari*s and four sets of kinship triads (Krishna, Balarama, Ekanamsha), date to 1st century CE.

Figure 12.1a Kinship Triad, Mathura, Uttar Pradesh, 2nd century CE. Courtesy: Government Museum, Mathura.

Figure 12.1b Kinship Triad, Atranjikhera, Uttar Pradesh, 9th century CE, State Museum, Lucknow. Courtesy: Author.

This evidence is rich enough to have been described by Doris Meth Srinivasan as "a sudden burst" in the number and variety of Vaishnava icons;[8] it is another matter that a "burst" of this kind in an artistic medium cannot in fact have been sudden and must have been preceded by considerable practice and faith. The reference in Panini's *Ashtadhyayi* (5th century BCE) to images of Krishna available for sale may be recalled as also the fully developed rendition of the lord and his elder brother on coins from Aikhanum, Afghanistan, from a little later.

In any case, art historians agree that sculptures in stone would never have been the first representations; they would typically have been preceded by centuries of work in non-stone materials such as clay, wood and cloth (*yamapata*). When translating remains in stone into evidence of the presence or absence of a sacred tradition, we must take into account this 'prehistory' of art.

❧ ☙

Especially so for Krishna worship that was characterised by its multiformity. In other words, it was constituted of multiple contexts that derived from different popular traditions of Mathura such as *yaksha*s, *naga*s and the *devi*. This points to the local and earthy make up of Krishna veneration. No one of these cultic alliances for Krishna exhausted the whole; they all combined in complementary roles that rounded out the worship of Vasudeva. The theologically significant combinations in which he occurs are best exemplified in the conception, both iconographic and textual, of the kinship triad: the siblings Balarama, Krishna and Ekanamsha.

Of this triad, Balarama/Samkarshana was a *naga* deity,

complete with his irascible temperament, fondness for liquor, association with water, and agricultural insignia such as the plough—all seen not only in the *Harivamsha*[9] but also in his images. Thus the Samkarshana stone image from Junsuti, Mathura (2nd cent BCE) stands under the canopy of a seven-hooded snake, resembling a serpent king as well as of course invoking Balarama's reincarnation of Vishnu's Sheshanaga.[10] No less ancient was the worship of *yaksha*s, the massive image from Parkham at Mathura being an excellent example. Krishna himself has been shown in one sense to be the *yaksha* of Govardhana, performing the primary *yaksha* function of protection (*yogakshema*) of his people.[11]

Krishna and Balarama's sister Ekanamsha provides perhaps the most fascinating element of an otherwise masculine pastoral or martial divinity. She is repeatedly named in *HV* as Vindhyavasini. Significantly, she, together with Manasa devi (snake goddess closely related to Govardhan hill), Vrinda devi (goddess of the woods) and Ganga devi, are folk goddesses that are worshipped even today in the Mathura region.

HV (2.2.52, 2.3.5–8, 2.3.10–12, 2.3.31, 33, 2.4.46–48) describes Ekanamsha as the dark-complexioned goddess propitiated with liquor and meat, resident of hills, caves and forests, one who removes the fear of disease and death, and is worshipped not only by forest peoples such as Shabaras and Pulindas, but also by the Vrishnis—the family of Krishna Vasudeva. The unbroken centrality of the worship of the goddess in Mathura is to be seen not only from the large number of terracotta *saptamatrika*s found there from the post-Mauryan period,[12] but that till today the *Vraj parikrama* (circumambulation), ostensibly a Krishnite ritual, includes a number of *devi* shrines.[13]

Add to this the central element of nature worship, vividly on display in *HV,* embodied in the bucolic Krishna himself and his identification with cows (*gopala, govinda*) in a literal as well as theological fashion. And then there is the Govardhana myth, whereby the worship of the divine hill (*giriyajna*) and of the divine hero by the people of Vraj are interlocked.

Further, the close association of Krishna and Balarama with the Vrinda woods, the Bhandira tree, and the Kalindi/ Yamuna river that flows through Vrindavana in the biography expounded in the *HV* is crucial. Witness some of this juxtaposition of myth and nature in the text: Gokula, the pastoral village (*ghosha*) in Vraja in which dwelled Nandagopa, the chief cowherd and adoptive father of Krishna Gopala, is encountered immediately on crossing the river Yamuna, located as it was on the bank opposite to Mathura city (this is described in the fifth chapter called *Nandavrajagamanam*). It

Figure 12.2a Govardhana hill, Mathura, Uttar Pradesh. Courtesy: Ananta Vrindavan Das.

Figure 12.2b Govardhana hill. Bird's eye view. Courtesy: Ananta Vrindavan Das.

is here that crawling about Vraja, Krishna's infancy pans out, and he performs in the first seven years of his life (*HV* 2.8.1) his first *līla*s, or acts of playful wonder, such as the overthrowing of the cart-shaped demon (*shakatabhanga*) (*HV* 2.6.6), the uprooting of the Yamalarjuna trees (*HV* 2.7.17–18), and the killing of Putana (*Putanavadha*), Kamsa's evil wet-nurse sent disguised as a murderous bird to bring an end to the divine baby's life (*HV* 2.6.26).

Thereafter, it is an important turn in adolescent Krishna's assumption of the leadership of the cowherd community (*gopa*s) when, on observing the exhaustion of the pastures in Gokula, he recommends the shifting of their village and all its cows to Vrindavana, the woods lying farther along the banks of the Yamuna. This passage of transfer from Gokula to Vrindavana deserves to be quoted here. It illustrates the text's ability and intent to chart and sanctify the surrounding environs of Mathura in both general terms and specifics such as flagging particular topographic or ecological landmarks such as the Govardhana hill, the Yamuna river in her local name as Kalindi and the Bhandira tree, all of which play their own roles in taking the pastoral-cum-divine narrative forward. Clearly, the landscape of the Mathura region is interwoven into the mythology in inseparable ways right from the *HV*. This is how Krishṇa describes the entire landscape:

It is heard that there is a beautiful forest named Vrindavana. That forest has adequate green grass. There are trees with delicious fruit and the water is good to taste. There are no thorny bushes; it has all that a forest should have. There are many *kadamba* trees in that forest on the banks of Yamuna. A cool breeze blows there. All seasons are present there simultaneously. The *gopi*s (cowherdesses) can roam freely.

Then he speaks of the hill and the river thus:

There is a great mountain named Govardhana not very far from the forest.... It looks splendid like Mt. Mandara in Nandana *vana* (heavenly woods). In the middle of the forest, there is a banyan tree with huge branches. Called Bhandira, it dazzles like a blue cloud in the sky.

The river Kalindi runs through the middle like the parting on the forehead of a married woman, like the river Nalini that runs through Nandana *vana*. It will be a pleasure for us to walk around there and see Govardhana, Bhandira, other trees and the beautiful Kalindi (*HV* 2.8.22–28).

After charting the mixed ecological terrain thus—forested, hilly and riverine—the text in the next chapter narrates movement onwards to a pastoral world. Witness:

Thus gradually, moving forward, the *vraja* reached Vrindavana. The residences were built over a vast area for the benefit of cows. The carts were parked around the boundary in the shape of a semi-crescent. In the middle, the breadth was one *yojana* and the length was two *yojana*s.... Pegs were driven into the ground. Churning ropes were tied on the pegs. Poles were erected and carts were tied to these poles. Buttermilk pots were hung on the poles with ropes. For cover, mats of grass were spread. Nests were built here and there on the trees for birds. Places were cleared for building cowsheds.... Some *gopi*s were lowering water pots from their heads. Some were enjoying the beauty of the forest. Some were walking around pulling down the branches of trees.... Some were cutting firewood and trees with axes. Because of all this, that place of *vraja*, surrounded by forest, appeared enchanting.... The cows which gave plenty of milk entered Vrindavana, which was full of bird-song.

Where Madhusudana (Krishna), the benefactor, is present, there the calves, cows and people can never face difficulty. Thus the cows, *vraja* and the young Samkarshana began to live with delight in the place liked by Krishna (*HV* 2.9.20–35).

It is Vrindavana that proves to be the playground of Krishna and Samkarshana's adolescent games and carefree jaunts with other *gopa*s and with *gopi*s, including the circular dance of Krishna during the season of the rains with all the cowherdesses coveting his attention (see later). Note also, in the text's description of Vrindavana that follows, the presence of other trademark motifs of the Krishna myth cycle such as the lord (and his brother in Gokul) playing the flute (*HV* 2.8.5,

2.11.12). This, together with the dalliance with the *gopis*, were themes that were seized on and elaborated—but not inaugurated or invented—by the 9th century CE *Bhagavata Purana*, the 12th century CE *Gitagovinda* of Jaideva, and the 16th century *Mathuramahatmya* of Rupa Gosvamin, the Chaitanya follower. Here are some excerpts from the simultaneous textual elaboration of the landscape and the mythology:

> One day while wandering in the forest with the cows, the Lord saw... the huge banyan tree, named Bhandira, appearing like a mountain... Krishna along with other cow-tending boys of the same age had a good time under the tree, like he used to in heaven before. When Krishna played under the Bhandira tree, his cow-tending boys brought him many toys of the forest. Some others with joyful minds sang. Some others who liked Krishna's *lila*s sang about them. When the boys sang, Krishna played a whistle made of palm leaves. Sometimes he played flute (*venu*) or the *vina*" (*HV* 2.11.23–27).

Elsewhere in the text:

> The chastisers of their enemies, Krishna and Balarama, would sometimes challenge each other for a duel, sing together, search for trees, and sometimes call the cows and calves by their names (*HV* 2.14.3). There, the two brothers... engaged in exercise by swinging and throwing stones. Along with their cow-tending friends, the two lion-like valiant brothers, roamed as they liked joyfully, displaying various fighting methods there (*HV* 2.14.10–11).

And then the iconic love dalliance of Krishna is also described:

> Krishna, who is knowledgeable about time, in his prime

Krishna in Mathura **195**

youth, invited the young *gopis* in the night, and experienced joy with them. Even though prevented by their husbands, brothers and mothers, the *gopis*... searched for Krishna in the night. All of them stood forming a circle and each one enjoyed herself with one of him. In this manner, pairs of Krishna and a *gopi* each were formed. The *gopis* sang the tales of Krishna; fixing their eyes on him, they imitated his *lilas* and walked like him.... In this way, Krishna enjoyed the company of ornamented *gopis* in circles in the moonlit nights during the autumn (*HV* 2.20.18–35).

Moreover, Vrindavana is also the site of other divine acts by Krishna and Samkarshana that were meant to rid Vraja and the earth of evil dangers such as the horse-demon Keshi (*HV* 2.24, 6–65) and the bull-demon Arishta (*HV* 2.22, 31), as well as Pralamba, the *daitya* (*HV* 2.14,12). These acts indeed earn the two deities some of their many epithets (Keshava and Baladeva respectively).

Similarly, but more spectacularly, it is the banks of the Yamuna (*yamunatire*) that witness the quelling of the serpent-demon Kaliya in the episode titled *kaliyadaman*. Yet again, effectively evoking and involving the quintessential riverine identity of Mathura and Vraja, the episode is described thus in the *HV* (2.11.28–39):

One day, while tending the cows, Krishna... went to the banks of the Yamuna which had trees covered with creepers and bushes. He saw the river which appeared curved because of waves. A pleasant wind was blowing touching the surface of the water. Good pathways led to the river. The water was good to taste.... The atmosphere was filled with the sounds of swans, *karandavas* and cranes. The river was full of aquatic animals and a variety of water-borne flowers. The water appeared greenish due to them.

Wandering along the banks of that great river, Krishna saw a huge lake the breadth of one *yojana*. The huge water body was calm and silent like an ocean without any movement. Aquatic animals and birds avoided it. On the unapproachable banks, there were big holes where serpents lived. The entire lake was covered with the fire and smoke emanating from the poison of the serpents. The water was not fit for drinking. It was impossible for the birds to fly in the sky over that lake. If a blade of dry grass fell on the water, it was immediately burned. For a distance of a *yojana* all around the lake, it was difficult even for the *deva*s to walk.

The dramatic contrast between a pristine and auspicious water body and a dour and ominous one is striking in the textual representation. It leads Krishna to the performance of another one of his famed feats. This is described thus:

Seeing that vast lake, Krishna thought: "This lake is the residence of serpent Kaliya, black like the *anjana* stone. It is Kaliya that has polluted the entire Yamuna.... Thus it is my duty to destroy the king of serpents, so that the water of this river becomes useful for Vraja. People will be able to roam in this area again. The river will become sacred and a source of happiness. For this reason, I took birth as a cowherd (*gopajanma*) and started residing in Vraja. It is for destroying the wicked who stay on the wrong path (*nigrahartham duratmanam*)."

Now, the *HV* was composed probably between the 1st and 3rd centuries CE and is believed to contain material that was still earlier. As such, it is particularly noteworthy that, as we have just seen in detail, the text already purposively names and charts as elements of this sacred terrain adjoining the city of Mathura places such as Vrindavana, Gokula, Govardhana and Yamuna, the iconic river that flowed right through the environs of Mathura and the narrative played out therein. It bears stating, then, that Vaudeville's claim that it was the Gauḍīyas and Vallabhites, coming more than a millennium after the *HV*, who were responsible for the discovery and inauguration of these very sites of sacredness and veneration is not quite tenable. All this evidence shows that these sites in and around Mathura were not figments nor *lila sthala*s inaugurated by Chaitanya or Vallabha in the 16th century. These were already in place textually and on the ground as an immutable part of the natural and mythic geography. Significantly, even today *prakriti puja* takes precedence over *murti puja* in connection with Krishna worship in Vraja.[14] Can such traditions and practices in ancient times be expected to have left durable traces in stone and archaeology?

Moreover, hills, groves, pastures and the river, defined not only the spatial imagination of the Krishna cult in *HV*, but rooted it in the precise topography of Mathura as we know it. This is because early Mathura was indeed situated at the junction of different habitats—rural, urban, pastoral, hilly, forested and riverside. Also, archaeologists tell us it was a non-nucleated and multi-mound phenomenon, wherein many of the 90 archaeological sites are located outside the fortification wall, in concentric semi-circles radiating out from it for several kilometres. Mathura thus needs to be understood as a composite landscape inclusive of this urban annexe. Is it so very curious then that legends of Krishna too were enacted in the environs just outside the city but very much within its cultural complex?

How is this rich naturalistic history of Krishna worship to be understood? As a remote, unconnected past? Or as seamless continuities, without appreciating which we cannot know its local rootedness? The latter approach is consistent with both archaeology and text for early Mathura. Theories of medieval manufacture, on the other hand, fail to do justice to either kind of evidence.[15]

Notes

1   Charlotte Vaudeville (1996) 'Braj, Lost and Found', in Vasudha Dalmia edited *Myths, Saints and Legends in Medieval India,* New Delhi: Oxford University Press, pp. 47–71. The words 'occupation' and 'colonisation' are used by Dalmia in her Editor's Preface to explain the import of Vaudeville's theory. Vaudeville was actually anticipated by H. Goetz, who first suggested back in 1932 that Mathura did not appear to be an object of veneration until Chaitanya's time. Cited in Vaudeville, 'Braj, Lost and Found', p. 48, note 3.

2   V S Agrawala (1951) *Catalogue of the Brahmanical Images in Mathura Art,* Lucknow: UP Historical Society, p. 4, and Doris Meth Srinivasan (1989) 'Vaishṇava Art and Iconography at Mathura', in D M Srinivasan edited *Mathura: Cultural Heritage,* New Delhi: Manohar Publications, p. 384. Agarwala enumerated fourteen images, while Doris Srinivasan later put the figure at thirty. For kinship triads, see Srinivasan, 'Early Krshṇa Icons' in D M Srinivasan edited *Mathura,* p. 127.

3   H C Raychaudhuri (1936) *Materials for the Study of the Early History of the Vaishṇava Sect,* Calcutta: University of Calcutta, and Suvira

Jaiswal (1968) *The Origin and Development of Vaishṇavism,* Delhi: Munshiram Manoharlal.

4   Suvira Jaiswal, *The Origin and Development of Vaishnavism,* p. 170.

5   Vinay Kumar Gupta (2023) 'Vrishnis in Ancient Art and Literature', *Vestigia Indica: BSSS Journal of History and Archaeology,* 1, 1, p. 186.

6   Vinay Kumar Gupta (2020) 'A Glimpse Into the Archaeological Antiquity of Vrindavan', *Heritage: Journal of Multidisciplinary Studies in Archaeology,* Thiruvananthapuram: University of Kerala, p. 183.

7   Suvira Jaiswal, *The Origin and Development of Vaishnavism,* pp. 79–80.

8   D M Srinivasan (1989) 'Vaisnava Art and Iconography at Mathura', in D M Srinivasan edited *Mathura,* p. 384.

9   All references to the *Harivamsha Purana* are taken from A Purushothaman and A Harindranath translated *Harivamsha Purana, Visnu Parvan,* based on Pandit Ramachandrashastri Kinjawadekar edited (1936) Chitrashala Press edition, http://mahabharata-resources.org/harivamsa/harivamsa-cs-index.html. The *mushala* and the *hala* are also seen as Balarama's weapons in the battle against Jarasandha fought at Mathura *HV* 2.35.60. His white complexion and blue garments are mentioned earlier during his stay at Gokula as a child *HV* 2.8.2 and in Vrindavana *HV* 2.14.5.

10 N P Joshi (1972) *Catalogue of the Brahmanical Sculptures in the State Museum,* Lucknow, pt. 1, Lucknow: The State Museum, Fig. 13; D M Srinivasan, 'Vaisnava Art and Iconography at Mathura', p. 389; V S Agrawala (1940) *A Short Guide-Book to the Archaeological Section of the Provincial Museum,* Lucknow: Provincial Museum, p. 14, fig. 1.

11 Charlotte Vaudeville (1996) 'The Cowherd God in Ancient India', in Vasudha Dalmia edited *Myths, Saints and Legends,* p. 26.

12 N P Joshi (1986) *Matrkas: Mothers in Kushana Art,* New Delhi: Kanak Publications. Images of other goddesses such as Laksmi, Vasundhara and Durga Mahishasuramardini are also found from the Kushana period.

13 Charlotte Vaudeville, 'Braj, lost and found', p. 65.

14 Ibid., p. 52.

15 For full details of the evidence discussed in this essay, see Shonaleeka Kaul (2015) 'Early Mathura: Sacred Imagination and Diverse Traditions', *Indian Historical Review*, vol. 42, 1 (June), pp. 1–16.

The Many-Splendoured City: Sensory Renditions of the Urban Multiverse in Sanskrit Texts

Sanskrit literature is replete with representations of the city. However, scholars have tended to disregard these as conventional, idealised and stereotypical rather than possessing anything of value for the urban historian. Rare have been the voices advocating a more sympathetic and literature-sensitive perspective, where the strength of these representations is shown to lie in the symbolic realm, yielding an intuitive grasp of structure otherwise unavailable to the modern scholar, or in capturing the "citiness of the city" beyond its physical contours.[1]

In this essay, I bring to bear a symbolic reading on the material phenomenon of the city in early Sanskrit literature, bringing it alive in all its complexity and vibrance. In particular, I explore sensory renditions of the city which flesh out its physical and behavioural dimensions. In my book *Imagining the Urban: Sanskrit and the City in Early India*, I suggested that literature's treatment of the city functions like a tourist guide map, which selects particular sites or routes to frame cities as attractive places and to project select urban qualities. These can be interpreted as outstanding or prototypical features of the city in the textual imagination. And there is an added aestheticisation both in the way the senses are invoked to describe places and in the choice of such parts of the city as are in themselves aesthetic points such as shopping malls, promenades, gardens and recreation centres.

There is no reason to argue that these are not meaningful selections; they may be out of a deference to literary factors such as the cultivation of *shringara rasa* (beauty), or *kavya*'s aim of creating joy (*priti*) or delight (*harsha*). The representational choice could also be suggested by the ancient poet's internalised cognitive map of surrounding urban reality. The fictive type of the texts notwithstanding, an authenticity can therefore be assumed to inform literary depictions of the city. Of course, it is only a universalised or essentialised picture of the urban phenomenon that we can hope to get here.

❧ ❧

When the sage Kapila Gautama asked his disciples, a group of royal princes, to found a great city, he flew into the air, holy water-pitcher in hand, sprinkled off an extensive area on the ground, and ordained the territory thus enclosed by the stream of water as the site for the prospective settlement (*Saundarananda*, henceforth *Saundara.*, I. 33).[2] Among other things, this account of the beginnings of the city of Kapilavastu in the *Saundarananda* illustrates the idea of the city as a precisely delimited zone. And in our texts, it is the city wall (*prakara*) or rampart (*vapra*) that marks off that zone. Indeed, almost every time a *kavya* or an epic refers to the walls of a city, it is the sheer magnitude of the fortification and/or its consequent strength and invincibility that are conveyed, typically by hyperbole (*atishayokti*) and simile (*upama*).

The walls of one city in the *Mahabharata* (henceforth *Mbh.*) are said to "reach up to the heavens" (*Mbh.* I. CCIX,

p. 407). The enclosure of another in the *Shishupalavadha* (henceforth *Shishu.*) is "much too high for the [surrounding] sea waves to triumph over" and even the entry of clouds is obstructed by the walls of the fort, so that they are forced to shed their moisture outside (*Shishu.* III. 40–41). The rampart enclosing Kapilavastu in the *Saundarananda* (I. 42) is said to be "as vast as mountains as if it [the city] were a second Girivraja".

Another kavya, the *Buddhacarita* (henceforth *BC*) mentions that a number of hills surrounded Girivraja, or Rajagaha, the capital of Magadha, and served as natural fortification (*BC*. X. 2). This is also attested in Pali literature and by excavation. The comparison therefore lends a double significance and specificity to the otherwise simple simile drawing on the size and strength of mountains. *Kavya* descriptions thus offer eloquent impressions.

Size, or rather height, and strength are qualities they also attribute to gates (*dvara, gopura*) that intersect the city wall at regular intervals. The gates are usually one in each of

Figure 13.1a Gates of Kushinagara depicted at Sanchi Stupa, Madhya Pradesh, 2nd century BCE. Courtesy. Wikimedia Commons.

Figure 13.1b Conjectural reconstruction of Kushinagara. Courtesy: Percy Brown, *Indian Architecture: Hindu and Buddhist,* 1942.

the four quarters and often several more. Their being closed at night with heavy bars, and it being impossible to force them open easily even by using elephants, are mentioned in the *Buddhacharita* (V. 82). They are also described in the *Shishupalavadha.* (III. 26) as decorated with arches (*torana*), so that Krishna's soldiers, following him out of Dvaravati, have to lower the banners and standards they carry to avoid breaking these against them.

The hues in which the fort structures are depicted may be an indication as to the construction materials used. For example, the gateways of Hastinapura being "dark as clouds", if it is not meant just poetically, could imply reference to the use of clay or black rock (*Mbh.* I.CIX. p. 233); the turrets of Kapilavastu as white and city walls of Ujjayini or Indraprastha as "white as clouds/moonrays" may likewise have meant the use of limestone for building or plastering.[3] A unique depiction of this kind pertains to the rampart of Dvaravati, which the *Shishupalavadha.* (III. 33, 37, 27) describes as "golden, effulgent like submarine fire (*kañcanavaprabhasa*)". Invoking submarine fire seems to be a reference to the supposed seaside location of Dvaraka, which may also be responsible for another description of the rampart in the same text as being full of sea shells. The unique golden appearance of the fort can possibly be explained in light of a reference earlier in the text to the soft, golden earth in the city which glittered like a peacock feather, reminiscent of sand. So it can be argued that the description is of an earthen rampart built out of the dense piling of coastal soil or sand that gave to it a yellowish tinge which, in poetic language, was transformed into "golden effulgence". The fort and rampart of Lanka in the Valmiki *Ramayana* (V. 2.14–17) are described as golden for probably the same reason.

❦

The fortification wall was the emblem par excellence of the city as a delimited site. But did the limits of the city always and in every way coincide with the boundary wall? Our texts suggest that it was not quite so. Even where walls exist, *kavya*s furnish enormous evidence of urban-related phenomena taking one outside the city on a regular basis. The notion of "outside the city" is denoted by several phrases such as *nagarabahya, upanagaram* and *puropakantha* ("near the city"). Even as it reflects a consciousness of what was 'city' and what was not, it also points to the significance in the life of the city of the areas just outside it.

These included the cremation ground (*shmashana, janadahasthana*), described in the *Malatimadhava* (henceforth *Malati.* V. p. 46) as a vast, dark and smelly area with cries of spirits and goblins and peopled by practitioners of dark magic. The *shmashana* also seems to have served as execution ground (*vadhyasthana*) and probably adjoined forests.[4] It may have thus constituted something of a backwater to the city, additionally because of its inauspicious and diabolical associations.

The *Arthashastra* (II.IV. p. 54) lays down that the cremation ground shall be situated either to the north or to the east of a settlement. It also provides for a second cemetery to the south (or "to the right") for the people of the highest caste (*uttarah purvo va shmashanavatai dakshinena varnottamanam*). This is reminiscent of the reference to *dakshinashmashana* in the *Mricchakatika* (X. p. 348), where Charudatta, the *brahmana* merchant, is taken for execution. It has been suggested that varna-based differential access to the cemetery implies that though it was outside the physical limits of the city, the cemetery was not outside its social world.[5]

In a related prescription, the *Arthashastra* (II. IV. p. 54) ordains that the heretics and *chandalas* (outcastes) shall live on the periphery of the cremation ground. The city thus appears to be imbued with a degree of social exclusivity. The hero of the *Avimaraka*, forced by a seer's curse to live a certain period as an outcaste (*antyajakulapravasa*), is shown dwelling outside the city of Vairantya (II. pp. 260, 284). However, as with the cemetery, so with these excluded social groups: the fact that they were located close to the city, even if outside it, points to their being linked to the world within the city walls. This was by virtue of the services they provided the city, such as cremation and execution. The so called "heretics" too, at least the alms-seeking varieties, would depend on the urban populace for sustenance via *dana* (donations).

*Kavya*s give evidence to this effect: In the *Mricchakatika*

(X. p. 353–55) a pair of *chandalas*, escorting Charudatta to the cremation/execution arena, parade with familiarity right through the city. Buddhist monks and nuns as well as Jaina mendicants are also shown routinely traversing the streets of a city, when not actively participating in the affairs of city-dwellers.[6] This is so much so that an aspiring renunciant in the *Mricchakatika* (II. p. 94) says he will be able to freely roam the king's highway after his ordination as a monk. And, in the *Mudrarakshasa* (I. p. 25), a spy who is asked to mingle with the populace within a city chooses to disguise himself as a Jaina monk.

Constituting a contrast with this ascetic/monastic complexion is the fact that, for the citizens of the city, the single largest purpose of these urban peripheries seems to be that of leisure and pleasure. There were those locales for sport outside the city that occurred naturally or in the wild, namely forests (*vanavihara*), rivers/streams/the sea (*jalavihara/jalakrida*), and mountain caves. And then there were those groves or gardens (*udyana, upavana, purakanana*) that suggest they were portions of the surrounding forest that were reclaimed by the city and semi-cultivated into a secure and accessible recreational annexe. These were frequented by the urban hoi polloi in addition to royal visitors, bringing into being what may be described as an "early Indian garden culture".[7]

Such groves were distinctively named and could be demarcated by a wall with gates (including a wicker gate *chhidradvara*) and guards (*Mrcch*. VIII. p. 264). They were ornamented and manipulated spaces, fitted with appurtenances: stone seats and pavilions, tanks and wells, and artificial pleasure hillocks. It is in this sense, one supposes, that groves are said to be "constructed" by kings and monied individuals. Further, though they are on more than one occasion described as open to the public (*sarvasadharana*), it seems they were at the same time claimable as the possession of an individual linked to the royal family or could be closed to the public when a royal was visiting.[8]

These groves were resorted to for conviviality, regarded in the nature of pleasure parks or sportive gardens. This is indicated by the synonyms applied to them: *lilavana, kelivana, akrida* and *pramadavana*. The sport consisted not only of the love dalliance of couples, much like modern day city parks, but of group excursions (*goshthiyana*) or community gatherings and festivities (*utsava*) as well. Prominent among these were the *kamadevamahotsava* or *vasantotsava* (spring festival) with its erotic tones. On such occasions, the groves could witness considerable congregations of urban origin (*Malati*. I. p. 14). They appear to have had much traffic even in the normal course, particularly from elite sections of the city. This is suggested by a reference in the *Mricchakatika* (VII. p. 249) that the sight of a carriage would arouse no suspicion in the Pushpakarandaka grove area because it was well frequented.

Finally, two instances from the *Dashakumaracarita* (VI. p. 122) and *Mudrarakshasa* (III. p. 184) suggest that groves outside the city could provide conducive conditions for carrying out the act of suicide, and as in one case in the *Mricchakatika* (VIII. p. 277), murder! There is also a reference to the confidence to speak of one's troubles that the secrecy in a grove generated (*Dasha*. Purva. IV. p. 38). Taken together, these point to the privacy and space that the extra-city territory afforded.

Thus we get two simultaneous impressions: that of the enclosed city and then of the open city. The city grounds, referred to in the texts as *upashalyam* ("near the boundary"), *purangana* ("city yard") or *purabhuva* ("city grounds"), can be understood as linked to the city by a series of contrastive qualities: morphological (open area versus built-up zone), lifestyle (sport versus business, asceticism versus worldly pursuits), ambience (privacy versus crowding) and social character (outcaste versus caste society). However, given the frequent and regular intercourse between the two segments of the urban phenomenon, the contrasts defined a spatial-functional whole. And so the city grounds extended and not merely adjoined the city.

Within the ancient Indian city, one finds a utilitarian organisation of space with numerous functions represented, namely, residential, commercial, recreational, institutional, transit-related (roads), religious and administrative. Neither palace nor any ceremonial centre is depicted as the nucleus. In fact the impression is not that of a settlement nucleated in any sense. A linear or rectilinear orientation seems to be more the case, and so an element of axiality rather than nuclearity can be said to characterise the urban layout, as captured in *kavya* literature. Chiefly responsible for the impression of axiality is the phenomenon of the royal road (*rajamarga, nagara-rathya*).

The *rajamarga* emerges as the quintessential focus of the city. Rows of all prominent buildings (*prasadamala*) converged on the royal road, situated along both sides of it.[9] Every sector of the city, and the area outside it as well, was

connected via the royal road (or the streets branching off it)—
veritably an urban artery or spine. And nearly everything that
took place publicly in the city and was worth mention took
place on the royal road. This could be regular urban activity
such as evening promenades by the culturati, or the occasional
spectacle such as a festive or royal procession, or, more rarely,
sensational events such as a famous man being taken away for
execution, or the charge and subsequent taming of a rogue
elephant. Indeed, on such occasions the highway seemed to
become one with the whole city which collected upon it.

Together these activities, and a whole array of humdrum
goings-on (vividly described for instance in the *BC.* X. 4–7),
constituted the royal road as a site of urban rhythms. By
urban rhythms, one can imply anything from the regular
comings and goings of people about the city to the vast range
of repetitive activities, sounds, and smells that punctuate life
in the city, arising out of the teeming mix of city life.[10] In the
process, some essences of the city can be experienced here.

The overwhelming characteristic of this highway is its
crowds. There were horses, elephants, chariots and other
vehicles passing through,[11] and of course teeming pedestrians.
Not unlike the modern cosmopolis, among them were all
manner of people, including the drunk, the poor and the
handicapped (*pratyangahinavikalendriya*), in addition to a
host of monks, merchants, courtesans, *vita*s (libertines), gentle
folk and the hoi polloi, strolling, chatting, lounging about or
at work.[12] Indeed, as the *Padmaprabhritaka* (p. 54) pithily
puts it: "On the royal road the touch of strangers is easy to
come by" (*rajamarge sulabhamaviditajanasamsparsham*). The
contrast with night time, then, is striking, with darkness and
desolation descending together on the *rajamarga*. The beloved

on a tryst, guards on patrol and the occasional thief are at this time the only ones to be seen walking the road.[13]

Then, the king's palace is represented as a sprawling complex, comprising several buildings and sections: the residential apartments of the king, queens and princes, the pillared audience hall (*sabha*) the music hall (*sangitashala*), painting hall (*chitrashala*), drinking hall (*panabhumi*), fire room (*agnigara*) or temple, gymnasium (*rangatam*), treasury (*koshagriha*) and considerable open spaces devoted to water tanks, stables for elephants and horses, and particularly pleasure gardens, housed with peacocks. These were often attached to the women's apartments (*grihopavana* or *antahapuropavana*). A passage in the *Dashakumaracarita* (III. pp. 77–78) describes fairly elaborately landscaped royal greens catacombed with tree-lined paths and avenues. It has been suggested that this presented a sort of botanical simulacrum of the palace itself, mirroring its elaborately choreographed space.[14] This may account for the impression of a concentric layout that the hero Avimaraka, gazing on the palace from atop its boundary wall, seems to get:

Oh, what a magnificent palace!
Huge as it is, it is delicately constructed—
One building seems to rise out of another.
I could believe the whole complex structure
Was straining to leave the earth and soar into pure sky.
(*Avi*. III.XII. p. 74. Emphasis added.)

The rest of the city consisted of buildings, standing in rows, arranged in quarters (*catvara*), localities or neighbourhoods. Two separate descriptions in the *Chaturbhani* (*Ubhayabhisarika*. p. 5; *Padataditaka*. p. 115) of rows of mansions, "as if calling to one another like the ten mouths of Ravana", imply a considerably dense use of space. This is explicitly indicated in the description in the *Ramayana* (I. 5,17; V.2.53) of the houses in Ayodhya being "built in close proximity to one another without the slightest gap between them" while the houses of Laṅka are also "crowded up against each other". The spatial and architectural density accords well with the houses on the royal road being depicted with their side doors opening on it, so that the longer front facade can be imagined to have looked on to side streets and alleys that intersected the main road.[15] Some windows nonetheless faced the main street and one of the common motifs in textual descriptions (as also sculptural relief) is women crowding their windows to get a view of goings-on in the street below.

These buildings are regularly noted for their height: similes drawing on clouds and mountain peaks, and claims about structures "propping up the sky", are commonly resorted to. This suggests that, as with the palace, these were many-storeyed structures, a point explicitly brought out by references to the "upper storey", "topmost room" (*valabhi* or *harmyashikhara*), and "lofty windows" of houses, as well as by the colourful description of a woman standing high on her mansion resembling a city banner with her clothes aflutter in the breeze.[16]

In the *griha* building, the open outer courtyard is what one entered from the street through a gate in a baked brick wall. It could also be accessed from the premises of the house through the side-door of the private garden that seems to have adjoined it. The garden housed domestic peacocks and a pleasure pavilion and has in one study been described as "the moral and material prerogative of the elite".[17] The texts provide incredible detail:

for example, in smaller houses, the outer courtyard seemed to have the form of a verandah-like extension (*pradvarangana*) before the doorsteps (*Pada*. pp. 153, 158).

The outer courtyard was something of the public domain of the private residence where those entering the house were received, guests or strangers entertained, and where an itinerant roadshow man could perform for the viewing pleasure of the inmates. The men of the house could also sleep the night there.[18] The outer court led into the inner one (*abhyantara-chatuhshalakam*). Here one entered into that part of the dwelling to which the genteel womenfolk (*kulastri*) in our stories normally appear confined and which perhaps thereby symbolised the domestic *sanctum sanctorum*. As I have discussed elsewhere, however, literature also shows that women routinely found ways and means of subverting the sequestration that such architecture was intended to ensure.[19]

Then, some of the main non-residential buildings that appear as a regular feature of the urban scape were the courtesans' houses, the drinking booth (*panagara*) and the gambling hall (*dyutasabha*). The *vitasabha* or *goshthishala* was in the nature of a clubhouse where connoisseurs could meet for an invigorating literary exchange or attend a musical concert (*sangitakam*). All this suggests the projected quality of life in the city as public and congregational, as well as relatively free of strictures.

The major shops (*mahapanam*) were located along the royal road, described as well-divided, conjuring the image of shops oriented to the grid pattern of a main road intersected at regular intervals by streets and alleys. A vivid reminder of these aisles separating blocks of shops is the reference in the *Mricchakatika* (II. p. 99) to dogs fast asleep at night in the various lanes between shops. It is likely that the market extended along some of these inner lanes, for example, in the *Padataditaka,* the *pushpavithi* or flower range led off the main market road (*Pada.* p. 118).

It also appears that shops, either *en bloc* or individually, had a verandah extending at the front, not unlike modern-day Indian bazaars, where perhaps goods for sale were exhibited, which would explain their being so visible from the main road as, for instance, in the *Avimaraka* (II. p. 279; III. p. 298). The texts emphasise that the saleable commodities within these markets were "the cream of many lands and seas", "articles of every variety [and] quality that man can desire".[20] And multitudes of men gathered there "from all regions" to buy and sell these. This made the marketplace "impassable due to the great crowd" (*mahajanasammardadurgamaṃ vipanimargam*) (*Pada.* p. 117–18).

꧁꧂

How did it *feel* to be in the city? In literature, an evocative collage of sensory perceptions evokes the urban ambience as a series of full-blooded sensory experiences. What you were likely to see, hear or smell in the city would depend considerably on where in the city you were. If you were standing near the gambling hall, you would be within earshot of a place "adorned with abusive words"! (*Dhurtavitasamvada.* p. 31). If you were turning off the main market and approaching the flower street, it would be the "combined fragrance of various flowers" that would accost you (*Padmaprabhritaka.* p. 82). And if you were in the marketplace, you would experience the following:

How wonderful is the mingling of great noises! ... Flowers, as if laughing with their beauty, are being sold; cups are passing round in the drinking booth, city birds are swooping on the butchers' shops while the buyers ... are looking at them with anxious eyes ... The people rubbing shoulders and haggling over various articles and making purchases, are proceeding like soldiers in their files. Gamblers, after earning their *mashaka*s (coins), are on the way to the courtesans, attended by servants carrying flowers, cooked meat, cakes and wine." (*Pada.* pp. 117–18).

There, you would also hear a cacophony, including "from the smithy a nasal sound, like the wailing of ospreys the sound of bell metal articles on the lathe, and like the hard breathing of a horse galloping, the sound of serrated cutters pressed against conch shells". You would possibly also hear the drums, flutes and brass gongs playing in accompaniment to a bit of intoxicated revelry near the drinking booth (*Pada.* 118–19). Similarly, the courtesans' quarter presented a site for multiple sensations:

The breeze, charged with the sweet smell of garlands and of liquor, blows like the breath of the courtesans' quarter ...Smokes of *agaru* (incense) from the windows of the houses are creating, as it were, a cloudy day; the door-fronts are smiling with flowers scattered there; the music of the clinking *kanci* (girdle) is creating excitement in men of passion; the jingling of anklets is its (the quarter's) voice... Its (the quarter's) rows of buildings seem to be roaring, constantly resounding with the playing of drums which scares away the pigeon couples. Craftsmen there are being ordered. Some servants are spreading flowers, some preparing scented oils of many kinds, some pounding colours, some making garlands. One hears here the sound of the *vina* (lyre). There goes round the wine cup..." (*Dhurta.* p. 34–35).

A crowded miscellany of effects thus appears as the projected quality of urban space. This is brought home also by descriptions of the city as seen from the royal road. The protagonist in the *Padmaprabhritaka* (p. 72, verse 9) thus exclaims:

> How wonderful is the supreme splendour of Ujjayini (*aho! ujjayinyah para shrih*) ... Here, there are recitations of the Vedas, the noises of chariots, horses and elephants, twangs of bowstrings, acting of plays, reading of poems, wrangling of the learned men, buying and selling of goods come from beyond the four seas. At some places there is the talk of *vita*s [libertines] and at others, practice of all the arts; and the rows of houses are all agitated with the cries of sporting birds, and resound with the tinkling of bangles and girdles.

The opening exclamation to the description conveys the awe and marvel that seem to have constituted the centre of feelings about the city. Further, the essential noises enumerated in the excerpt recur in descriptions in other texts, and are added to by "the noise of butchers chopping meat", "chatter in different rooms [of houses]", and the ubiquitous palace gong, or conch and drums, that "reverberate in the expansive vaults of mansions and spread loudly in the sky", proclaiming morning, midday and evening hours every day.[21] This entirely auditory rendition of the city not only shows that it was considered possible to capture the urban experience by its sounds in themselves, but that noise, perhaps an element of any human settlement, was most compellingly so of a city.

A further imaginative rationale behind such a representation is that it emphasises an intensely heterogeneous ambience, deriving from a multiplicity of occupations and functions performed in relative proximity, including ritual, military, academic, recreational, commercial, cultural and residential. This thoroughly differentiated and interactive use of urban space points to the teeming mix of life—of people and activities—that this space contains. *The physical effect is therefore also a social fact.* In the same vein, the crowds that populated the city enacted it as the site of a new set of physical and sensory relationships. The press, excitement and chaos of so many people with so many purposes, all in one place, is an identifiable quality in the descriptions. It transforms, for example, the main road, which is a place of everyday business and not frightening in itself, into a "human jungle" (*purushakantara*) (*Pada.* p. 143). Physical effect and social fact combined to create an altered psycho-sensorial experience of the city. Here variety, noise, crowding and hectic activity dominated, while on special occasions such as festivals, these phenomena were only accentuated by a sensuousness—colour, fragrance, noise and beauty.

Interestingly, the behavioural traits of the urban community that inhabited the city tallied with the physical and sensory qualities of the urban experience. Liberality, education, aesthetic sensibility, athletic and recreational skills, and social etiquette are highlighted as representing urban living, a picture of cultural and ethical sophistication. However, the texts also indicate that a city need not possess any unitary visage or reputation. Thus the *Kuttanimata* (176,

p. 79; 180, p. 83) describes Pataliputra as the *kulagriha* of Sarasvati (goddess of learning), but also as being the *asura-vivara* (habitat of demons) for being home to sensuous women. It describes Varanasi as home to many scholars, but also famous for its courtesans and fashionable ladies (*Kuttani*. 3, 5, 7–8, 12, 15, 17, pp. 172, 243). Similarly, the *Harshacarita* (III. 107–8) says of a city:

Sages call it a hermitage.

Courtesans a lovers' retreat.

Actors a concert hall.

Foes the site of death.

Seekers of wealth the land of the philosopher's stone.

Aspirants to knowledge the preceptor's home.

Singers the home of *gandharva*s.

Merchants the land of profit.

Bards the gaming house.

Good men the gathering of the virtuous.

Libertines the rogues' meet.

Wayfarers the reward of their good deeds.

Treasure-seekers the mine.

Quietists the Buddhist monastery.

Lovers the haunt of *apsaras*.

Troubadours the festival congress.

Brahmanas the stream of wealth.

Poetic effect apart, it is being suggested that the early Indian city sported multiple, even contrary, images. This, as we know, was consistent with the profusion of social types, activities and sensations the city hosted. Its very structure made it the object of plural perspectives, bringing into being a living, throbbing multiverse.[22]

Notes

1   See A K Ramanujan (1993) 'Towards an Anthology of City Images' in Vinay Dharwadker edited *The Collected Essays of A K Ramanujan*, New Delhi: Oxford University Press; B D Chattopadhyaya (1997) 'The City in Early India: Perspectives from Texts', *Studies in History*,13, 2, pp.181–208; Shonaleeka Kaul (2010) *Imagining the Urban: Sanskrit and the City in Early India*, Delhi: Permanent Black.

2   References are to the following translations: *Works of Kalidasa*, vol. I and II (2002) edited and translated by C R Devadhar, Delhi: Motilal Banarsidass; *Kautilya's Arthashastra*, (1961) translated by R Shamasastry, Mysore: Wesleyan Mission Press; *Avimaraka, Love's Enchanted World* (1970) translated by J L Masson and D D Kosambi, Delhi: Motilal Banarsidass; *Ashvaghosha's Buddhacarita or Acts of the Buddha* (1992) translated by E H Johnston, Delhi: Motilal Banarsidass. *Glimpses of Sexual Life in Nanda-Maurya India*, the *Caturbhani* (1975) edited and translated by M Ghosh, Calcutta: Manisha Granthalaya; *Dashakumaracarita of Dantin* (1979) translated by M R Kale, Delhi: Motilal Banarsidass; *The Harshacarita of Bana* (1968) translated by E B Cowell and F W Thomas, Delhi: Motilal Banarsidass; *The Jatakamala, Garland of Birth Stories, of Aryashūra* (1971) translated by J S Speyer, Delhi: Motilal Banarsidass; *Bana's Kadambari* (1968) translated by M R Kale, Delhi: Motilal Banarsidass; *India as seen in the Kuttani-Mata of Damodaragupta* (1975) Ajay Mitra Shastri, Delhi: Allied Publishers; *The Mahabharata of Krishna-Dvaipayana Vyasa*, vols I–XII (1981) translated by K M Ganguly, New Delhi: Munshiram Manoharlal; *Bhavabhūti's Malatimadhava* (1967) translated by M R Kale, Delhi: Motilal Banarsidass; *Mricchakatika of Shūdraka* (1962) translated by M R Kale, Delhi: Motilal Banarsidass; *Mudrarakshasa of Vishakhadatta* (1983) translated by M R Kale, Delhi: Motilal Banarsidass; *The Ramayana of Valmiki: An Epic of Ancient India*, vols I-VII, (1984–1996) general editor R P Goldman, Princeton: Princeton University Press; *Saundara Nanda* (1928) edited and translated by E H Johnston, London: Oxford University Press; *Shishupalavadham, Mahakavi Shrimaghapranitam* (1955) translated (into Hindi) by Haragovinda Shastri, Banaras: Chowkhamba

Vidyabhawan; *Vasavadatta: A Sanskrit Romance by Subandhu* (1965) translated by Louis H Gray, New York: Columbia University Press.

3   *Saundara.* I. 43. This could be a reference to the colour of buildings within the city rather than that of towers. *Kadambari*, 102, p. 210.

4   *Mudra.* I, p. 36; VII, pp. 154, 158; *Dasha.* IV, p. 86; *Mricch.* X, p. 348.

5   B D Chattopadhyaya, 'The City in Early India', p. 190.

6   *Mrichh.* II, p. 94; *Malati.* I, p. 10 (of the Sanskrit text); *Kaumudi.* II, p. 36; *Mudra.* I, p. 25 (of the Sanskrit text).

7   Daud Ali (2003) 'Gardens in Early Indian Court Life', *Studies in History,* 19, 2, p. 222.

8   *Mricch.* VIII, p. 257; *Avimaraka* henceforth *Avi.* I. p. 230.

9   *Avi.* III, p. 303; *Raghu.* VI. 67; *B.C.* III. 13; *Pada.*, p. 115.

10   Ash Amin and Nigel Thrift (2002) *Cities: Re-imagining the Urban,* Malden, Massachusetts: Blackwell Publishing, p. 17.

11   *Mricch.* VI, p. 223; VII, p. 245; *Ubhayabhisarika* henceforth *Ubhay.* p. 5.

12   *Jatakamala* henceforth *Jataka.* XVII, p. 145; *B.C.* III. 4; X. 4–7.

13   *Megh.* I. 37; *Caru.*VI. p. 26; *Mricch.* I, pp. 39, 65; *Dasha.* II, p. 54; *Avi.* III, p. 297, 300.

14   Daud Ali, 'Gardens', p. 238.

15   *Malati.* VII, p. 70; *Pada.*, p. 136; *Mricch.* I, p. 39; VI, p. 221.

16   *A.S.* III. VIII, p. 189; *Padmaprabhritaka* henceforth *Padma.* p. 90; *Malati.* VII, p. 70; *Dhurta.* p. 39; *Malati.* I. p. 6; *A.S.* III. VIII, p.189; *Shishu.* XIII. 36.

17   Daud Ali, 'Gardens', p. 223.

18   *Mricch.* III, p. 109, 117; *Dasha.* VI, p. 112; *Mudra.* I, p. 31.

19 Shonaleeka Kaul, *Imagining the Urban*, Chapter 4.

20 *Padma.*, p. 72; *Pada.*, p. 117.

21 *Pada.* pp. 110, 115, 139; *Malati.* II, p. 24; VII. p. 69; *H.C.* V. 137; *Charu.* III, p. 32; *Jataka.* XII, p. 118; *Kad.*. 28, p. 11.

22 For much more on the complex characterisation of the city as a multiverse, see Shonaleeka Kaul, *Imagining the Urban.*

Kama Culture: A Social History of Erotics in Early India

14

Most studies on erotic representations from early India focus either on their ritual-cultic role or on their putative courtly settings, thereby only inadequately deferring to the wider social milieu in which such representations were produced and to which they might relate. This essay argues that there is evidently a strong connection between erotic representation and urbanism in cultural material from early India. As a significant illustration, it looks at a body of classical Sanskrit literature called *kavya*—aesthetic poetry, drama and tale—and allied texts such as the *Kamasutra*, which concertedly display this connection. It samples an array of the eroticised characters and patterns of behaviour these texts locate in and identify with the city, in the process characterising the city as a centre of *kama* culture—a culture of desire and eros. This essay then proposes various explanations for why the city is so represented, including the role of aesthetic conventions and civilisational discourse on the one hand, and of socio-sexual attitudes, moral conflicts and behavioural unorthodoxy peculiar to the early Indian city, on the other.[1]

There are a number of art reliefs from the post-Mauryan period onwards that depict what can be described as amorous, erotic or even, to some, obscene activity, a sexual content so obvious that, ironically, we believe it requires some sort of explanation. A clear and detailed idea of the archaeological context of these finds—i.e. where exactly in the settlement structure/spread they were found and in conjunction with what else—would go some way in suggesting what function they likely served in early Indian society or how they are to be understood as located in the culture of that time. As with other aspects of early historic archaeology in India, however, such a horizontal understanding of sites remains by an large a desideratum. What can be observed with certainty, though, is that most of these images have been recovered from the sites of flourishing cities of the time such as Kaushambi, Chandraketugarh, Tamralipti, Mathura and Nagarajunakonda, a fact that squares well with the sophistication that some of these images display.

Figure 14.1 Loving couple (*Mithuna*), Mathura, Uttar Pradesh, 2nd century CE. Courtesy: Metropolitan Museum of Art Cultural Commons.

Figure 14.2 Amorous couple, Nagarajunakonda, Andhra Pradesh, 2nd century CE. Courtesy: Metropolitan Museum of Art Cultural Commons.

Figure 14.3 Loving couple, Odisha, 13th century CE. Courtesy: Metropolitan Museum of Art Cultural Commons.

Figure 14.4 Amorous couple, provenance unknown, 13th century CE. Courtesy: Metropolitan Museum of Art Cultural Commons.

This correspondence between erotic representation and urbanism is not, I believe, incidental. Nor is it confined to the field of visual arts. This essay offers a glimpse of other cultural material produced in early India that is striking, among other reasons, for exhibiting precisely the same connection between erotics and the city. I refer to narrative or creative literature in Sanskrit known as *kavya*, highly aesthetic poetry, drama and prose, the composition of which was governed by elaborate codes and conventions. Looking at *kavya*s might provide us with insights into urban socio-sexual thought and behaviour in early India and its relationship with cultural portrayal.

After all, these texts, composed throughout the first millennium CE and after, locate themselves in the quintessential cities of early India such as Pataliputra and Ujjayini, with which they self-consciously engage and provide critical commentaries, and thereby resonate with an urban referentiality. The fact that the Sanskrit plays (*nataka*) were often performed at street crossings and temple courtyards and other such very public and congregational sites within cities means that their rendition of the city and their take on it would have stood the test of contemporary reception by an equally urban audience.

Then again, as A K Ramanujan famously put it, once the specific density and refractive index of the literary medium are understood, the special research potential of literature lies in its vision, its intuitive grasp of structures and the realm of symbolic values the writers express, which provides a repertoire of perceptions otherwise not available to the social scientist.[2] How texts conceptually organised space was never free from an understanding of society itself. This essay in fact demonstrates one way in which we may interpret this integral relationship between urban space and society via the rubric of erotics.

The findings presented here are based on a reading of over two dozen classical *kavya*s authored during the first millennium CE by Kalidasa, Bhasa, Shudraka, Dandin, Magha, Bana, Bhavabhuti and Damodaragupta among others. The citations are from celebrated works such as *Mrichchhakatika*, *Malatimadhava*, *Avimaraka*, *Dashakumaracharita*, *Meghaduta* and *Kuttanimata*, and also, seminally, from a set of four less known but no less remarkable monologue plays, the *Chaturbhani*, that is the *Ubhayabhisarika*, *Padmaprabhritaka*, *Dhurtavitasamvada* and *Padataditaka*. These represent sparkling erotic comedy in Sanskrit, a language usually identified with scripture and theology. Along with these texts, I cannot but draw on a text that is not a *kavya*, the *Kamasutra*, because it embodies a defining discourse on early Indian erotics, and because it closely informs *kavya* depictions and is really an allied text (*samana tantra*).[3]

Kama Culture

Common to this body of textual evidence is also the fact that in their themes, locales and vantages, these texts all centre around great cities of the Second Urbanisation (the prolific rise of urban centres in north and central India between circa fifth century BCE and fifth century CE), and were mostly composed in the second half of that period too or later. These works thus may be seen as constituting a pre-eminently urban literature. Therefore, it is worthwhile to keep in mind that their representations may come close to being the self-perception or self-projection of an urban culture, albeit from a by and large elite perspective. (There is controversy over whether early historic urbanism in India declined by the middle of the first millennium CE. However, it has been argued that *kavya* does not show any perceptible break in the urban tradition relating to the transition to the early medieval.)[4]

In the event, it is significant that *kavya*'s overarching characterisation of the city, indeed its idiom for the city, is what I call *kama* culture or culture of desire, an ethos centred on the ethic of pleasure and eros. This extends not only to the embracing of a full-blooded materialistic hedonism attested in the literature, but pointedly and prominently to the pursuit and cultivation of erotic activity. Indeed, representations of the city are awash with the theme of love and sensual pleasure, directly stated or implied and insinuated.

It is instructive to clarify and emphasise at this point that this concern for the sensual is a concern for the erotic rather than for the procreative or the socially sanctioned, marital form of sex, which would be the purview of traditional socio-legal texts such as the *Dharmashastras*. It therefore departs quietly but significantly from the socio-sexual norm. Thus, men and women, but especially men, are typically shown with paramours. This is best seen in the character-type of the *nagaraka* who is the protagonist of the *Kamasutra* and the effective hero or *nayaka* of the *kavyas*.

The *nagaraka* (from the word *nagara* or city) is the man about town who is trained to be a connoisseur at good life in general and good sex in particular. Though a *grihastha*, a householder, as the *Kamasutra* (I. 4.1) clearly indicates, he practises his refined cultural and sexual skills with public women, i.e. the courtesans (*ganikas*) in the main, as in the *Mricchakatika* and the *Kuttanimata*.[5] Or he may go to work on a beloved, the *abhisarika*, who slips out after dark for a surreptitious rendezvous with her lover, as in the *Meghaduta* (I.37, II.9) or *Avimaraka* (III. p. 302). Occasionally, the more daring *nagaraka* is also to be seen with other men's wives, including queens, as in the *Dashakumaracharita* (III. p. 76).

The feminine counterpart to the *nagaraka* appears to be the *ganika* or courtesan. A complex character type, as culturally cultivated as the *nagaraka*, she is even more obviously engaged in erotics than he is, and is shown to be publicly celebrated and coveted in the city for the combined package of pleasure and culture she offers. Both she and the *nagaraka* are identified with the city through epithets such as *nagarasyavibhushanam* (ornament of the city).[6] The *ganika* is the heroine of the *Mricchakatika* as well as of a major story from the *Dashakumaracharita*. The red light district (*veshamarga*) is the object of avid descriptions in these texts.[7]

Yet another urban character in the texts that brings out fairly self- reflexively the erotic tone lent to the city is the *vita*, the libertine or voluptuary. The monologist of the *Chaturbhani*, the *vita* is a master eroticist who admonishes both the *nagaraka* and the *ganika*—and lovers at large— on *kamatantra* and is seen making a full-time living out of bringing lovers together and arbitrating love disputes. The *vita* is an uncompromising votary of the open pursuit of sexual pleasure in the city in the texts.

In addition to these eroticised specific models of masculine and feminine behaviour, a series of other motifs recurrently played in *kavya*s reiterates the representation of urban space as the centre of a sensuous culture of desire. Interestingly, some of these seem to be the very motifs in early Indic erotic sculptures.

Thus the city seems always full of beautiful women and men who look like *Kama*, the love god.[8] Women are always in love dalliance or busy preparing for it by enhancing their beauty through *shringara* (make-up and finery), and the men flock to the courtesans' quarter or flirt with maids on the highway or in pleasure haunts.[9] Drinking and gambling, music and dance are among the favourite depicted occupations.[10] The home of all the arts (*sakalakalah dadhanah*),[11] the city is always in festival (*satato utsavam*).[12] Love itself is celebrated as an *utsava*,[13] while the worship of *Kamadeva* is one of the popular festive occasions.[14] Pleasure groves are cherished urban assets frequented in droves.[15] The city is likened to Bhogavati, the capital of the *asura*s, the very name of which means a place possessed of all manner of enjoyments; it is also likened to Amaravati, the heavenly city, for the pleasures it affords[16]— pleasures that could seduce even the ascetic.

Indeed, remarkably, some monks in the city may be seen in the texts frequenting sex workers, while nuns may indulge in love themselves when they are not running love errands for others as messengers or *dutis*.[17] Described as served fearlessly by *Kamadeva* (*madanena vitabhayamityadhishthita*),[18] 'where the tremulous delights of amorous union' abound (*kaminidhuvanalila, vividhavilasacitrasurata*),[19] the city is the pre-eminent, if not the only, place to obtain the fruits of desire (*phalamavikalam kamukatvasya*).[20]

Now, to what do we attribute this singular emphasis on erotics in textual depictions of the city? To begin with, we must concede that the felt need to ask this question bespeaks a certain presumption that erotics as the subject of open representation is an oddity, a transgression perhaps of an unspoken rule of moral propriety. In taking that position, are we projecting onto the past more recent norms and expectations? Or does this presumed clash with social norms in fact trace its lineage back to early times? I return to this question below. For the moment, explanations at different levels are possible. We can invoke literary convention, behavioural discourse as well as the sociology of early Indian urban spaces.

Kama and Rasa

For instance, it is possible to argue that *kavya*s favour the erotic theme out of a predisposition to the *rasa* theory. *Rasa* means 'flavour' or 'taste', and refers to the abstracted and universalised essence of emotions or *bhava* that Sanskrit rhetorical treatises from the *Natyashastra* (2nd century CE) onwards lay down as one of the defining features and ends of *kavya* composition. The erotic flavour corresponds to the *shringara rasa*, which is perhaps the most popular of nine *rasa*s, and it is reasonable to suppose that the conventional election of this *rasa* is what is responsible for the amatory focus of the urban plots and representations in our texts. In other words, erotic representations, wherever they occur, may be only a matter of literary convention.

I have argued elsewhere, however, that literary convention or rhetoric is not an 'only'.[21] It should not be dismissed as a mechanical technique or a barren construct, but be seen as codifying a meaningful, if somewhat schematic, set of representational choices. The *rasa* theory, for instance, stands for a repertoire of universal emotions (anger, love, fear, pity, comedy, horror, calm, courage and wonder)— emotions that in turn presuppose, stem from and provoke corresponding kinds of human behaviour. The question therefore would still be: Why do *kavya*s privilege *shringara rasa* or the erotic flavour over eight other types of sentiment and conduct when depicting the city? And in doing so, are they doing something self-consciously unprecedented or radical?

Kama and Trivarga

It is possible that in the process of emphasising the *shringara rasa*, what the kavyas are doing is displaying a referential involvement with certain discursive ideological systems such as the *trivarga*, the traditional aims of life—*dharma* (piety/society), *artha* (profit/power), and *kama* (pleasure/sex). (The fourth goal, *moksha* or liberation, does not relate to the social world as such, but to transcending it.) Tellingly, the *Kamasutra* starts by a salutation to *dharma, artha* and *kama* (I.1.1).

Please note that these ideas as referents are traditional and traditionally sanctioned, and established in the Epics or *itihasa* and the law books or s*mriti* literature as a framework that embraces all the fundamental life possibilities. They may be said to perform an integrative function, bringing together and reconciling what Greg Bailey has termed normative and pragmatic values and modes of behaviour.[22] It is worth considering that *kavya*s may be performing *kama*, i.e. desire or pleasure, as a specific cultural position, locating themselves in this discourse and thereby opening up for analysis the disjunctions between formally prescribed and actual behaviour. That they would do so testifies to their role as social narratives or commentaries.

Kama and Urban Society

If I am right that the *kavya*s assume this role, what occasions their doing so? In other words, was there anything about the city that may have prompted this exploration of the connection between social norm and practice, specifically with regard to sexual behaviour? In answer to this question, I would begin by noting that in this regard, not one but several sustained views emerge from the texts. One of these is that the *Kamasutra* and *kavyas* both display an exclusively urban contextualising of erotics. The *Kamasutra* (I.4.2) ordains that to live the highly sensual and refined life of a *nagaraka*, one ought to live in one kind of urban centre or another (*nagarepattanekharvate va*). As noted before, the word *nagaraka* is itself derived from the word for 'city'.

Moreover, the *Kamasutra* (V.1.52, 54) shows a fairly low opinion of sexual activity in the countryside when it maintains that the wife of a villager, like the wife of a man who is jealous, putrid, impotent, unmanly or deformed, among others, 'can be easily had [by the *nagaraka*] without any effort'. This implies sexual ignorance or abstinence, or both, on the part of the male villager. The same is hinted at in the *Kuttanimata* for both men and women of the countryside,[23] while the *Dhurtavitasamvada* (p. 46) categorically declares that living in a village puts an end to amorous passion (*gramevasa madanantakarina*). Witness also the terms in which the *Meghaduta* (I. 16, 27, 29, 47 and 49) describes the difference between urban and bucolic women. Thus the cloud messenger is told:

...peasant women (*janapadavadhu*), unversed in eyebrow play (*bhruvilasanabhijña*), drink you in with eyes moist with happiness, knowing that the harvest depends on you.

This is in direct contrast with the tremulous eyes of the city (Ujjayini's) women (*paurangana*) that dart at the play of lightning. And the eager eyes of Dashapura's women accomplished in the graceful play of curving eyebrows.

For Kalidasa, these city women are those who 'proceed to their lovers along the king's highway at night when it is too dark to see' and at daybreak lie with 'tired limbs after passion's ecstatic play' (*Megh.* I.31, 33, 37). The projected perception is that city women possessed the art and artifice of love dalliance, of which peasant women were innocent, and that the concerns and pursuits of the latter did not revolve around amour but those of the former did.

The Ambivalence of Urban Space

Having established the realm of the erotic as an urban preserve, the *kavya*s then seem to address the nature of that preserve. This is the second impression that emanates from the texts. For all the sensuality of characters and activities in the city, is the city really conceived as a site of unexpurgated and unencumbered gratification? In fact not. Both the *Kamasutra* and *kavya*s appear to be seized of a subterranean tension, a consciousness of a countervailing ideology that, far from idealising or celebrating the free and full pursuit of erotics, as they themselves seem to do, disapproves, censures and opposes it. This is no doubt the voice of traditional social morality, which can conveniently if loosely be designated as the dharmashastric perspective as opposed to, say, a kamashastric one.

I have suggested elsewhere that this viewpoint represents an ideology of anti-pleasure, an approach to sexuality that firmly subordinates libidinal concerns to social ones and assimilates permissiveness to social vice.[24] Further, at the level of discourse, it is this view that seems to have been the dominant view in the historical social reality of early India, a fact suggested by, among other things, our texts themselves and the anxiety with which they seem to defer to this view after all. You hear its voice in all kinds of ways.

Thus rhetorical descriptions of the city of Kusumapura in the *Vasavadatta* use the technique of *shlesha* or paronomasia/

pun to say: 'It is pure even through its drinking haunts because of its temples...', 'there are outpourings of manly vigour in tremulous delightsomeness, but there is no desertion of justice among citizens', 'there is redness of the lower lip among young girls, but there is no base inclination among subjects' (*Vasav,*121, 128, 129, pp. 79–82).

Similarly the *Kadambari* says of the residents of Ujjayini: 'Though handsome, (the men are) content with their wives; ... though they seek love and wealth, they are strictly just'; 'though free intercourse with women is allowed, it is of irreproachable conduct; ... though it is hung with strings of pearls, it is most adorned by its temples; ... though it glows with colour, it is white as nectar.' The text also tells us that 'its [the city's] sin is washed away by the perpetual recitation of sacred books' and 'it is purified with the smoke of a hundred sacrifices' (*Kad.* 103, 105, 108, p. 211–13).

Of course it is possible to see these examples as standard literary word play or idealisation, but I do believe a deeper meaning, a deeper conflict is readily discernible in such wordplay. Through such devices, *kavya*s are engaging with the larger issue of urban social behaviour, acceptable and otherwise.

Moreover, concrete instances are available of the curtailing voice of social morality resounding even in the eroticised world of *kavya* characters, sometimes despite themselves. Thus, even the figure of the *abhisarika*, said to be the woman who has discarded modesty (*hitva lajjam*) and, intoxicated by lust, sets off for a tryst with her lover, is always shown doing so surreptitiously, after dark. Thus also, young women such as Malati and Kurangi, in love outside of wedlock in the *Malatimadhava* (II. p. 20) and the *Avimaraka* (II. p. 269) respectively, are shown to feel fear (*bhaya*) and shame (*lajja*) and to give a thought to modesty and family pride (*kulamana*) when they pine for their lovers.

And men such as Carudatta and Samarabhatta, attached extra-maritally or otherwise to public women or other paramours in the *Mricchakatika* and *Kuttanimata*, or Pururavas in the *Vikramorvashiya*, are told by their friends and relatives of the undesirability of their liaisons, especially when they have chaste and good wives at home.[25] Such men themselves are shown displaying deep public embarrassment at courting public women and are hard-pressed to conceal the fact from society at large (*Mricch.* IX. 329). The *Dhurtavitasamvada* (p. 58) spells it out: "A person attached to a sex worker is not respected by people (*lokasya veshyam prati sakto manushyah pujyo na bhavati*)." Thus also we meet a figure such as Pavitraka in the *Padmaprabhritaka* (pp. 80–81), who has a secret affair with a sex worker but, being the son of a dispenser of justice (*dharmasanikaputra*), pretends in public to be a man of uncompromising purity. The narrator's reference in this context to the 'armour of hypocrisy' (*mithyacarakañcukam*) tells its own tale.

At the very least then, *kavya* representation of sexual behaviour in the city is not that of unalleviated indulgence; glimpses of the ambivalence of urban sociology, of the normative counter-thrust, so to speak, to the erotic ideal of the texts, are also to be spied. From this, it is reasonable to infer that the urban space was a behaviourally contested one. And personifying the tension or ambivalence is the figure of the *ganika* who is depicted as standing at the centre of a series of social paradoxes enacted in the city: She is regarded as mercenary and deceptive, yet desirable and sought after.

She is coveted, but the act of coveting her is publicly a matter of shame. She is culturally accomplished and celebrated, but socially degraded. Her accessibility, facility and independence characterise and highlight the city's ethic of unfettered pleasure, but also expose the city's dominant, normative structures that demand her social degradation, as being those of anti-pleasure. The *ganika*, in fact, also described as *prakashanari* (the exposed woman) and *svadhinayauvana* (mistress of her youth), due to the ambiguity of her location (public) and functions (pleasure and desire), straddles the divide between the public and the private sphere in the city.

Does this apparently mitigating consciousness of socio-moral constraints in the city detract from my observation about *kama* culture being the dominant textual ideal? On the contrary, it may help clarify our understanding of the nature of *kama* that the authors of our texts sought to attribute to the city, and possibly also guide us towards the imperative behind cultural representations of the erotic.

Kama Culture as Civilising Discourse

For this, I turn to the *Kamasutra* that appears equally seized of the portentous clash between the tenets of *kama* and *dharma*, the latter the basis of social order which is imperative even for the proper cultivation of *kama* (I.2.25). Being a *shastra*, and a pragmatic one at that, it comes out early in support of *dharma*, clearly recommending the subordination of *kama* (as well as *artha*) to *dharma* (also of *kama* to *artha*) whenever these are in conflict (I.2.14).[26]

And yet, the *Kamasutra* is nothing if not a freewheeling enunciation and celebration of *kama*. What is the *Kamasutra*'s *via media* then? It lies in a two-fold transformation of the concept of *kama*: It liberates *kama*, "rescuing erotic pleasure from the confining morality of reproduction," as Wendy Doniger and Sudhir Kakar put it.[27] Having liberated it, it sublimates *kama*, and not only by pronouncing on it as a *shastra* and integrating it into a schema of normative behavior, the *trivarga* (I. 1.2). More so, it sublimates *kama* by rendering it as a ritual, method or form of art, cultivated and controlled and extolled. Indeed, the seven chapters of the *Kamasutra* are precisely an explication of love-making as an art and craft.

Accordingly the *Kamasutra* (I.2.11) defines pleasure as consisting in 'engaging the ear, skin, eye, tongue and nose, each in its own appropriate sensation, all under the control of the mind and heart driven by the conscious self (*shrotratvakcakshurjihvaghranam atmasamyuktena manasa dhishthitanam sveshu sveshu vishayeshvanukūlyatah pravrittih kamah*)'. I submit that it is in this sense that the city is projected as *kama*-centric in the *kavya*s. Refined pleasure, pursued as art and not pure instinct, with the zeal and approach of a connoisseur, defines the city as a civilisational centre where urges of 'nature' can be mastered and exalted to 'culture'. This gives the term *kama* culture a double significance.

Indeed, it is in this light that the high cultural accomplishment of the *nagaraka* and the *ganika*, which is a major part of the characterisation of these figures in the texts, assumes importance. Such cultural accomplishment consisted in literary work, reading aloud, improvising poetry, knowledge of metres, staging plays, singing, dancing, playing instruments, painting and decoration, preparing wines, gambling, make-up and etiquette (*KS* I.3.15). These were among the sixty-four arts 'that should be studied along with the *Kamasutra*' by men and women alike.

It is clear, moreover, that these arts were to be put into practice by *nagaraka*s and *ganika*s when they were engaging with each other as social and sexual partners. Thus, of the *ganika* it was said (KS I.3.17–18) that she who 'distinguishes herself in these arts and has a good nature, beauty and good qualities' would be sought by men and approached for sex. For his part, the *nagaraka* could be expected to make 'gentle conversation', 'exchange thoughts about works of art,' and show 'courtesies that charm the mind and heart' with women during love dalliance (*KS* I.4. 12, 20). Personifying this ideal are Charudatta and Vasantasena, the toast of the city of Ujjayini, in the *Mricchakatika*.

The pursuit of culture in common by these men and women seems to create in the texts a uniquely urban zone, best represented by the *goshthi* or cultural conclave, where they could freely access each other socially and sexually, something traditionally denied by social norms—a niche public-private sphere of heterosexual interaction where the cultivation of culture seemed to provide the stage (and perhaps veneer?) for pleasure to play itself out.

❧ ❧

Sanskrit *kavya* thus presents a complex commentary on early Indian urban sociology. The combination of pleasure and culture, of the erotic and the aesthetic, whether in literature or art, emerges as symptomatic of urbanism. It provided perhaps a sexually active but traditional society a forum for self-expression, a tacit site for a parallel, alternative discourse where the erotic could be free of the often repressive concerns of social morality, yet without resorting to rebellion, licentiousness or anarchy. That the city occasioned such a discourse was because it developed as the centre par excellence of cultural pursuit and patronage—the home of all the arts, as *kavya* put it.

However, relatedly, as I have elaborated elsewhere, this was also because the city saw the ascendance of essentially amoral structures of power such as commercial wealth and the monarchical state. Equally, the early Indian city, as the nodal point of multi-faceted and long-distance convergence of men, goods and ideas (as we glimpsed in Chapter 13), came to house such intense social heterogeneity as would render attenuated the hold of any homogenising behavioural norm. As I have discussed in my book *Imagining the Urban*, it is again Sanskrit *kavya*s, unplumbed social representations, that give us glimpses of the city's demographic and ideological heterogeneity and unorthodoxy. These in turn perhaps yielded in *kavya* an understanding of the city as a multiverse, where spheres of abundance and deprivation, hedonism and prudery, culture and crudeness, patriarchal conformity and subversion, coercion and resistance, tradition and transgression all coexisted and overlapped.[28] Cultural representations of erotics can perhaps best be understood as located in such a multiverse.

Notes

1   This essay first appeared with the title 'Kama Culture: Erotics and the Sociology of Urban Space in Early India' in *Kalakalpa: IGNCA Journal of Arts* (2022), VII, 1, pp. 23–42. Reused here with permission.

2   A K Ramanujan (1993) 'Towards an Anthology of City Images', in Vinay Dharwadker edited *The Collected Essays of A K Ramanujan*, New Delhi: Oxford University Press.

3   It has been suggested that the *Kamasutra* looks like a work of dramatic fiction, a play in seven acts. "The man and the woman whose … lives are described here are called the *nayaka* and the *nayika* (male and female protagonists), and the men who assist the *nayaka* are called the *pithamarda*, *vita* and *vidushaka* (the libertine, pander and clown). All of these are terms for stock characters in Sanskrit dramas … according to yet another textbook, the one attributed to Bharata and dealing with dramatic writing, acting, and dancing, the *Natyashastra*." Wendy Doniger and Sudhir Kakar translated (2002) *Vatsyayana Mallanaga Kamasutra*, Delhi: Oxford University Press, p. xxv. Also, Sheldon Pollock is of the opinion that the *Kamasutra* may have been but a sourcebook for poets composing erotic works, again suggesting the closeness of the text and the *kavya* genre. Cited by Doniger, p. xxviii).

4   For a discussion of the debate and why literature does not support the idea of urban decline, see Shonaleeka Kaul (2018) 'Texts and Transitions: Early Indian Literature and the Problem of Historical Change' in Bhairabi Sahu and Kesavan Veluthat edited *History and Theory*, Delhi: ICHR and Orient BlackSwan.

5   The following translations have been used in this essay: Manmohan Ghosh edited and translated (1975) *Glimpses of Sexual Life in Nanda-Maurya India*, the *Chaturbhani*, Calcutta: Manisha Granthalaya; M R Kale translated (1962) *Mricchakatika of Shudraka*, Delhi: Motilal Banarsidass; Chandra Rajan (1989) *Kalidasa, The Loom of Time, A Selection of his Plays and Poems*, New Delhi: Penguin

Books; Ajay Mitra Shastri (1975) *India as seen in the Kuttani-Mata of Damodaragupta*, Delhi: Allied Publishers.

6   Multi-text references are kept in the fend notes so as to not disrupt the flow of the text. *Mricch.* I. p. 49, II. p. 89; VIII. p. 277; p. 295; X. p. 359; *Dasha.* II. p. 46.

7   *Kuttani.* 743–754, p. 243; *Pada.* p. 121, 153.

8   *H.C.* III.107; *Vasav.* 114–5, p. 76–77; *Shishu.* III.42, 58, XIII.29; *Raghu.* VII.5; *Megh.* I.27, 47; *Kuttani.* 5–8, p. 243; *Kad.* 103, p. 210, 110, p. 214.

9   *Avi.* II. p. 279, III. p. 301–302; the *Caturbhani* are replete with such references.

10 *Ubhaya.* p. 3,13,19; *Caru.* III. p. 25; *Pada.* p. 148; *Malati.* I. p. 4, 7; *Kuttani.* 68, p. 207, 82, p. 220, .795,1013, p. 159; *Dasha.* II. p. 53–54; *Mricch.* II. p. 73; *Dhurta.* p. 31–32; *Abhijñan.* VI. p. 167.

11 *Shishu.* III. p. 60; *Dhurta.* p. 30.

12 *Shishu.* XIII.67; *Mudra.* III. p. 37.

13 *Ubhaya.* p. 8.

14 *Kuttani.* 886–904, p. 159–60; *Malati.* I. p. 7.

15 *Megh.* I.25, II. 8; *Kuttani.* 17, p. 75, 91; *Saundara.* I.49, III.17; *B.C.*III.2; *Jataka.* XXI.45, p. 175; *Mriccha.* IX. p. 341; *Vasav.* 119. p.78; *Dasha.* Purva. II. p. 19; *Dasha.* VI.104, 106; *RItu.* VI.23; *Padma.* p. 97.

16 *Kuttani.*17, p. 75, .180, p. 83; *Megh.* I.30, etc.

17 *Ubhaya.* p. 9; *Padma.* p. 84, 85; *Pada.* p. 133–134; *Dasha.* II. p. 60; I. p. 119; *Malati.* I. p. 7; *Kaumudi.* II. p. 55 ; *Kuttani.* 562, p. 97; *KS* I.3.14; I.4.35.

18 *Shisu.* III.61, XIII.38; *Kad.* 102, p. 211; *Vasav.* 111–112, p. 75.

19 *Vasav.* 46, p. 56; .128, p. 82.

20 *Megh.* I.24.

21 Shonaleeka Kaul (2010) *Imagining the Urban: Sanskrit and the City in Early India*, Delhi: Permanent Black.

22 Greg M Bailey (1994) *Bhartrihari's Critique of Culture*, La Trobe Asian Studies Papers, Research Series 2, p. 30.

23 Some villagers are shown attracted by the glittering city life but ignorant of how to go about partaking of it—*Kuttani*. 397–399, p. 123. The village woman is compared unfavourably with the *nagarika*, the courtesan of the city—*Kuttani*. 863, 111.

24 Shonaleeka Kaul (2009) 'Pleasure and Culture: Reading Urban Behaviour through *Kavya* Archetypes' in N Lahiri and U Singh edited *Ancient India: New Research*, Oxford University Press, New Delhi, 252–279. Ortner and Whitehead speak of kinship-based societies in particular displaying 'the power of social considerations to override libidinal ones'. They are cited in Pat Caplan edited (1987) *The Cultural Construction of Sexuality*, London and New York: Tavistock Publications. p. 17.

25 *Mricch.* X. p. 403; III. p. 129; *Kuttani*. 301–324, p.111; *Vikram.* II. p. 29, 31, 35; p. 61.

26 The only exception made was for the king and the courtesan, for whom *artha* was rated higher than the other two—*KS* I.1.15.

27 Wendy Doniger and Sudhir Kakar, *Kamasutra*, Delhi: Oxford University Press, pp. xl–xli. Shonaleeka Kaul, *Imagining the Urban*, p. 256.

Recovering 'Other' Voices: Animal History in the Hitopadesha

15

This essay is an abbreviated exploration of the representation of animals in a seminal, dedicated textual tradition from early India in Sanskrit, best identified with the influential 2nd century CE *Panchatantra* and its later retelling, the 9th century CE *Hitopadesha*. It will focus on the latter, less known work. The *Hitopadesha* is an epigrammatic text in mixed prose and verse peopled by a large number of birds and animals. It was composed in the 9th or 10th century CE, perhaps in eastern India, by one Pandit Narayana, and was sponsored and promoted by a yet-to-be-identified ruler called Dhavalachandra, who the poet acknowledges briefly at the end of the composition. Beyond this, as is common for much of Sanskrit literature, we do not know anything about the author and his context.

We do know, however, that the *Hitopadesha* belonged to a major genre of ancient Indian thought known as *niti,* which was the knowledge and art of prudent conduct. This essay delves into this tradition to illuminate the mutually constituted fields of animal history and Sanskrit literature and how the latter could not just recover experiences of non-human animals, but even accord them an instrumentality in the political and ethical culture of early India.

Figure 15.1
Manuscript of the
Hitopadesha circa
18th century from
Nepal. Courtesy:
Wikimedia
Commons.

Literally meaning 'good advice', the frame story of the *Hitopadesha* is a king's need to educate his lazy and worthless princes in statesmanship, warfare, and worldly wisdom more generally. Here is where you begin to glimpse the consciously appointed role of animal stories in elaborating political and strategic instruction. A pandit, Vishnusharma, brings home to the uninitiated princes the subtle teachings of prudent politics (*niti*). '*Niti*' is usually translated as 'principles of polity and/or morality'.[1] But I argue that *niti*, as represented in a collection of stories such as the *Hitopadesha*, went well beyond the political and the moral to embrace the simply practical. Prescribing canny and pragmatic responses to a range of situations, ambitions, problems and dilemmas, *niti* is really the knowledge and art of prudent conduct. And the *Hitopadesha* disseminates this didactic knowledge or instruction in the form of illustrative stories and maxims involving the lives of humans and, more prominently, birds and animals.

This happens over four books or sections titled *Mitralabha* (Winning Friends), featuring a tortoise, a crow, a deer and a mouse, *Suhrdbheda* (Losing Friends), which revolves around a bull, a lion and a couple of jackals, *Vigraha* (Waging War) and then *Sandhi* (Brokering Peace), the last two books set amidst the avian world of swans, ducks, peacocks and so on.

The reference to political and strategic thought in the book/ section titles is easy to see—making allies, sowing dissension, fighting battles and suing for peace. And that is indeed the overt project of the *Hitopadesha*—to teach politics. But then, is the presence of animals in this work merely by way of allegory, where animal life is but a metaphor for human life and concerns? This is typically what fables are supposed to be and scholars of the *Panchatantra-Hitopadesha* tradition have supposed it to be.

However, I argue that the *Hitopadesha* tales are also materially, and not only metaphorically, human-animal stories, yielding a sense of animals as animals and their experiential realities. In the process, they also challenge the conventional view of Sanskrit literature as privileging only particular forms and ways of life—the human, the courtly, the urban and so on—while marginalising others—the non-human, the rustic and pastoral, and the untamed. The *Panchatantra-Hitopadesha* tradition, in recovering the latter, invites us to renegotiate our understanding of the scope of Sanskrit itself.

⁂

A large number of non-humans figure in these lively stories, but significantly, so do humans such as kings and their ministers, husbands and their wives, wives and their lovers(!), masters and servants, ascetics and householders and so on. The *Hitopadesha* thus represents a multi-species genre, not a purely phantasmagorical world of marvellous talking birds and animals, but a real world of real humans and animals, where the attribution of speech to the animals—anthropomorphism, if you like—does not take away from their reality, but is a heuristic conduit for it. That literature put words in the animals' mouths does not mean that such words cannot be true to animals themselves. As Susan McHugh puts it, "the animal story is a human story but it is also an animal story".[2]

Further, the numerous sub-stories that constitute the *Hitopadesha* install birds and animals as not just characters but narrators, even of human stories, inaugurating a striking literary agency of the animal. Moreover, where the non-human narrators break their story to bring in human tales, the pattern of the fable is effectively reversed, for here humans are introduced to exemplify the lesson that animals are trying to impress on each other and not the other way around.

The joint human-animal narrative space, I believe, stirs up the conventional *modus operandi* of a didactic work by creating, together with the use of humour and satire, an overt lightness and childlike quality of literary treatment that enables the project of the gnomic text: namely, to show us how to live with ideals in a less than ideal world.

⚜

Indeed, though didactic and instructional, the *Hitopadesha* is highly realist literature depicting contradictions, complexities and ironies of the lived world, whether human or animal, and not idealised stereotypes or caricatures where animals stand in for humans. The didacticism of the *Hitopadesha* is, paradoxically, an irreverent and unorthodox project to which animals are central. Hence I have named this the antinomic didactic in my book on the Hitopadesha.[3]

It is not therefore a "moralising subjection" or "domestication" of non-human species for the purpose of asserting human values and hierarchies, which is what Jacques Derrida feared fables are all about.[iv] Far from being conservative and reproducing social hierarchies, the *Hitopadesha* could be antinomian and transgressive. It destabilised and problematised figures of power and human ideals and behaviour rather than sought to reinstate them. This is a big difference from how fable is usually defined as moral tales. The *Hitopadesha,* for all its didacticism, and in so far as it related to humans at all, is not some sanctimonious moral fable, but a complex and wry take on social reality.

Thus, even in a story commissioned by royalty, the king, whether human or animal, is routinely shown as unwise, haughty, dependent or gullible. In fact, the last two books of the *Hitopadesha* are entirely about a couple of impetuous kings and their armies, albeit of the feathered variety—a peacock called Chitravarna and a swan called Hiranyagarbha—and the easily provoked, needless war between them. It is only through the wise counsel and strategies of their respective ministers—also birds: a duck and a vulture—that peace is ultimately secured. The satire on kings as risky liabilities is a constant in these tales.

The figure of the brahmana, who stands at the head of the socio-ritual caste hierarchy and represents learning and scriptures, is also satirised in the parodical story of the old tiger who pretends to be pious and righteous only to ensnare unsuspecting passersby as prey (1.2). Notably, the author of the *Hitopadesha*, Narayana, and the narrator, Vishnusharma, were both *pandits* or learned brahmanas, thereby displaying Sanskrit's sagacious capacity for self-satire in the tiger story, something that the literary culture is hardly given credit for by modern scholars. This story concludes with the observation:

How does reading the sacred books
Emancipate a villain?!
Nature and temperament alone are supreme
In shaping a person (*svabhaveva atra atirichyate*) (1.2.17)[5]

And, then, sensationally, women are represented as highly libidinous and resourceful characters who go after what they want despite social censure, such as indulging in extramarital affairs. This may be read as misogyny by some, but may also reflect considerable female agency in early India, something that is visible in other Sanskrit literature as well, including *kavya* and *dharmashastra*.[6] An example is the adultery tale which the crow narrates. A young and sensuous woman is married off to an old and lustful merchant who is unable to satisfy her, driving her to take a young and vigorous lover. The text unabashedly declares:

> Women have twice the appetite of men
> Four times their brains
> Six times their courage
> And eight times their libido! (2.7.119)

> Aged men are hardly virile.
> Their wives are taken with other men
> And regard the husband
> As a necessary evil, just like medicine! (1.6.109–10)

But:

> While living beings lust for life and wealth,
> The aged man desires a young wife more than life itself!
> An old man can neither enjoy sense-pleasures
> Nor renounce them.
> *He is like an old, toothless dog*
> *Who cannot chew the bone*
> *But helplessly licks at it.* (1.6.111–12. Emphasis added.)

Note the invocation of a real animal condition of geriatrism to mock its human variant! The *Hitopadesha* is remarkably candid and unsentimental about social ideals, inclining perhaps towards representing social reality more, which is always complicated. Its purpose is not merely to mock this class or that, for kings, brahmins and women are all also praised elsewhere in the text. Rather, strong social satire confounding ethical subjectivity is here underwritten by an important practical observation about life: to contrast the ideal with the real and the sacred with the profane, since the world where people must act was both real and profane.

⚜

Taking this further, the *Hitopadesha* appears as something of a survival guide for the innocent, the good and the weak—a constituency the text invokes often and which is, crucially, a trans-species constituency. Which is to say that the animal world is as vulnerable as the human, if not more—the ultimate subalterns! And the *Hitopadesha* attempts to educate precisely the vulnerable and the subaltern on how to make it in an unequal world, using nothing but the power of intellect (hence *niti*).

No matter how much more mighty the villainous enemy, the *Hitopadesha*'s ringing call is '*matireva balad gariyasi*' or 'the mind is superior to might' (2.4.86/87), also phrased as '*upayen hi yacchakyam na tacchakyam parakramaih*' or 'strategy can achieve what valour cannot' (1.9.202, 2.7.120). And these central lessons are seen brilliantly demonstrated in the text by *animals*, especially those emblematic of frailty and endangerment viz. the sparrow whose nest is washed away by the sea (2.10), the crow whose eggs are eaten by the snake (2.8), the hare offered up as a meal to the lion, rabbits crushed in elephant stampedes (3.4), aquatic life dying or migrating as ponds dry up (1.8) or as fishermen move in on them (4.2), the mouse stealing grain from a village hut (1.5), the deer caught in a hunter's trap (1.4) and even the tiger unable to hunt from old age (4.11).

I hardly need emphasise that these are very actual situations and threats that animals face, being the quintessential underdogs in the chain of beings that they are. There is nothing anthropomorphic about this representation! And in foregrounding such narrative plots, the *Hitopadesha* effectively

Figure 15.2a Birds ensnared in hunter's net: Story from the *Hitopadesha*.
Courtesy. Wikimedia Commons.

Figure 15.2b Rabbits trampled in an elephant stampede: Story from the *Hitopadesha*. Courtesy: Wikimedia Commons.

decentres human perception and foregrounds the animal's gaze.

Animals are also depicted embodying the host of emotions and mental processes that go along with the struggle for survival, namely, love, care, fear, hunger, suffering, grieving loss of loved ones, cunning, presence of mind, loyalty, pack coordination, empathy, altruism, etc. This, to my mind, exemplifies animal personhood and defies human exceptionalism in favour of a species continuum in the realm of affect.

⁂

In yet other stories, not only the affective but also the ethical is centrally brought into relation with the animal. Consider the famous story of the loyal mongoose who puts his life at stake in a bloody battle to fight off a snake that would have bitten his master's infant (4.3). His heedless master, however, on getting back home, sees all the blood. Suspecting the mongoose had bitten his child, he beats his poor pet to death. Even if it is not the explicit purpose of the story, which is to convey the lesson 'act with thought and not haste', the animal is clearly shown as superior in emotion and ethics to the human here.

Or take the story of the washerman's donkey tied up in the yard, braying in desperation to warn his sleeping master of a thief entering the house, only to have the washerman, peeved at the noisy disruption, bash up the poor beast to death (2.3). Again, it is not the animal who is shown incapable of thought, affect and commonsense, but the human. When you see this assessment together with the depiction of morally flagrant behaviour by men and women earlier, a distinct disturbance of the human effected by the *Hitopadesha* emerges in clear relief. And this is why I say that the characterisation so far of this genre as anthropocentric fables meant to fortify the human needs to be seriously rethought.

The same human-displacing effect applies to the story of the domesticated bull, Sanjeevaka, yoked to an ambitious merchant's cart passing through the forest (2.1). Along the way, Sanjeevaka stumbles and breaks one leg. He is promptly abandoned and left to die there by his human master, underlining the latter's ethical equivocality.

In a further lesson, the beleaguered bull is shown willing himself to survive, healing, and going on to lead a life of strength, freedom and plenty in the forest. This remarkable recovery symbolises a rewilding or return to nature, which is shown as more nurturing and full of possibilities as compared to the human world. There is in this story without doubt an authorial intention to represent the animal as he is himself, his compulsions in the domesticated state, his redemption in

Figure 15.3 The lion kills Sanjeevaka as the jackals look on: Story from the *Hitopadesha*. Persian manuscript. Courtesy: Wikimedia Commons.

nature, but also, when the bull is eventually killed by the lion, the perils of a life in the wilderness. Again we are reminded of how the *Hitopadesha* is not some anthropocentric vision, with no place for the true animal.

꧁ ꧂

Thus we can arrive at thriving animal histories in early India, foregrounding both the individuality of non-human lives and their interdependence and entanglement with the human, be it in material terms or by jointly partaking of complex affective-ethical discourses. Further, far from a homogenising human view, Sanskrit literature as represented by the *Hitopadesha* displays vis-a-vis the animal world a capacity to closely observe and bear witness to the experiences of 'Others', in this case animals, who are seen as both victims and exemplars.

Notes

1   M R Kale edited and translated *Hitopadeśa of Nārāyaṇa*, Delhi: Motilal Banarsidass, jacket description; Patrick Olivelle (2009) *Pañcatantra: The Book of India's Folk Wisdom*, UK: Oxford University Press, p. x.

2   Susan McHugh (2009) 'Animal Farm's Lessons for Literary (and) Animal Studies', *Humanimalia: A Journal of Human/Animal Interface Studies*, 1 (1), p. 29. https://www.depauw.edu/humanimalia/issue01/mchugh.html

3   Shonaleeka Kaul translated (2022) *Hitopadesha by Narayana: A New English Translation*, Delhi: Aleph.

4   Jacques Derrida 2002 'The Animal That Therefore I Am (More to Follow)', *Critical Inquiry*, 28 (2), pp. 369–418.

5   All translations are from Shonaleeka Kaul, *Hitopadesha.*

6   See Shonaleeka Kaul (2009) 'Pleasure and Culture: Reading Urban Archetypes in Kāvya Literature' in N Lahiri and U Singh edited *Ancient India: New Research*, Delhi: Oxford University Press, pp. 252–79, and Patrick Olivelle (2005) 'Rhetoric and Reality: Women's Agency in the *Dharmaśāstras*' in his *Language, Texts, and Society: Explorations in Ancient Indian Culture and Religion*, Florence: Firenze University Press, pp. 247–60.

Journeys in History: Personal and Professional

16

The bulk of this essay first appeared in a volume of autobiographical narratives by social scientists in India.[1] As such, it traces my personal and professional development as a historian through only my first three books (2010–2018) on early Indian cultural history. In sections titled Portrait of the Historian as a Person, Portrait of the Person as a Historian, and The Historian and the World, the essay identifies the moving forces behind the revisionist questions I investigated and the novel methods that were put forth in those works. It articulates and advocates the importance of holding space for temperamental over ideological affinity in the practice of history, for originality and freshness, demonstrable rigour as the claim to truth, and an apolitical humanism.

❧

The writing of history, by definition, depends on records of some fashion or the other. Rarely, however, do historians keep a record of *themselves* and *their* own role in the writing of history. It is uncommon to find reflections by scholars in the field on themselves, either as individuals or as working professionals, much less on how the two identities may relate to each other.[2] This is a task typically left to others, if at all, often in the form of celebratory *festschrifts* if the historian was influential enough, and after the scholar has retired from active service.

This apparently self-effacing tendency on the part of academics may be interpreted as a responsible admission of their subjectivity and as a statement on the difficulty of honest self-critique. Closer thought, though, reveals that a bigger reason for the absence of public introspection by historians on their personal positions and motivations may be history's enormous investment as a discipline in the ideal of objectivity. In this charged perspective, the historian, as an objective relayer of truth—which is somehow thought to be directly apprehendible from historical sources, despite the latter's often fragmentary and mediated testimonies, and despite something called the historian's own imagination[3]—is above board and self-evident in what they say and show. Why, then, the need to go within?

Above board and rigorously demonstrable the historian's work must certainly be, but is everything about it entirely self-evident and self-contained? Are the choices the historian makes, in terms of themes, sources, regions, paradigms and methods, purely professional and rational or does the accidental, the fortuitous, the temperamental or the intuitive play an important role? Is the historian's worldview not reflected in the way they view the world, past and present, and if it is, then what goes into the making of their worldview? Again, sterile academic ingredients? Or a good dose of political/social and personal ideologies and experiences or even a self-conscious rejection or reworking of these?

The answer to these questions, in the spirit of the questions, would perhaps be that it is a case of to each his own, and it would be erroneous to generalise. Yet that is precisely what the volume of autobiographical narratives in a sense sets out to do. Rather like in sociology and anthropology (though not so much in history), it seeks to probe the inner workings of the mind and life of some, self-reflexive members of the community of social scientists with a view to arriving at or surmising thereby what may be applicable to all social scientists. The extrapolative leap is something to beware of. But the very exercise of bringing scholars to this rather sensitive task of publicly and cogently baring themselves and their processes in ways that they have not before, and on lines that they may not even have thought before, is ground breaking. The least that it will make for is a forthrightness in academic discourse, a fostering of the ability to theorise the Self, and a greater acceptance of non-conformist, independent scholarship that is true to its own imperatives rather than to *a priori* schools of thought and camps, which do predominate in academia.

What follows is a trepidatious attempt at a case study of my own work up till 2018, which includes a research and teaching career of 17 years and a publishing tenure of 12 years, three books and over three dozen academic articles in international journals, volumes and national print media. In this essay I shall confine myself to tracing the course of my research interests and their wellsprings in the three books alone, drawing at length from the prefaces and introductions of each; I imagine that the volumes can be said to represent the thrust and trajectory of my engagement with history so far (as would the articles, but in a dispersed manner) and also point to my current, new projects.

Portrait of the Historian as a Person

What makes the task attemptable for me is the fact that I happen to be from the beginning someone who was inclined to, and thought it a part of the historian's academic project to, describe the genesis of the work that they were presenting to the world. As the Preface of the third book puts it: "A work of history should perhaps begin by telling its own history" (2018: xi). In the first book, perhaps, this duty of historicising the historian was not as self-conscious, and perhaps I did it as a way out of not knowing what else to say in the prefatory comments that publishing protocols required me to provide! But there was almost certainly much more than that at work even then. This is because at one point in the preface to *Imagining the Urban: Sanskrit and the City in Early India* (2010), I wrote, with something of the earnest decisiveness of a young historian discovering herself, that "for me history, the discipline, has been a private, individual experience; its rigour a personal satisfaction, its discoveries self-edification".[4]

Till today I have readers, including students, tell me how taken they were by this intimate and personal, almost conversational tone and track of the introduction to the book, and the rest of the book as well. This was something that is far from usual in tomes written on history, a subject sadly associated more often than not with dry, ponderous and impersonal monologues and data substituting for communication. I might add that I seemed seized of this implication of departing from history's 'weighty' stance when I went on to write in that preface: "I can't help believe that this is a nice, intimate way to feel about, and go about, a subject otherwise notorious as scholarly, heavy and boring."[5]

262 Bharata Before the British

What was it about *Imagining the Urban* that made it such a personal adventure for its author? The answer is its very genesis in a deeply temperamental, childhood love for Sanskrit literature and an unaccountably irresistible inclination to ancient India. Here is how the preface tells it:

> *Imagining the Urban* was first conceived more than a decade before it came to be written. Considering I had barely entered my teens then, this calls for explanation. My fascination for cities in early India, and with Sanskrit culture, started with a television serial telecast on Doordarshan. Chandra Prakash Dwivedi's *Chanakya* made an impression on me, as it did on many people, for its directorial soundness, gravity of content and chaste, eloquent dialogues. But it was its representation of the city, mostly Mauryan Pataliputra, the locale for the exciting developments that issued forth from the Machiavellian yet moralistic mind of Chandragupta's prime minister, that took me into a different world, a world from long ago. That early urban ethos, and a desire to revisit it, stayed with me, and must have mingled with my fondness for Sanskrit and its beautiful imagination, which developed at about the same time in school.
>
> Years later, when actually conceiving of a project for my PhD, it occurred to me that *I could pursue my romantic inclinations* and bring together the city and Sanskrit texts. This I did…"[6] (Emphasis added.)

Note how history *could* be the coming together of "romantic inclinations" for this writer! Sacrilege?! In a discipline that prides itself on dispassion, here was a no-less-proud admission of the crucial role of passion for the subject in giving birth to original and creative explorations in history. Indeed, 8 years after it appeared, it may be fair to now repeat what many readers, scholarly and lay, observed over this time, namely, that *Imagining the Urban* broke new ground by presenting, for the first time, a behavioural history of early Indian urbanism as a *mentalité*, and by rehabilitating Sanskrit poetry and drama (*kavya*) as not just a legitimate historical 'source' but a sophisticated and hyper-critical, symbolic representation of contemporary attitudes to morality, authority and tradition through the construction of literary archetypes.

Portrait of the Person as a Historian

One of the issues that the book addressed, in the process, was the social location of Sanskrit literature and the debate about Sanskrit as an elite, reified and socially conservative language. On the strength of the internal evidence of *kavya*s, it argued against such a reductionist approach to language and culture that sheared these down to power effects. It argued instead for the irreverent, even radical potentialities of Sanskrit literature on account of a series of antinomian and thought-provoking plots and characters that would emerge from the woodwork if only the texts were read closely and not foreclosed by *a priori* labels such as elite and courtly. But it so argued also on account of the public and performative, materialising contexts of the Sanskrit plays in particular: the book posited that mixed, heterogenous and heterodox audiences such as the ones these plays seem to have enjoyed, would bring to the Sanskrit composition expectations and interpretations that were just as unorthodox, and which the literature clearly satisfied, given its historical success and popularity. (See Chapter 7.)

This concern for paying attention to what I would later call "culture's varied contexts of consumption" can be seen to have carried over into my second book, an edited reader which was an anthology of seminal published works, titled *Cultural History of Early South Asia* (2014). The novelty of this volume's presentation of early Indian cultural history, and the principle behind selecting the representative essays in it (including by some greats such as A K Ramanujan and Ananda Coomaraswamy), was the broadening out of the study of cultural forms such as painting, sculpture, poetry and architecture—beyond the moment of their production to that of their multilayered reception. In other words, the volume urged looking beyond issues of patronage, which has received enormous attention from social historians of Indian art only to influentially establish a rather confining view of culture as political legitimation.

Instead, drawing on the field of cultural studies and reader reception theory, which were being applied perhaps for the first time to a study of early India, the volume proposed the need to look at the consumption of culture and the role that a cultural form which catered to communitarian consumption played in shaping the traditions and identities of its communities. This, it has to be said, was a fresh approach to the writing of Indian cultural history, one which ambitiously sought to invert the prevailing pyramid of top-down interpretive approaches. And it did not happen by accident. As the preface to the Reader explains, the necessity of newness in an undertaking such as the one this volume represented was an imperative. This deserves to be cited at some length also for the manner in which it lays out the thought process and dilemmas that may go into the making of a book. I quote:

> Compiling a cultural history of early India (which I later expanded to South Asia for reasons explained in the Introduction) was not an obvious or easy mandate. Any

number of masterly works on different aspects of India's vast and varied cultural past had been published over the last century…Though obviously the potential for fresh research was nowhere near exhausted, fresh research is not quite what a Reader based on already published, representative works purports to do. So what could we say that would be new and yet only introductory? What tack or line should the Reader adopt that would acquaint its readership with fundamental contributions to the regions' art history, and yet do so *in a way that questions and opens up received wisdom,* and initiates, hopefully, a new understanding of early cultural processes? (Emphasis added.)

I decided that the answer may lie in democratising somewhat the study of art and culture in early India. This would take two forms—namely, broadening the choice of objects selected for study, and more so, the questions asked about those objects. Hence readers will find the inclusion of ornaments, on the one hand, and folklore, on the other, in this collection of essays; these were and arguably continue to be widespread forms of cultural production that emanate from people's daily lived lives, but have rarely been incorporated in standard surveys of South Asian cultural history. Then, apart from commonplace culture, this volume also takes up more visible and conventionally regarded cultural forms such as temples, stupas, sculptural reliefs, or of a different order, drama and poetry composed in ancient times. But here too, it seeks to broaden the perspective and nudge the focus beyond their production to *the much wider phenomenon of their consumption or reception.* What did an art form mean to its audience? Indeed who constituted its audience, its community of response, its clientele and user base? How did art speak to their lives—to their beliefs, practices and identities? And how did the dialogue between culture and its communities contribute over the centuries to the formation of South Asian traditions?[7] (Emphasis added.)

Cultural History of Early South Asia, looking at art as dynamic processes of meaning and communication in the past, identified at least three contexts of consumption: art as not only objects of aesthetic enjoyment and utilitarian value but, most of all, as creations of rhetorical or philosophical moment.[8] This emphasis on meaning and representationality, as also on what a cultural form such as a text meant and did for its community, may be identified, in retrospect, as the bridge between this volume, *Imagining the Urban* before it, and my third book that appeared four years after the *Reader.* That this is a recognition in hindsight is crucial: this was not a planned thrust, and yet it is clear that threads from one piece of work by a scholar often develop and find resonance in another, and when seen all together, over a substantial period of time and body of work, a cogent alternative paradigm or way of thinking and doing the subject may take shape. In retrospect, this appears a lucid, organic process; in reality, given the chaos of a creative life, it could well be regarded as magical!

The third book, *The Making of Early Kashmir: Landscape and Identity in the Rajatarangini* (2018), returns to the theme of decoding spatial representations in Sanskrit *kavya*, a theme which showed up in the context of the city in the first book and now was about the region. But there is a connection with the second book too, as mentioned, in that *The Making of Early Kashmir* heroises the question of what a cultural form—

the iconic *Rajatarangini*—meant for its community, the Kashmiris, and how it shaped their world and their Self in charting the formative 2000+ years of Kashmir's history. This is, to my knowledge, the first work to evolve such an approach to the regional process—certainly for Kashmir, but perhaps also for most of South Asian Studies.

The book also makes bold to ask what history really was in premodern South Asia and how modern historians may have made nonsense of it in imposing 19th century Enlightenment positivist criteria on Indic texts that were fundamentally humanist in their vision and concern. It is a thoroughly revisionist work, then. In the three chapters, devoted to time, space and identity respectively, *The Making of Early Kashmir* opens up fundamental questions: What is history and in what modes may we receive it? How does a land become a homeland? And how are cultural identities formed? It explores these questions via the discursive and material practices that shaped Kashmir up to the 12th century CE.

Reinterpreting the first work of Kashmiri history, Kalhana's *Rajatarangini*, this book argues that the text was history not *despite* being traditional Sanskrit poetry but *because* of it. It elaborated a poetics of place, implicating Kashmir's sacred geography, a stringent critique of local politics, and a regional selfhood that transcended the limits of vernacularism. Further, in drawing not only on texts but also *longue durèe* testimonies from art, material culture, script and linguistics, all brought together within a joint interpretive framework but never in the spirit of empiricist corroboration, this work offers a nuanced answer to the question that has vexed historians for long: What is the relationship between literature and reality? How do textual and material cultures speak to each other?

While all my work would seem to be in response to these two questions, *The Making of Early Kashmir* presents a more intensely integrated multi-source-based history than before, and one that is also interdisciplinary in the questions it poses (history, identity and ethics) and concepts it uses (narrativity, connectivity and landscape) to answer them. Thus the Introduction begins with:

> This book is a cultural history/anthropology/geography of early Kashmir. The reason it dons many hats is that the phenomena it investigates, the questions it raises, and the perspectives it employs do not belong to any one discipline. They do all relate, however, to the broad field of culture. *Culture has been understood in its essence as shared meanings and values.* And after the recent 'cultural turn' across the social disciplines, it is understood to be discrete and irreducible to other spheres of human life such as the economic and the political. This book is an attempt to identify and interpret the values and meanings associated with the region called Kashmir....[9] (Emphasis added.)

When all these propositions and attempts that the book represents are seen together, *The Making of Early Kashmir* is informed by the position that if we are to ask meaningful and creative new questions about the past, historians must have an open mind to innovation and shun biases for or against different tools and methods of knowing the past. And cultural history can lead the way in this. As a matter of fact, however, this inclination towards "purposive innovation" and towards the ascendancy of culture is first seen in the Introduction to *Imagining the Urban*,[10] and represents perhaps the main thread of my research trajectory and my idea/project of history ever since.

The Historian and the World

But if it's a book on Kashmir, which also challenges many entrenched assumptions and misconceptions about its origins and cultural identity, can it escape political readings and entanglement? Perhaps the prior question should be: Is a book of this order written necessarily with reference to politics? Should it be? How does the historian—and here one means the honest, well-meaning historian without hidden agendas—deal with a subject so volatile and tragic? Is it the task of the historian, in the first place, to enter the fray, so to speak? Or is it for them to only represent their sources as faithfully as possible, whatever the result?

The fact that I am a Kashmiri by birth can also be expected to complicate the situation. Or so it is assumed. This deserves a moment of consideration for its serious implications for the working of any 'social scientist', especially in the rather charged times in which we live. Does the personal location of a historian preordain and seal the professional choices they make? I was once asked by a veteran colleague in a job interview, no less, whether I could be accused of being an outsider in writing this book! To this day, one is unsure why he didn't equally presume me, a Kashmiri Pandit (KP), to be an 'insider' to the situation in Kashmir. In both cases, however, my reply then—howsoever idealistic—would remain my testament today: the social/ethnic background of a historian should not be relevant to the rigour of their work.

For some practising historians of modern Kashmir, however, the lure of the political may be too strong to resist. One such worthy in a published academic piece chose to racially profile me because I was born a Kashmiri Hindu.[11] Clearly, she was concerned less by the battery of historical evidence *The Making of Early Kashmir* marshalled—none of which she could counter—than by this evidence disproving a couple of her own, previously published takes on modern Kashmiri identity, which were based on an obvious and perhaps understandable lack of familiarity with premodern Kashmiri history. Rather than respond to that academically and let it inform anew our understanding of the evolution in regional identity from the ancient to the modern, this historian took pains to make a personal charge instead. In the piece presumptuously titled 'Narratives from Exile: Kashmiri Pandits and their Construction of the Past', she asserted that the conclusions that this pioneering book on ancient Kashmir and its Indic culture came to were due to the extra-academic factor of my belonging to the minority Hindu community of Kashmir that was hounded out of its homeland by terrorists in the 1990s.

Unfortunately for this attempt at labelling and imputing ulterior motives—a rather common practice when scholarship withers and other concerns take centre stage— neither was I a member of any KP family that had to flee Kashmir in the 1990s nor were the conclusions I arrived at on the basis of overwhelming historical evidence from two thousand years ago mine alone. A number of respected Sanskritists, epigraphists and archaeologists were conversant with some of the evidence before, even if they had not joined the dots themselves to yield the big picture, and had been cited in my book. Some of them also applauded the volume when it came out for representing "empirically rich and theoretically sophisticated" work.[12] Yet other reviewers called it "an incredibly potent piece of scholarship" and "a milestone in the study of the region and the most authentic statement yet on the origins of the

Kashmiri identity".[13] Inconveniently for the racial profiler, all these scholars were Americans, Europeans or others, and not Kashmiri Hindus![14]

⚘ ⚘

While it is true, as Levi Strauss put it, that "history is never simply history, always history-for, history written in the interest of some vision",[15] the million dollar question is: What should that vision be, or what are the ends of history-writing? I have argued that in Classical Greece and even more so in early India, the didactic and the injunctive were inseparable from the historical: individual and societal ethics and values were the fulcrum of the early Indian literary and historical vision. Yet this civilisational investment in ethical instruction has been forgotten and does not figure in modern ratings of works on history.

There does linger today in a different avatar the image of the historian as educator, neigh, emancipator of the masses who are children of a lesser truth. While the risk of the hubris of the professional towards the 'uninformed' masses is clear and present, we do live in an age of disinformation and unsubstantiated or even fake narratives—a hyper-politicised world. So, the onus of producing and making available authentic versions of truth and knowledge does and should lie on the responsible historian. But the rigour of their truth, rather than their ethnicity or ideology, should be the judge of its authenticity.

Let us close by turning now at some length to how the preface of *The Making of Early Kashmir* deals with all these issues raised above. I quote:

I first picked up Kalhana's *Rajatarangini* in 2005...My PhD had been on Sanskrit *kavya* (highly aesthetic poetry and prose) and it was to read another *kavya* that I turned to the *Rajatarangini*. *In retrospect, this intuitive approach was propitious.* For, swimming against the tide of its enormous reputation as a work of objectivist history rather than poetry...I went on to argue that the *Rajatarangini* was indeed a *kavya* first, and thereby perhaps history.

A second instant observation on my first reading of the text has also stood the test of 12 years of time to remain the centrepiece of my thinking and analysis on the *Rajatarangini* that is presented in this book. This is the conviction that ethics is the fulcrum of Kalhana's literary and historical vision. This was however not something that most of 200 years of modern scholarship ... had believed—they who had looked upon the moral, didactic and rhetorical tendencies of the poem as an eminently disregardable indulgence typical of convention-bound, brahmanical Sanskrit poets. Though the preaching of the ancients may have little interest for the intellectuals of today, to deny the centrality for those poets of this preoccupation with a critical idealism and call to action is, to my mind, to miss the moving spirit and *raison* of an entire thought-world.

From ... 2012 to the completion of this book in 2017... this book became an investigation of larger discursive questions that possess, I would like to believe, an enduring primacy across the humanities and social sciences as also a striking resonance for contemporary Kashmir and the world. These questions are: What is history and in what modes may we receive it? How does a land become a homeland? And how are cultural identities formed? That the three questions are in fact intertwined and inform one another is perhaps at the core of the answers to them that this book proposes. Howsoever obscured, *the ancient past cannot be erased or wished away.* It shapes a land and a people in intrinsic ways; it shapes their collective self. *An identity divorced from history may descend into delusion.*

...I discovered a disturbing reality. Indians knew so little about Kashmir... The world knew even less—perhaps only the tales of violence and strife that have been doing the rounds of certain diplomatic and academic circles for the last thirty years. However, and undoubtedly the saddest of all, many young Kashmiris in the valley today, reared on a schizophrenic narrative, seemed to know or care the least about the rich origins and legacy of their land. *Though hardly written with that object, it is hoped that TMEK will go some way in forcing our collective attention back* to the ancient history of a region that once spearheaded virtually all intellectual and cultural movements in the Indian subcontinent with trademark erudition and brilliance.[16] (Emphasis added.)

Four comments follow on the four paragraphs excerpted above, with special reference to the lines italicised:

One: The author *tells* her readers how the book came about—where it started and how it took the shape it did. This is in keeping with the full disclosure approach seen in my first two books, as we know by now. What is more, there seems to have been nothing remotely political in the generative process.

Instead, the role of the intuitive is indicated, rather along the lines of the individual historian following her heart that *Imagining the Urban* inaugurated.

Two: There is a pronounced critique of the historians' establishment and a consciousness of being thoroughly revisionist. Again, this is the novelty and innovation paradigm, mediated by a thought-out, demonstrable rigour of course.

Three: When the historian appeals gently to the futility of trying to erase or wish away a possibly inconvenient past, and points to the dangers of a descent into delusion by a community that does so—she is subtly speaking truth to the power of disorder and mayhem perpetrated by insurgent violence.

And relatedly, four: There is an acknowledged ambivalence of the position of the historian in her admission that though the book was not written for any political effect or intervention, there was retrospectively still a hope for the stakeholders in the conflict to rise to Kashmir's historical truths and embrace these to heal again.

In all these ways, the historian may negotiate the world, both within and without.

Notes

1   Achla Pritam Tandon, Gopi Devdutt Tripathy and Rashi Bhargava
      edited (2021) *Social Scientist in South Asia: Personal Narratives, Social
      Forces and Negotiations,* London: Routledge, pp. 230–39. Reused
      here with permission.

2   A notable exception to my mind is Uma Chakravarti, the feminist
      historian, who in the introduction to her collection of articles
      *Everyday Lives, Everyday Histories: Beyond the Kings and Brahmanas
      of 'Ancient' India* (2006) Delhi: Tulika Publishers, traces her life's
      journey as a civil activist and is explicit in its correlation to her
      themes as a historian. See my review of her book Shonaleeka Kaul
      (2006) 'Peopling History', *Frontline,* 23, Nov.18–Dec.1, pp. 72–74.

3   The idea and inevitability of the operation of the historian's
      imagination in the writing of history was spoken of by R G
      Collingwood (1946) *The Idea of History,* Oxford: Clarendon Press.
      More sophisticated treatments of the same followed by the likes of
      Leon Goldstein and others. As a part of the post-modern revolution,
      and specifically the literary turn executed within it by the likes of
      Hayden White and Paul Ricouer, a great deal more has been said on
      this inescapable, non-empirical aspect of the discipline of history.

4   Shonaleeka Kaul (2010) *Imagining the Urban: Sanskrit and the City
      in Early India,* Delhi: Permanent Black, and New York: Seagull
      Books with University of Chicago Press, pp. ix, x.

5   Ibid, p. x.

6   Ibid., p. ix.

7   Shonaleeka Kaul edited (2014) *Cultural History of Early South Asia:
      A Reader,* Delhi: Orient BlackSwan, pp. xi, xii.

8   Ibid., p. 1.

9   Shonaleeka Kaul (2018) *The Making of Early Kashmir: Landscape
      and Identity in the Rajatarangini,* Delhi: Oxford University Press, pp.
      1–2.

10   Shonaleeka Kaul, *Imagining the Urban,* p. 38.

11   Mridu Rai (2021) 'Narratives from Exile: Kashmiri Pandits and their Construction of the Past' in Sugata Bose and Ayesha Jalal edited *Kashmir and the Future of South Asia*, New York, pp. 91–115.

12   Sheldon Pollock in his endorsement of *The Making of Early Kashmir*, book jacket.

13   See Nathan McGovern (2020) Book Review, *International Journal of Hindu Studies*, 24, 2, August; Manu Devadevan (2018) 'Quest for Kashmir', *Frontline*, June.

14   This is not to say that Westerners are above politics when it comes to Kashmir and India. Another scholar, Luther Obrock, who found it difficult to digest the overwhelming evidence of Kashmir's historical Indic connections, again, chose to put this down to my personal "desire" to see Kashmir as Indic rather than deal with the facts. See John Nemec (forthcoming) *Kings and Brahmanas*, New York: Oxford University Press, chapter 4, for calling out the baselessness of Obrock's slant and endorsing the analysis that *The Making of Early Kashmir* puts out.

15   Claude Levi-Strauss (1966) *The Savage Mind*, London: Weidenfeld and Nicholson, p. 257.

16   Shonaleeka Kaul, *The Making of Early Kashmir,* pp. 11–13.

Decolonising the Mind: Pipedreams for Indian Academia

It would be appropriate to conclude this collection of essays that attempt a new history of early India with a piece on the very system with which all histories, old or new, of India are condemned to contend. This is Indian academia and here are a few of the changes that would make it a much more valuable place to work and be.

First, there is a need to free Indian academia from bureaucratic strangleholds. For instance, if you look at the rules for promotions in public universities ever since the 6th Pay Commission was introduced in 2006, there would appear to be an inverse relationship between quantity and quality. The earlier system of promoting teachers just by virtue of their having lived out a certain number of years in the system allowed many individuals to slip into a complacent disregard for research and continued learning. However, the UGC's Academic Point Index (API) system now in currency, in the hands of recalcitrant universities, may have the scope for harassment built into it.

Teachers must garner a certain number of points every year in a variety of academic and "extra-curricular" activities, and compile enormous folios of "proof" of all this over the years, sometimes retrospectively, for every single promotion. These folios they must submit, in numerous copies each, to the powers-that-be. The latter then adjudicate on what is indeed admissible and what is not—a deficit of trust that becomes inevitable when achievements are assessed mechanically.

Yet, despite putting in the long years demanded (perhaps the longest anywhere in the world) and meeting, even exceeding the API required, there is no guarantee of getting your promotion, given arbitrary interpretations of the rules and unaccounted-for delays (15 years in a leading central university recently) by largely unsympathetic or helpless institutional bureaucracies.

Many feel the system may be, ironically, ranged against the genuine scholar-teacher, who could take five years to research and produce a great book, but will be awarded a mere 8–12 points for all that (according to the 2018 rules), even as their colleague, publishing an expedient article in one of the dozens of journals which have mushroomed overnight to cater to the API industry, can lap up 10–30 points per piece. Similarly, a host of administrative duties, membership of committees, and financial grants are essential if you have to meet the required points, whether or not they do anything to make you a better teacher or scholar.

Promotions apart, there is also pressure on faculty to spend longer and longer hours in 'office', whether or not there are classes, and to teach larger and larger numbers of students, whether or not they show up. Oftentimes, pressed to fill seats, professors are required to supervise PhDs that have no connection to their own expertise. This is to the detriment of students and the discipline alike. Moreover, their own reading and writing is something that many conscientious teachers end up having to do on their own time as a result, after they return from the workplace, during holidays and miniscule vacations, as if research were their personal affair and irrelevant to teaching. Scarce sources of funding, especially in the humanities, and impossible sabbatical rules—in striking contrast to best Western practices to which we otherwise aspire—exacerbate the situation. Most academics simply give up.

Any wonder then that the average standard of scholarly output has dropped here? Or that our course curricula are languishing and many students regard admission to Indian degree programmes as "time pass", or stepping stones to institutions abroad, rather than rigorous and creative opportunities to excel in their own country? This is the real crisis of higher education in the public sector.

At the other end of the spectrum are commercial monopolies, redressing which would be another pipedream. Consider the profiteering private-run educational institutes across the country. They cater only to students who can pay their exorbitant fees, and often poach on public universities for their teaching staff—people who, much like government doctors, flee to private pastures for fat pay cheques and different degrees of glamour. Left to their fate in the process are the lakhs of students who cannot afford these expensive teaching shops and have no alternative but to go to subsidised—and sadly stagnating—government academies.

This is not to say that all private universities that have come up in the last twenty years or so are not propelled by noble impulses or do not have a worthy vision of ameliorating the ills of higher learning. Some would appear to. But what is worth pondering over is that if these are to remain privileged islands in the sea of Indian humanity thirsting for and deserving of quality education, can they do justice to their own cause? Not just places of learning, scholarly knowledge in general seems subject to commercial controls of access today, what with the steep price of academic books and journals and prohibitive copyright fees. The bulk of these profits by far goes to the publishing houses, not the author, who may have little say or share in the matter.

Surely what is needed today is more equitable structures of both knowledge production and dissemination. The internet and social media have certainly opened up new avenues, but they also bring with them risks such as fake news, unsubstantiated narratives and disinformation. It is mainstream Indian academics itself that must reform if authentic versions of truth and knowledge are to be widely available. Let us see now what direction such internal, qualitative change may need to take.

We inaugurated above a list of aspirations for higher education in India, starting with the need to free the field of bureaucratic strangleholds, on the one hand, and of commercial monopolies over knowledge production and dissemination, on the other.

Concomitantly, in this age of internet-driven fake narratives and disinformation, the need for qualitative self-reform by the academy, especially in the humanities, to facilitate the emergence of authentic versions of truth and knowledge, was also asserted.

However, what defines an authentic version of knowledge? Indeed who defines what knowledge is, in the first place? And who may be regarded as an authority? These are ethical as well as political questions. Even as it is essential to reform Indian universities and infuse in them greater rigour and quality, it must also be recognised that a good bit of the teaching done at these formal centres of higher learning today, especially in our metropolises, tends to rely on imported Euro-American theories, concepts, methods and ideologies.

Vastly engaging and erudite though these are, only a few of them may illumine culturally specific historical processes and worldviews of the non-West, while others may well inflict varieties of epistemic violence on endogenous ways of knowing. On the other hand, how many local Indian thinkers, past or present, ancient or modern, can you name who are taught and applied in mainstream Indian universities today—pedagogical spaces which otherwise resound with Foucault, Heidegger and the like?

Indeed, illustrative of colonial epistemic hierarchies is my own discipline of history, which continues to creak under the burden of 19th century European Enlightenment notions of scientism, objectivism and materialism, as if history were a physical science rather than a humanistic field. This has led to the delegitimising and rejection of vast swathes of traditional Indian literature and thought for their emphasis on human values, aesthetics, ethics, liberation or other subjectivities. Sterile facts versus meaning and values are two different civilisational *weltenschauungs*. In championing Western notions of history today that have become dated in the West itself, we are perpetuating an imperialism and backwardness that are of our own making.

Mind you, this is not a call for nativism or some brand of indigenist reaction. Far from it. This is a call for radically rethinking anachronistic and etic approaches to India and letting our profound and prodigious knowledge traditions, in every one of the hundreds of languages and dialects we have, speak for themselves. This will enrich and refresh international academic discourse as well, just as all other thought from the Global South is doing, and the world will thank us for it—for being what India always was in the past: an intellectual giant.

⚜

Within the country as well, this is the way forward: There has to be dialogue between Anglophone academicians and vernacular scholarship, and on equal terms. And here, in the vernaculars, one includes the whole range from classical pan-Indic languages such as Sanskrit to regional languages and dialects, and from texts and literary cultures to oral traditions and folk narratives.

All too many students from small towns and villages of India come to study in the megalopolises diffident and on the back foot, because they don't know English or don't know it well enough. No doubt multilingualism is the need of the hour in the globalised world we inhabit, and we encourage students to learn English, but there is nothing intrinsically superior in this language over others. Our students need the confidence to know that language is a skill, not a liability, and must be the medium for trans-cultural conversations, mediating faithfully between their own thought-worlds and international ones. If this conversation has to be in English for now, so be it; what is even more important than decolonising the tongue is decolonising the mind.

That said, the Colonial 'Other' is not the only occupying force when it comes to Indian intellect. Academic circles, again in the social sciences and liberal arts particularly, are also in the thrall of a different kind of regime: the warring twin camps of Left and Right politics. There seems to be little intellectual engagement of substance between the two, but plenty of disdain, name-calling and power-lust. Worst of all, there is negligible space for independent scholarship that does not conform—and is promptly branded! It is high time to emancipate Indian academia from the tyranny of these labels.

One has no doubt that there are a large number of scholars in this country doing fresh and creative work, especially studying our vibrant regional traditions on the latter's own terms, who are tired of being asked to see and show things through the prism of politics. But they are invisibilised and disenfranchised more often than not. Here is an exclusionist conspiracy of silence within the very bastion of freedom that academics like to believe they represent.

To those who speak for education's powers of resistance and calling out oppression, here is the challenge within. Will we overcome it? One can only hope so. For, as Nelson Mandela said, "to be free is not merely to cast off one's chains, but to live in a way that respects and enhances the freedom of others".

ABOUT THE AUTHOR

Shonaleeka Kaul is India's leading cultural and intellectual historian, specialising in Sanskrit literature. She is Professor, Centre for Historical Studies, Jawaharlal Nehru University, and has also been the Malathy Singh Distinguished Lecturer in South Asian Studies at Yale University (USA), the Jan Gonda Fellow in Indology, Leiden University (The Netherlands), and Visiting Professor of History at the South Asia Institute, Heidelberg University (Germany).

Kaul is a prolific and path-breaking author. She has published 8 internationally acclaimed books so far, each demolishing colonial shibboleths about early India and putting out a fresh, rigorous and compelling new understanding of it. These include *Imagining the Urban: Sanskrit and the City in Early India* (2010), *The Making of Early Kashmir: Landscape and Identity in the Rajatarangini* (2018), *Eloquent Spaces: Meaning and Community in Early Indian Architecture* (2019), *Retelling Time: Alternative Temporalities from Premodern South Asia* (2021) and *Myths and Places: New Perspectives in Indian Cultural Geography* (2023). *Looking Within: Life Lessons from Lal Ded, the Kashmiri Shaiva Mystic* (2019) and *Hitopadesha* (2022) are translations by her.